Four Russian Serf Narratives

Wisconsin Studies in Autobiography

William L. Andrews
General Editor

Four Russian Serf Narratives

Translated, edited, and
with an introduction by

John MacKay

The University of Wisconsin Press

This book was published with the assistance of
the FREDERICK W. HILLES PUBLICATION FUND
of YALE UNIVERSITY.

The University of Wisconsin Press
1930 Monroe Street, 3rd Floor
Madison, Wisconsin 53711-2059
uwpress.wisc.edu

3 Henrietta Street
London WC2E 8LU, England
eurospanbookstore.com

1   3   5   4   2

Printed in the United States of America

Library of Congress Cataloging-in-Publication Data
Four Russian serf narratives / translated, edited, and
   with an introduction by John MacKay.
      p.   cm. — (Wisconsin studies in autobiography)
   Includes bibliographical references and index.
   ISBN 978-0-299-23374-7 (pbk.: alk. paper)
     ISBN 978-0-299-23373-0 (e-book)
         1. Serfs—Russia—Biography.
   2. Serfdom—Russia—History—19th century—Sources.
         I. MacKay, John Kenneth.
   II. Series: Wisconsin studies in autobiography
         HT807.F68   2009
          306.3′65092247—dc22
                  [B]
              2009008140

To

MY PARENTS

Our fathers all were poor,
Poorer our fathers' fathers;
Beyond, we dare not look.

Edwin Muir, "The Fathers"

Contents

Illustrations

Acknowledgments

While preparing this volume, I received help from more people than I can properly acknowledge, including audiences who heard various sections at conferences and colloquia. I am deeply grateful to them all.

I could not have completed the project without the Morse and Griswold Fellowships awarded by Yale University; the aid offered by the staff at the State Archive of the Russian Federation (GARF) and the Russian State Archive of Ancient Documents (RGADA); and the helpful staff at Yale's Sterling Memorial Library. A special thanks to Abraham Parrish of Sterling's Map Collection, who prepared the map.

For specific and particularly crucial assistance, I thank Peter Kolchin, James Heinzen, Dale Peterson, Vladimir Alexandrov, Harvey Goldblatt, Paul Bushkovitch, Laura Engelstein, Irina Golubchikova, Robert Stepto, Laurence Senelick, Lina Steiner, and Benjamin Harshav. For guiding some of my previous serfdom-related work to publication, I am also grateful to Gad Heuman, Jason Haslam, Julia M. Wright, Denise Kohn, Sarah Meer, Emily B. Todd, and Miriam Fuchs. A very special thanks to the anonymous readers who reviewed the manuscript for University of Wisconsin Press, as well as to Adam Mehring, Amy Freitag, Sheila Leary, Nicole Kvale, and Raphael Kadushin at the Press for all the work and attention they lavished on this project. My deepest gratitude to William L. Andrews, who guided this book to completion and whose work on slave narratives has been a constant inspiration to me in my research into serf writings.

For all their support, companionship, and patience, I thank all my colleagues at Yale, the members of Yale's Working Group in Marxism and Cultural Theory, my friends and family, my students, and above all, Moira Fradinger. The book is dedicated to my parents, Jack and Betty MacKay, whose stories about the past led me to think about the lives of rural laborers in the first place.

Four Russian Serf Narratives

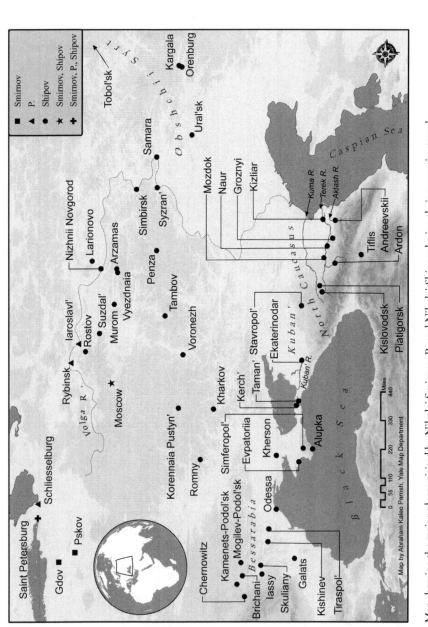

Map showing the major places visited by Nikolai Smirnov, P., and Nikolai Shipov during their respective travels.

Introduction

Serfs as Writers

The four works gathered here under the heading "Russian serf narratives" were composed by Russian serfs and former serfs between 1785 and about 1911; two of the texts were composed before and two after serfdom's abolition in 1861. Readers will notice immediately that the narratives are very diverse in character. Chronologically they range from Nikolai Smirnov's 1785 deposition, written by Smirnov in a desperate effort to save his own life after a botched escape attempt;[1] to the long narrative poem *News about Russia* (composed sometime before 1849 by an anonymous peasant poet known as Petr O., or simply as P.);[2] to Nikolai Shipov's 1881 account of his repeated attempts to escape bondage (culminating in his liberation in 1845, highly unusual for being mediated by a period of captivity in what is now Chechnya);[3] and finally to M. E. Vasilieva's fragmentary account of her girlhood in serfdom on a rural estate in the Russian heartland (1911).[4] The two longest narratives (by P. and Nikolai Shipov) are presented in abridged form, although enough is offered of their texts to give a good sense of their life stories and authorial personae. Together these four texts printed here make up the only collection of autobiographies written by serfs published in a language other than Russian.[5]

Why has so little attention been paid to the writings, autobiographical or not, of serfs and former serfs who lived within the territory of the Russian Empire? The sheer rarity of such writings is, to be sure, the main reason: although there exists no adequate estimate of the percentage of serfs able to read and/or write, we can safely assume that the numbers were not large, though perhaps not disproportionately low if compared with the numbers of literate working and peasant people in other European countries in the early nineteenth century. Thus scholars have identified only a few serf autobiographies in total—around twenty—although surely other autobiographical texts and fragments repose in police and estate archives awaiting discovery.[6] Moreover, we need to confront the whole issue of the authenticity of such rare and improbable writings, which actually involves the intertwined but distinct questions of (1) whether a given text was "really" written by a serf or former serf, and (2) whether the text offers a "truthful" picture of serf life in Russia. The second question immediately brings up one of the paradoxes of the testimony of enslaved, imprisoned, and otherwise dishonored and oppressed people in general: that a serf consigns his or her life to paper already makes him or her "atypical," and yet how can we obtain an adequate picture of the institution of serfdom, and particularly of the kinds of subjectivity it helped to generate, without such "insider" accounts? (This paradox touches on at least one of the narratives in this book very acutely, for precisely that author who seems to have led the most classically "Russian-serf" sort of existence—the poet P., who worked with a plow alongside other peasants—produced what is surely the most idiosyncratic of all of the narratives collected here, the long poem *News about Russia*.) Meanwhile, the first question haunts even the present volume to some extent, and it is possible, though unlikely, that the narratives of P. and M. E. Vasilieva (about neither of whom I have uncovered any historically confirming data) are inauthentic—that is, not "really" written by "real" serfs.[7]

Both the paucity of serf narratives and the question of authenticity recall the very different but suggestively comparable situation in regard to slave narratives in the United States. The fierce political struggle waged by antebellum U.S. abolitionist groups provided both an audience and a rationale for American slave narratives between 1845 and 1865, with the result that no other group of unfree laborers in history produced anything like a comparable quantity of autobiographies. As is well known, the same polemical context led to heated and long-lasting debates about the value and veracity of slave narratives as historical sources, debates that found resolution (in favor of the narratives) only in the 1970s.[8] The relative though not complete absence in pre-reform Russia of a similarly combative public atmosphere of debate does much to explain the scarcity of written serf testimony.[9] What little we do have from the serfs was published well after their emancipation and is therefore (with the exception of the protest poem *News about Russia*) less charged with immediate political urgency and more conventionally autobiographical, if strikingly varied. As far as the twentieth century goes, the Works Progress Administration slave narratives project of the late 1930s was carried out at a time when, in the Soviet Union, the Russian peasantry as a whole was either enduring the last stages of the violent and traumatic state-driven collectivization project or (usually as a consequence of collectivization) simply abandoning the rural areas for towns and cities.[10] In our own day, the highly active memoir publishing industry in post-Soviet Russia has only very recently produced a collection of nineteenth-century peasant autobiographies, in spite of intense interest in the lives of Russian nobles—who were, of course, the main proprietors of the serfs—and in the social and artistic world of noble estates.[11]

It would be wrong, however, to claim that serf testimony has been entirely ignored, whether in Russia or elsewhere. Even if no such testimonies were published in the years leading up to the abolition of serfdom, the idea of the serf as testimonial speaker (if not author) came to figure in literary works critical of serfdom, such as Alexander Radishchev's *Journey from St. Petersburg to Moscow* (1790), Alexander Herzen's story "The Thieving Magpie" (1847), and Ivan Turgenev's *Sketches from a Hunter's Notebook* (1852), although the narratives of bondspeople did not inform these fictions as deeply as they do, say, Harriet Beecher Stowe's *Uncle Tom's Cabin* (1852). The notion of a "serf intelligentsia" first appeared in the late nineteenth century, and a number of autobiographies (including those of Shipov and Vasilieva) were published during this time and later.[12] The Soviet period was marked by continued if fitful interest in the culture of serfdom, particularly until 1933 or so and then again in the post-Stalin period, especially in the 1970s. Soviet historical studies of serfdom tended to focus on issues of exploitation at the expense of other aspects of the institution; it was largely left to Western historians of Russia, perhaps affected by the new legitimacy of slave narratives in U.S. historical study after 1970, to incorporate the testimony of bondspeople into their accounts of serfdom.[13] It was in the United States, too, that the first book-length translation of a serf autobiography (Aleksandr Nikitenko's) was published just eight years ago.[14]

The translation of the present volume was prompted not only by a consciousness of a lack of testimonial material about Russian serfdom but also by an awareness of the relatively new importance of slave narratives for the study of eighteenth- and nineteenth-century literature (especially U.S., but also British, French, and Hispanic literature), for the study of autobiography, and for the study of modernity (and its relationship to bondage) more generally.[15] My own training is in literary studies rather than history, and it was during the process of coming up with a syllabus on the comparative study of U.S. and Russian literatures that the absence of serf autobiographies first came to my attention. For the title of the book, I deliberately chose to designate these texts as "narratives" rather than "testimonies" or "autobiographies," not in order to assert that they are somehow "the same" as U.S. slave narratives but rather to signal them as contributions to the growing field of comparative slavery studies, which overlaps with both the historical and the literary-cultural studies disciplines, and wherein the discursive category of the "slave narrative" has become central. The nineteenth century was, after all, the great age of slave emancipations, and there was considerable awareness of the American and Russian situations among the various international "enlightened" reading publics in the lead-up to the abolitions (1861 in Russia, 1865 in the United States).[16] It might prove profitable to think of these Russian texts as participating in a very broad and emergent discursive context in which modernization and territorial expansion were coming to be thought of as inextricably linked to bondage, with all of its complex, violent history and manifold consequences.

The Narratives

As indicated before, the narratives included here are strikingly different from one another both in terms of style and of the stakes involved in their composition. The earliest (1785) is by the remarkable Nikolai Smirnov (1767–1800), a serf belonging originally to Andrei Mikhailovich Golitsyn (1729–70), a prominent member of one of the foremost Russian aristocratic families. As it happened, all the villages belonging to this particular Golitsyn household were managed by Smirnov's father (also a serf, of course), who was able to pay for his son's education in (among other subjects) "Russian grammar and spelling," "the basic rudiments of the French and Italian languages," "English, history, geography, mythology, iconology [. . .], the rudiments of physics and chemistry [. . .], draftsmanship, painting, architecture, geodesics and the fundamentals of mathematics."[17] Unable to enroll in Moscow University, Smirnov studied informally with at least one professor from that institution, namely Semyon Desnitskii, the founder of Russian secular jurisprudence and a former student of Adam Smith in Glasgow. Clearly endowed with an extraordinary desire and aptitude for learning, Smirnov was in fact destined to work for his father, helping to manage the various villages as a scribe and accountant. When his repeated requests for manumission were rejected one after another, he decided to flee, first stealing 3,500 rubles from his father, then trying escape Russia by posing as "the Italian merchant Camporesi." Eventually he hoped to join up (or so he claims) with the three young Golitsyn sons, who were on a "Grand Tour" of Western Europe. Deceived and robbed by a couple of con artists, Smirnov contracted an illness and was captured in Saint Petersburg. He indicates that he expected clemency; however, after pronouncing hanging as its initial verdict, the chamber of the criminal court decided that Smirnov should be given ten blows with the knout, have his nostrils ripped open, be branded (presumably on the forehead), and sent in shackles to perpetual hard labor in Riga. It was at this point that Smirnov composed his narrative, as both an explanation of his deeds and a desperate, if somewhat ambivalent, expression of penitence.

News about Russia was apparently written by a serf from the Iaroslavl' area, who refers to himself only as "Petr O." or more often simply "P." The tale, written in four- or five-foot iambs and rhyming consistently within changing stanzaic schemes, is loosely centered on the serf narrator's failed attempt to marry a free peasant girl. The simple frame structure of the poem is deeply complicated by the generous insertion of dream visions, songs, and especially "side" narratives told in what appear to be semi-fictionalized voices other than the narrator's. Thus, *within* a tale told by one character, another character will begin to tell a tale about someone else, who will also in turn set off on his or her own independent narrative, until the reader finds himself at several removes from the main narrator, P. This proliferation of story can be confusing at times, as each tale threatens to sprout into a theoretically infinite number of branches. It also makes *News about Russia* into a kind of omnibus testimonial work, where a host of serf voices are linked into a single structure—rather like the famous matrioshka dolls, one inside the other. The cumulative effect of the poem yields the representation of a large, diverse peasant population united in its antipathy to the landowning class and its allegiance to the tsar. We might think of P.'s creation as a *narrative* counterpart to the *symbolic* construction of the African American community achieved in Frederick Douglass's "Narrative," when the "root" given to Douglass by the conjure man Sandy Jenkins (prior to Douglass's decisive physical encounter with Edward Covey) becomes a token of black people's collective opposition to white domination.[18]

The author of the remarkable "multiple-captivity" narrative, Nikolai Shipov (b. 1802) was a serf peasant who, along with his father, was much engaged in trading rams and other livestock. He attempted both flight and the purchase of himself and his family out of serfdom, to no avail. Shipov was literate, however, and in 1844 he found an odd statute in the ninth volume of the "Code of Laws," indicating that a serf captured by "mountain predators" would become free in perpetuity, along with his entire family, upon being liberated. Already accustomed to trading with non-Russian peoples in the mountainous northern Caucasus and elsewhere, he deliberately fell into Chechen bondage on February 8, 1845, escaping his captors—and serfdom—eleven days later.[19]

Finally we have M. E. Vasilieva's extraordinary late fragment, "Notes of a Serf Woman," published in 1911. Vasilieva's autobiographical self, named "Akul'ka" in the text, never emerges from her childhood, spent in the village of "Dubovoe."[20] The author includes no conventional comparisons between a previously enslaved and currently free condition; nor is the child-serf bent toward some future moment of liberation. The resulting text offers a harsh reflection on authority and submission, rather than a submissive performance for authority.

History and Society in the Narratives

Though this is not the place for a detailed account of the history and structural features of Russian serfdom—a large number of superb works on this subject exist[21]—some overview of the institution needs to be briefly offered.

At the time of the abolition of serfdom on February 19, 1861, under Alexander II, just under 40 percent of the Russian population, and roughly half the peasant population, had the status of "bound peasants" or serfs. This amounted to around twenty-three million people, whose status was in many ways comparable to that of chattel slaves, despite improvements since the end of the eighteenth century. The term "serf " (in Russian, *krepostnoi krestianin*) applies to a peasant legally bound to a plot of land and to landowner, and who passed this servile status on to his children. Almost all the remaining peasants in Russia lived on land belonging not to a landlord but to the state (to which they paid rent) and are designated in English as "state peasants."

In contrast to bondage in the Americas, serfdom was gradually superimposed on a peasant society and economy that already existed, in a lengthy process that lasted around three centuries, beginning right around the time that "similar forms of servitude had begun to decline in many parts of Western Europe."[22] Until the mid-sixteenth century, peasants who lived on noble landowners' estates were tenant farmers who paid rent (whether in goods, cash, or as labor) to their landlords, but were also free to leave them to seek out better conditions with other masters.[23] In 1497 this right was restricted to a two-week period after the completion of harvest. In 1603 peasants were prohibited from moving away from the landowners at all, and in 1649, under the new Law Code (*Ulozhenie*), fleeing serfs became permanently liable to be returned to their previous homes and owners, although the same code importantly allowed for serfs to be given permission to leave their landlords temporarily "to seek employment or to pursue other economic activities."[24]

All of these restrictions emerged because of shortages of agricultural labor, brought about in turn by the consolidation and eastward and southward expansion of the Russian state during the fifteenth and sixteenth centuries, as the principality of Muscovy (whose seat was, of course, the city of Moscow) became the center of power in the Russian lands. The landowners who benefited from this new expansion, most of whom came into their property starting in the late fifteenth century, were originally noble subordinates of the rulers of Muscovy, beginning with Ivan III (1462–1505). Rewarded with conditional grants of land, the landowners were obligated in their turn to fight in the ruler's army. The peasants who lived on the estates were to be the main support of these royal subordinates, especially as providers of agricultural produce. During the agricultural boom years of the late fifteenth and early sixteenth centuries, landowners began to compel their tenants to produce grain for sale on the market as well, mainly to the military and to the rapidly growing city population.[25] Thus, the area with the highest concentration of serfs was in the farmlands surrounding the major cities of European Russia, from Saint Petersburg in the north to around Voronezh in the south, and from Pskov in the west to around Nizhnii Novgorod in the east (see map on page 2).

Yet labor was always scarce, competition among landlords for workers quite intense, and the country vast and growing larger. As a consequence, landlords, especially smaller, poorer ones, petitioned the state for tighter restrictions on peasant movement.[26] These restrictions were reinforced in the wake of the disastrous reign of Ivan the Terrible (Ivan IV, ruled 1547–84), when war, social chaos, famine, and epidemics led to a large-scale depopulation of the Russian heartland.[27] In order to keep peasants from either seeking better deals with other landlords or from wandering away into the new areas opened by expansion, particularly during hard economic times, the peasants were thus gradually "bound" to land and owner.

As we can see from the examples of Nikolai Smirnov and Nikolai Shipov, these restrictions were not sufficient to prevent serfs from seeking freedom in the hinterlands or even beyond the bounds of Russia itself. And as I have already indicated, even legally, the "binding" of the peasants was never absolute, as they were often given permission to migrate away from their villages in order to work in crafts, trades, and factories (the peasant P. in *News about Russia* is a good example of just such a migrant serf, as are Nikolai Shipov and his father).[28] Clearly, a desire for personal advancement and autonomy from both the landlord and the authority of the peasant community motivated many peasants to work away from the village, as Nikolai Shipov's narrative reveals quite clearly. It was this ability to migrate that in some instances facilitated the emergence, much noted by economic historians of Russia, of large-scale serf entrepreneurship and even, on occasion, the amassing of great wealth and prestige (as serfs could own property, except other serfs). Such was the case of the serfs V. I. Prokhorov and Savva Morozov, who bought their way out of serfdom and became major Moscow industrialists.[29] Because the serf peasantry could regard the Russian lands as "theirs"—both because of the possibility of migration and enrichment within those territories and because of their sheer numbers, especially relative to serfowners—the geographical imaginary of Russian serfs is often different from that offered by U.S. slave narratives, where we find that the distinction between slave and "free" territories within the United States, while marked by ambiguities, structures the narratives through and through.[30]

Nonetheless, in spite of these possibilities for enrichment and advancement, serf peasants were decidedly subaltern subjects, and from the late fifteenth through the eighteenth century, noble landowners (in Russian, *poméshchiki*) were gaining more rights as the peasants were losing theirs. By the early eighteenth century, serfholders were moving serf peasants from one estate to another, converting them to domestic serfs, and sometimes buying and selling them with or without land.[31] More typically, however, the serfholder's power over his peasants was restricted to extracting payment of various kinds from them. Peasants would pay their dues either in the form of labor for the landlord, usually three days a week (in an arrangement known as *bárshchina,* best translated by the technical term "corvée"), or in the form of money or goods or produce of some kind (this was called *obrók,* "quit-rent"). Sometimes they paid both; to be obliged to pay obrók alone, as in Nikolai Shipov's case, was thought to be the lightest sort of obligation.

The state exacted its tribute as well, both in the form of direct taxes and, more onerously, by obliging service in the military. After Peter the

Great created a new system of recruitment in 1699, serfholders had to send some of "their" young men to serve in the army. Evidence suggests that the majority of peasants regarded the prospect of recruitment with horror, as it usually meant that the draftee would never return to his village (from 1699 until 1793, the term of service was for life); often, peasants would do anything in their power to avoid losing any of their family members to the recruitment, including paying another serf family to provide a substitute, if they could afford it.[32]

In the villages themselves, the basic social and productive unit was the peasant household. Those households often included two generations, usually blood relations, living under the same roof or in closely adjacent buildings, holding property in common and headed by the senior male in the household, the "patriarch."[33] On the village level, the important decisions on topics like the distribution of land among the various households, the distribution of obligations, recruitment, punishment for various infractions, and so on were made by the assembly of the peasant community, or *mir* (pronounced like "mere"). The meetings of this assembly, often raucous by all reports, were open to all villagers but only "the heads of households with land allotments" could cast votes.[34] Representatives from the assembly were the main mediators between the village on the one side and the master, the state, and judicial authorities on the other.

A small minority (about 4.8 percent in 1851)[35] of serfs worked in the households of the nobles as grooms, cooks, footmen, gardeners, and so on; one of our serf narrators, M. E. Vasilieva, lived her childhood and adolescent years as one of these "*dvorovye,*" or house serfs.[36] Inside these landowner homes was a world far removed from the one the rural peasants knew, especially in the early years of the nineteenth century, by which time the European cultural values imported into Russia by the great autocrats (Peter I and Catherine II above all) had penetrated deeply, even into provincial estate life. Noble landowners dressed in current European fashions, read European literature, and often spoke French rather than Russian among themselves. The resultant cultural gap helped to provide that strong distinction between peasant and landowner that virtually all systems of bondage require as part of their own self-justification. At the same time, some serfs received training in the arts, particularly music and painting, as part of their owners' construction of cultural enclaves for themselves and their noble neighbors.[37]

Of course, along with the French novels, serf choirs, and fancy-dress balls came various progressive streams of European thought that influenced some landowners and helped to erode support for serfdom. It is clear that the influence of the Enlightenment and antislavery thought, whether exerted through literary works, philosophical texts, or otherwise, had an impact upon those members of the educated Russian elite who initiated the process of considering and then implementing an emancipation plan in the late 1850s to early 1860s. Considerations of economics and *Realpolitik*—prompted above all by Russia's defeat in the Crimean War of 1853–56 (which exposed the weaknesses of the largely peasant army), and by the increasing sense that Russia's viability as a competitive "modern" imperial state was being compromised by the old serf order—played a major role as well.[38]

Our four serf narrators experienced, articulated, and in some cases diagnosed the contradictions inherent in this simultaneously serf-based and "Europeanizing" Russian society. Catherine II's contemporary Nikolai Smirnov was an eccentric but just as surely an inevitable product of the serf system: a bondsman of great talent who, due to his serf father's unusual privileges and position, was able to acquire great knowledge and remarkable skills through contact with the highest levels of Russian society. This clearly led both to an intense consciousness of his cultural difference from the serf peasantry to which he legally belonged and to his entirely individual quest for liberation through flight. Similarly, the opportunity afforded P. as an adolescent to work in trade in Russia's capital city exposed him not only to alternative styles of life but also to the secular poetic and dramatic forms—his verse suggests that he knew the work of Pushkin and Krylov—in which he tried to express his outrage at serfdom. Vasilieva's narrative takes place largely within a closed and seemingly eternal past of bondage and domination, but her subjective trajectory—especially on the evening of her move from Granny Ustina's cattle yard to the manor house with its footmen, green tubs, and newspapers—finely delineates the gap between peasant and post-Petrine aristocratic culture as experienced by a single consciousness.

It is in Nikolai Shipov's narrative, in which historical actors as important as Napoleon, Imam Shamil, Count Vorontsov, and Tsars Nikolai I and Alexander II themselves appear, that we encounter the richest quilting-together of the interlinked realities of serfdom, imperial expansion, and social and economic modernization. The majority of the soldiers who served in the conflicts against both Napoleon and in the north Caucasus were, of course, serfs (though Shipov doesn't say as much);[39] and Shipov connives to fall into Chechen bondage through his association with Jewish traders accompanying the army on its imperial crusade. Similarly, the entrepreneurial energy of Shipov was of great financial benefit to his owner Saltykov—who had previous owned and then imprudently freed an enterprising serf who later became wealthy—motivating his refusal to free Shipov under any circumstances, even as it was that very profit-making drive, and the worlds it exposed him to, that led Shipov to detest serfdom. Shipov is even able to link his personal emancipation in a prefigural way with the abolition of serfdom *in toto*—after all, he escaped (so he says) on February 19, 1845, exactly sixteen years to the day before Tsar Alexander's decree—and throughout shows his intense consciousness of the way his individual life intersected with more public history.

Indeed, Shipov's is the best example in this volume of a memoir written within the horizon of a developing national historical consciousness in Russia. Historian A. G. Tartakovskii has shown how, in the years following the War of 1812 and under the influence of figures like the poets Alexander Pushkin and Petr Viazemskii and the historian A. I. Mikhailovskii-Danilevskii, Russian intellectuals became concerned with preserving memoirs by individual writers both as a way of "strengthening the historical memory" of the now-modernizing nation and as a basis for the eventual creation of a richly detailed Russian history linking private and national narratives.[40] Shipov's narrative, like Vasilieva's, appeared in *Russian Antiquity* (*Russkaia Starina,* published in Saint Petersburg between 1870 and 1918), a journal devoted to the publication of diverse biographical and autobiographical writings that functioned as a repository—of great use to later scholars—of "historical memory."[41]

It is important to note, however, that the serf narrators writing before the 1861 emancipation, while less able to regard their writings as part of a larger "Russian" story, also conceive of themselves and their predicaments in relationship to the power of the Russian state. Thus we might contrast Shipov's historical consciousness with that of the pre-emancipation poet P., whose fundamental desire is to be an historical actor (he wants to "speak to the Tsar" about the situation of the serfs on behalf of his fellows) but is able to imagine historical change only in visionary and apocalyptic, if also collective, terms. Nikolai Smirnov, born in close physical if not social proximity to the centers of power, must have been aware of the vast state-driven historical shift underway in eighteenth-century Russia—not least because of his position between an "enlightening" nobility and a peasantry whose mental world was essentially that of the fourteenth century—even as his main task in writing was to fend off a lethal punitive threat issued by the state. This "state-consciousness," manifested often as expressions of devotion to the tsar, is one of the features distinguishing the ideological world of Russian serf narrators from their enslaved African American counterparts, for whom the state is largely absent as an imaginative horizon—although other collectivities and institutions, like fellow slaves, religious groups, and abolitionism, certainly play vital roles in the U.S. context.[42]

On the level of representation, the historical-social coordinates of the time are transmuted into distinct mappings of space in each narrative. Smirnov, for instance, contrasts the enlightened Europe he hoped to escape to with what was for him the nightmare of the peasant countryside. The treacherous space of the road—the space of both adventure and dangerous encounters with otherness, in Bakhtin's account[43]—undoes this dualism entirely, leading Smirnov to an unexpected terminus in prison and eventually exile. P., whose story basically begins in Saint Petersburg, offers a more ambivalent account of his own rural context, with joy and terror, peasant solidarity and mutual antagonism, energy and stagnation represented in almost equal measure. To be sure, the cause of the negative term in each of these binaries is found in the almost Sadean manor house of the "soulless" serfowner Bezdoúshin, a stand-in for the nobility as a whole.

For their part, the post-emancipation narrators Shipov and Vasilieva can stand as topographical antipodes, with Shipov as the maximalist and Vasilieva the minimalist. Shipov traces out an enormous map of the Russian empire, from the serf heartland to the less-regulated peripheries where he and his family find temporary freedom. Yet liberty in his narrative is ultimately a matter of actual legal status rather than geography—he ends up a captive, after all, in Chechnya—a point powerfully made when Vorontsov, the leader of the Russian forces in the northern Caucasus at the time, congratulates him on his escape:

> His Highness [Count Vorontsov] spoke very affectionately with me and asked about my time in captivity. At the end he said, with a smile:
>   "Well done! You escaped from them quickly—I suppose you didn't much like it there."
> And with that he rode away from me.[44]

Shipov's discreet and seemingly unconscious silence about the fact that he fell into Chechen captivity precisely in order to "escape from them"—that is, the serfholding nobility, of which Vorontsov was a member—only adds to the quietly stinging irony of the exchange. Indeed, the passage introduces a tension between Shipov's individual story of liberation and the grand and ongoing "national" history (of imperial and military glory), a dissonance of which neither Shipov nor his editors at *Russian Antiquity* may have been aware. Vasilieva (in her persona of "Akul'ka," the serf girl) makes the passage from the cattle yard to the manor house with the aid of the quasimagical donation of a dress to replace her peasant garb—and here we might recall Shipov's use of disguise to facilitate mobility as well, not to mention the inventive camouflaging described by U.S. slave narrators—only to find that the bright new space to which the dress gives her access is more oppressive than the "primitive" space from which she is abducted. The "modernity" of the manor house is exposed as grounded in cruelty and exclusion through and through.[45]

Yet the picture of Russian society offered by these narratives is not a single one. All of the writers are afflicted by "double consciousness," to use W. E. B. Du Bois's term: all of them are conscious of being part of a socially dishonored group even as they are acutely aware of their distinctness from that group. This is particularly true in the case of Smirnov, who clearly and understandably felt no affinity whatsoever for the peasants among whom he was destined to work. Although P. places all the blame for peasant evils on the serfowning nobility, *News about Russia* includes vivid depictions of peasant drunkenness, venality, cruelty, and passivity. In Shipov's case, fellow serfs envious of his family's wealth created almost as many problems for his family as his owner did. However, Shipov is also at pains to display his own integration within that community as a prominent and wealthy member (as, for example, when he dispenses gifts to the poor after his father's death); his extraordinarily meticulous account of his own peasant wedding seems to be informed by a true preservative impulse, as though the elaborate rituals he is recounting needed to be described to the last detail, given that they were already on the wane by the 1880s. Vasilieva's portrayal of the peasantry is perhaps the most positive of those on offer here, if also charged with ambivalence: if she represents serfs as essentially benumbed and passive sufferers, she also makes us sense their reserves of wisdom and ultimate consciousness of the nature and causes of their predicament.

The Narratives as Kinds of Writing

The authors of the four narratives want different sorts of responses from their projected audiences, and we can see in them a chronologically sliding scale of urgency. Smirnov, clearly enough, is concerned to save his own life; his situation requires that he represent his own consciousness in terms of a specific trajectory, from sin to penitence, and yet his explanation requires that he shows what led him into sin—namely, his situation as a serf. In treading this fine line between penitence and self-justification, Smirnov's deposition indicts serfdom as well as himself, and one can only wonder if Smirnov—whose command of extraordinarily complex sentence structure, poetic formulae, and narrative construction is nothing short of remarkable—was not conscious of this duality in his own text, although he was certainly terrified during the writing of it.

For his part, the poet P. represents himself as passing from a naïveté about his situation to a consciousness brought about specifically through the narrative device of hearing the stories of others, of the immensity of the problem of serfdom. As with Smirnov, it seems that he views his display of poetic skill as another basis for taking his text seriously. He uses the socially valued form of poetry to insert a legitimacy into his work that it would otherwise lack, which is especially important given his paradoxical decision to versify quite ordinary feelings and surmises—his thoughts while riding in a cart, for example, or the impression made upon him by some casual conversation—over the course of the poem.[46]

Indeed, in one way or another, writing itself is inevitably thematized in these serf writings, if only because it was literacy above all that both made the composition of the narratives possible and distinguished these serf narrators from the majority of their fellow bondspeople. Both Smirnov and Vasilieva achieved their knowledge of reading and writing by virtue of living in close proximity to their owners. In Smirnov's case, his father, a highly placed serf bailiff, was able to help finance his son's education; for Vasilieva, the separation from her earlier, pre-literate life is marked punctually by the sight of the newspaper she sees in the hands of her owner on the evening of her almost-surreal arrival in the manor house. On the other hand, Shipov and P. learned to read through church training and in the city, and Shipov's self-liberation from serfdom would have been impossible had he been illiterate; his perusal of the Russian legal codes seems at once a kind of patriotic interest in the laws of the fatherland and (because of the use he makes of them) a totally subversive and criminal use of his own literacy—"reading as poaching," in Michel de Certeau's terms.[47]

Finally, it should be noted that all of the authors here were in some sense Russian Orthodox believers—although Vasilieva does not in fact use any religious language—and throughout, the language of piety helps to legitimize their writings as testimony. Most Russian villages had a church, and Orthodox faith and ritual were central to the lives of the peasants. The serf narratives presented here, of course, present those religious sentiments through the prism of specific experiences and contexts. If Smirnov's rhetorical supplications involve constant reference to God's justice in having thwarted his "evil" intentions to escape, P.'s religious language is of a far more mythic and visionary cast, including constant reference to God's justice and occasionally—as in the case of African American religious discourse—to the Mosaic idea of liberation from bondage. The most recognizably pious writer is certainly Nikolai Shipov, who stresses his own piety (which extends to teetotaling, a surprising choice for a Russian peasant) in part to emphasize his Russianness and patriotism, in spite of his own transgressive use of Russian law and obvious fascination with and appreciation of cultural "others" within the Russian Empire.

Much more could be said about these texts as literary works, especially if placed more firmly within the necessary comparative context of juxtaposition with U.S. slave narratives, from which my characterization of them as "serf narratives" derives. Further investigation will be required to shed light on what we might call the contrasting formal mechanisms of slave and serf narratives (as distinct from their obviously different content), in order to give theoretical breadth to the notion of "slave narrative" as such. Eventually, comparative reflection on slave and serf narratives might have something to contribute to our notions of autobiography more generally, especially in its relation to notions of "subjective autonomy" and "collective solidarity"—and their putative opposites—as they emerged during the modern period.

Notes

1. The original text of the deposition is in the Russian State Archive of Ancient Documents, Moscow, section 7, file 2679, pages 66–67 recto and verso, from the year 1785. It was first published under the editorship of K. V. Sivkov under the title "Avtobiografiia krespostnogo intelligenta kontsa 18-ogo veka" in *Istoricheskii arkhiv* 5 (Leningrad: Akademiia Nauk SSSR, 1950), 288–299.

2. The poem was sent as a "letter of protest" to Tsar Nicholas I in 1849, and was first published in T. G. Snytko, ed., *Vesti o Rossii: Povest' v stikhakh krepostnogo kres'ianina* (Iaroslavl': Iaroslavskoe knizhnoe izdatel'stvo, 1961). The manuscript is in the State Archive of the Russian Federation (GARF), archive 109, file 100, from the year 1850.

3. N. N. Shipov, "Istoriia moei zhizni: Razskaz byvshago krepostnago krest'ianina N. N. Shipova," *Russkaia Starina* 30 (1881). An abridged version was published in 1933 under the editorship of N. L. Zhatkin (V. N. Karpov, *Vospominaniia,* and N. N. Shipov, *Istoriia moei zhizni* [Moscow and Leningrad: Academia, 1933], 363–523).

4. M. E. Vasilieva, "Zapiski krepostnoi," *Russkaia Starina* 145 (1911): 140–151. My translation and introduction appeared as "Notes of a Serf Woman by M. E. Vasilieva" in *Slavery and Abolition* 21:1 (April 2000): 146–168.

5. The only Russian collection appeared two years ago: *Vospominaniia Russkikh Krest'ian XVIII–Pervoi Poloviny XIX Veka,* ed. and intro. by V. A. Koshelev (Moscow: Novoe Literaturnoe Obozrenie, 2006). Of the nine narratives printed there (along with one village chronicle), only Nikolai Shipov's is translated in the present volume. The others are by L. A. Travin, A. G. Khrushchova, S. D. Purlevskii, A. Ia. Artynov, I. V. Vasil'ev, I. M. Kabeshtov, F. D. Bobkov, and M. E. Nikolaev. Purlevskii's narrative has been translated (with an excellent introduction) as Savva Dmitrievich Purlevskii, *A Life under Russian Serfdom: Memoirs of Savva Dmitrievich Purlevskii,* ed., trans., and intro. by Boris B. Gorshkov (Budapest and New York: Central European University Press, 2005).

6. In her 1983 study of the "serf intelligentsia," M. D. Kurmacheva identifies twelve autobiographies or portions of autobiographies that recount serf experiences. In addition to Smirnov's and Shipov's, she mentions the major autobiography of Aleksandr Nikitenko (mentioned in following paragraphs) and those of N. Shcherban', L. P. Nikulinaia-Kositskaia, F. D. Bobkov, I. A. Golyshev, I. K. Zaitsev, V. E. Raev, P. I. Gusev, G. Ia. Lomakin, and I. P. Spekhin (M. D. Kurmacheva, *Krepostnaia intelligentsiia Rossii: Vtoraia polovina XVIII–nachalo XIX veka* [Moscow: Nauka, 1983], 152–176); the recent Russian collection of peasant narratives includes seven others (see note 5). A number of these narratives appeared in the journal *Russkaia Starina* (*Russian Antiquity*), which also published the narratives by Shipov and Vasilieva.

7. Vasilieva's narrative has been cited as an example of serf autobiography by Peter Kolchin in his indispensable comparative study (*Unfree Labor: American Slavery and Russian Serfdom* [Cambridge, MA, and London: Belknap Press of Harvard University Press, 1987], 379), and *News about Russia* has been employed by both Kolchin and Daniel Field (in the latter's case, in the classic study of peasant "naïve monarchism," *Rebels in the Name of the Tsar* [Boston: Unwin Hyman, 1989]).

8. On these debates, see John W. Blassingame's introduction to his edited collection *Slave Testimony: Two Centuries of Letters, Speeches, Interviews, and Autobiographies* (Baton Rouge: Louisiana State University Press, 1977), xvii–lxv.

9. See Peter Kolchin's bibliographical note in *Unfree Labor,* 379; and David Moon, *The Abolition of Serfdom in Russia, 1762–1907* (Harlow and London: Longman, 2001), 29–36.

10. On the various sources of U.S. slave testimony and the problems associated with using them in historical study, see Blassingame, *Slave Testimony,* xl–lxv. On the situation in the Soviet Union in the 1930s, see Sheila Fitzpatrick, *Stalin's Peasants: Resistance and Survival in the Russian Village after Collectivization* (New York and Oxford: Oxford University Press, 1994).

11. See note 5.

12. Apparently, the first use of the term "serf intelligentsia" occurred in 1883, in Ekaterina Letkova's article of that title ("Krepostnaia intelligentsia," *Otechestvennye Zapiski* [November 1883]: 157–198); the term was employed in the Soviet period by E. S. Kots (*Krepostnaia intelligensiia* [Leningrad: Seiatel', 1926]) and M. D. Kurmatcheva (*Krepostnaia intelligentsiia Rossii*), among others. See Richard Stites, *Serfdom, Society, and the Arts in Imperial Russia: The Pleasure and the Power* (New Haven, CT, and London: Yale University Press, 2005), 35–36.

13. In addition to the works by Kolchin and Field, mention should be made of studies by Elise Kimerling Wirtschafter, especially *From Serf to Russian Soldier* (Princeton, NJ: Princeton University Press, 1990) and *Social Identity in Imperial Russia* (DeKalb: Northern Illinois University Press, 1997), where mention is made of Nikolai Shipov's narrative (70); and the essay by Daniel Brower and Susan Layton, "Liberation through Captivity: Nikolai Shipov's Adventures in the Imperial Borderlands," *Kritika: Explorations in Russian and Eurasian History* 6:2 (Spring 2005): 259–279.

14. Aleksandr Nikitenko, *Up From Serfdom: My Childhood and Youth in Russia, 1804–1824,* trans. Helen Saltz Jacobson, intro. by Peter Kolchin (New Haven, CT, and London: Yale University Press, 2001).

15. Particularly important works in these areas include William L. Andrews's *To Tell a Free Story: The First Century of Afro-American Autobiography, 1760–1865* (Urbana and Chicago: University of Illinois Press, 1988); and Paul Gilroy's *The Black Atlantic: Modernity and Double Consciousness* (Cambridge, MA: Harvard University Press, 1993).

16. Both Harriet Beecher Stowe and Tocqueville (see the end of the first volume of *Democracy in America,* with its famous comparison of America and Russia) had a global sense of the problem of slavery and emancipation. On the role played by Stowe's novel among the educated classes in pre-emancipation Russia, see my essay "The First Years of *Uncle Tom's Cabin* in Russia," in Denise Kohn, Sarah Meer, and Emily B. Todd, eds., *Transatlantic Stowe: Harriet Beecher Stowe and European Culture* (Iowa City: University of Iowa Press, 2006), 67–88; and R. D. Orlova's *Khizhina, ustoiavshaia stoletie: O romane G. Bicher-Stou "Khizhina diadi Toma"* (Moscow: Kniga, 1975). For a recent historical treatment that touches on the dialogue about slavery, see Norman E. Saul, *Distant Friends: The United States and Russia, 1763–1867* (Lawrence: University Press of Kansas, 1990).

17. See Smirnov, "Autobiography," 25.

18. Frederick Douglass, "Narrative of the Life of Frederick Douglass," in *Slave Narratives,* ed. William L. Andrews and Henry Louis Gates, Jr. (New York: Library of America, 2000), 329.

19. For more on Shipov's tale and the history of its composition, see Brower and Layton, "Liberation through Captivity," especially 263–264.

20. Vasilieva's story ends with "to be continued," suggesting that the journal intended to present additional installments. But no more appeared and I have been unable to locate any information either about the fate of those plans for future publication or (beyond what is contained in the narrative itself) about the putative author, "M. E. Vasilieva." The actual date of composition of the "Notes" is unknown; it was published in 1911, exactly fifty years after the emancipation of Russia's serfs under Alexander II.

21. Apart from the works by Kolchin, Field, Stites, and Moon previously referred to, the list of the most important English-language studies would include Geroid Tanquary Robinson, *Rural Russia under the Old Régime: A History of the Landlord-Peasant World and a Prologue to the Peasant Revolution of 1917* (Berkeley and Los Angeles: University of California Press, 1932); Jerome Blum, *Lord and Peasant in Russia from the Ninth to the Nineteenth Century* (Princeton, NJ: Princeton University Press, 1961); Steven L. Hoch, *Serfdom and Social Control in Russia: Petrovskoe, a Village in Tambov* (Chicago and London: University of Chicago Press, 1986); and David Moon, *The Russian Peasantry, 1600–1930: The World the Peasants Made* (London: Longman, 1999). Good summaries can be found in Boris B. Gorshkov, "Serfdom: Eastern Europe," in *Encyclopedia of European Social History,* 6 vols.,

ed. Peter N. Stearns (New York: Charles Scribner's Sons, 2001), 2:379–388; and M. L. Bush, *Servitude in Modern Times* (Cambridge, UK: Polity, 2000), 151–160.

22. Boris B. Gorshkov, "Introduction," in Purlevskii, *A Life under Russian Serfdom,* 3.

23. See Kolchin, *Unfree Labor,* 3.

24. Gorshkov, "Introduction," 3. See also Gorshkov's "Serfs on the Move: Peasant Seasonal Migration in Pre-Reform Russia, 1800–61," *Kritika: Explorations in Russian and Eurasian History* 1:4 (Fall 2000): 627–656.

25. Kolchin, *Unfree Labor,* 6.

26. Frontier landlords, usually particularly short of labor, often took advantage of peasant flight from the center and were therefore less opposed to it, while larger landlords were confident that they could offer better terms and, additionally, "had the muscle to defend their interests by force if necessary" (ibid., 8).

27. Ibid., 7.

28. Gorshkov gives the best account of peasant migrant labor in his "Serfs on the Move." Interestingly, the Central Industrial Area (the heartland of serfdom, which included Moscow, Iaroslavl', and Nizhnii Novgorod provinces among others) saw particularly high rates of peasant migration, in part because the poor soil fertility led peasants to seek other ways of making money to support their families and pay their rent (Gorshkov, "Serfs on the Move," 632). There were, of course, considerable variations in the character of serfdom across Russia and even from village to village, and local traditions and practices were of crucial importance. (The poet P., it will be seen, has an intense consciousness of himself as a peasant from the Iaroslavl' area.) These local differences have not been sufficiently studied, however, and I know of no great synthetic discussion along the lines of Ira Berlin's analysis of the geography of U.S. slavery in "Time, Space and the Evolution of Afro-American Society on British Mainland North America," *American Historical Review* 85:1 (February 1980): 44–78. For a brief discussion, see Gorshkov, "Introduction," 10.

29. Gorshkov, "Serfs on the Move," 654. See also Alfred J. Rieber, *Merchants and Entrepreneurs in Imperial Russia* (Chapel Hill: University of North Carolina Press, 1982).

30. See my essay "'And Hold the Bondman Still': Biogeography and Utopia in Slave and Serf Narratives," in *Biography* (Winter 2002): 110–129; here 124–126. The 1850 Fugitive Slave Law, which declared that slaves that had escaped to Northern states be returned to their Southern masters, complicated this territorial distinction.

31. Kolchin, *Unfree Labor,* 41. For an account of a master moving his serfs and his entire household from one place to another, see one of the greatest of all depictions of serf Russia—and a literary masterpiece—S. T. Aksakov's *Family Chronicle,* trans. M. P. Beverley (New York: E. P. Dutton, 1961).

32. Kolchin, *Unfree Labor,* 42, 76–77; Moon, *The Russian Peasantry,* 82–84.

33. Gorshkov, "Introduction," 8; and Jerome Blum, "The Internal Structure and Polity of the European Village Community from the Fifteenth to the Nineteenth Century," *Journal of Modern History* 43:4 (December 1971): 542–576; here 562–563.

34. Blum, "Internal Structure," 554–555. See also Gorshkov, "Introduction," 9; and Kolchin, *Unfree Labor,* 201–206.

35. Kolchin, *Unfree Labor,* 161.

36. Nikolai Smirnov also clearly grew up inside the Golitsyn home (see previous summary), but it is unclear whether he carried out any labor duties in his childhood and youth.

37. See Tat'iana Dynnik, *Krepostnoi Teatr* (Moscow and Leningrad: Academia, 1933);

Priscilla Roosevelt, *Life on the Russian Country Estate: A Social and Cultural History* (New Haven, CT: Yale University Press, 1995); and Stites, *Serfdom, Society, and the Arts in Imperial Russia.* In her narrative, M. E. Vasilieva recounts being taught ballet steps in the manor house alongside the daughters of her master.

38. On the emancipation process itself, see Daniel Field, *The End of Serfdom: Nobility and Bureaucracy in Russia, 1855–61* (Cambridge, MA, and London: Harvard University Press, 1976). For an excellent discussion of the variety of reasons behind the emancipation, see Moon, *The Abolition of Serfdom in Russia,* 19–55; for a comparison with the circumstances conditioning other emancipations (specifically the U.S. case), see Peter Kolchin, "Some Controversial Questions concerning Nineteenth-century Emancipation from Slavery and Serfdom," in *Serfdom and Slavery: Studies in Legal Bondage,* ed. M. L. Bush (London and New York: Longman, 1996), 42–67. It should be noted that it does not appear that serfdom was in itself an "unprofitable" institution in economic terms; rather, it would be better to say that the productive relations dominant within serfdom were felt by at least some to be a barrier to development. As Kolchin puts it (comparing serfdom with the profitable slave economy of the U.S. South), "Neither [serf Russia nor the slave South] underwent the kind of economic transformation experienced by England and the northern United States. The failure of any major slaveholding or serfholding society to go through this kind of transformation raises serious questions about the ultimate compatibility of capitalism and forced labor" (Kolchin, "Some Controversial Questions," 48).

39. Not until Tolstoy's *Hadji Murat* in 1904 can we find a truly lucid literary representation of this link between bondage and expansion, in the person of the serf soldier Avdeev. On the relationship between serfdom and empire in Russia, see Kolchin, "Some Controversial Questions," 1–4.

40. A. G. Tartakovskii, *Russkaia Memuaristika i Istoricheskaia Soznanie XIX Veka* (Moscow: Arkheograficheskii Tsentr, 1997), 337.

41. To be sure, Vasilieva's narrative, published thirty years after Shipov's in 1911, is both less clearly tied to "national" events and more unsparingly critical of the serf order and of the aristocracy in particular; perhaps her tone is conditioned by some of those socially critical attitudes that emerged in the wake of the tumultuous 1905 Revolution, which helped bring about a general politicization of society and heightening of class tensions.

42. On this topic, see my essay "Form and Authority in Russian Serf Autobiography," in *Captivating Subjects: Writing Confinement, Citizenship and Nationhood in the Nineteenth Century,* ed. Jason Haslam and Julia M. Wright (Toronto: University of Toronto Press, 2005), 57–85. In an important and little-known essay, Alois Schmücker has shown how Russian aristocratic memoirists of the eighteenth century represented their lives and their terms of state service as virtually co-extensive; see his "Anfänge und erste Entwicklung der Autobiographie in Russland (1760–1830)," in *Die Autobiographie: Zu Form und Geschichte einer literarischen Gattung,* ed. Günter Niggl (Darmstadt, Germany: Wissenschaftliche Buchgesellschaft, 1998), 414–458.

43. See M. M. Bakhtin, "Forms of Time and of the Chronotope in the Novel," *The Dialogic Imagination,* ed. Michael Holquist, trans. Caryl Emerson and Michael Holquist (Austin: University of Texas Press, 1981).

44. See Shipov, "Story of My Life," 194.

45. For more in-depth analysis of the spatiality of Russian serf and U.S. slave narratives, see my "'And Hold the Bondman Still.'"

46. For more on the relationship between style and rhetorical authority in these narratives, see my essay "Form and Authority in Russian Serf Autobiography."

47. Michel de Certeau, *The Practice of Everyday Life,* trans. Steven Rendall (Berkeley: University of California Press, 1984), 165–176.

Nikolai Smirnov

Autobiography

Among the documents of the Saint Petersburg Secret Investigation Office is a file from 1785 on the attempted flight across the western Russian border of the serf Nikolai Smirnov (1767–1800).[1] The file contains his deposition, in which he recounts how he came to decide upon flight and how he attempted to realize his plan.

Other documents in the file show that, after being captured, Smirnov was tried in the lower and upper courts and in the chamber of the criminal court. The first two courts maintained that for some of his crimes he deserved the death penalty, while the other courts asserted that the penalty should be public flogging with a knout, accompanied by the slicing-off of his left ear and exile to his masters' estate. The chamber of the criminal court pronounced hanging as its initial verdict. But in response to an old decree (of September 30, 1754) regarding abolition of the death penalty, they decided that Smirnov should be given ten blows with the knout, have his nostrils ripped open, be branded (presumably on the forehead), and sent in shackles to hard labor in Riga.

It was at this point that Smirnov composed his narrative as both an explanation of his deeds and as a desperate if ambivalent expression of penitence.

---

1. This original text is in the Russian State Archive of Ancient Documents, Moscow, section 7, file 2679, pp. 66–67 recto and verso, from the year 1785. It was published under the editorship of K. V. Sivkov under the title "Avtobiografiia krespostnogo intelligenta kontsa 18-ogo veka" in *Istoricheskii arkhiv* 5 (Leningrad: Akademii Nauk SSSR, 1950), 288–299.

❧

July 15, 1785—the deposition of the serf Nikolai Smirnov, arrested for attempting to flee across the border and other offences:

On July 15, 1785, a certain Nikolai Smirnov, a man belonging to the Princes Golitsyn and sent from the local Governor General Major Kanovitsyn, on being asked while in the premises of the general prosecutor about all his crimes and with what intentions he did them, asked to be allowed to write his account of them himself. This was permitted, and with his own hand he wrote first a draft, then a clean, final copy of the following:

My father and all my family are serfs belonging to the deceased Major General Prince Andrei Mikhailovich Golitsyn.[2] At the time of his death in 1770, his three young sons and all his property were entrusted, by order of her Royal Highness,[3] to the guardianship of his brother (the likewise now-deceased General Field Marshal Prince Alexander Mikhailovich Golitsyn),[4] the General in Chief Ivan Mikhailovich Izmailov,[5] Brigadier Nikolai Grigorievich Naumov, and Colonel Prince Dmitri Vasilievich Golitsyn.[6] Because Prince Dmitri Vasilievich had already died seven years earlier, the head chamberlain Prince Alexander Mikhailovich Golitsyn was appointed to his place by order of the Government Senate.

In 1778 the young princes went abroad to foreign lands for their education, and my father's brother went there with them. My father is the manager of all the estates and property of my masters, just as he was during the lifetime of the deceased princes.

---

2. Andrei Mikhailovich Golitsyn (b. August 15, 1729–d. February 23, 1770) was married to Princess Elizaveta Borisovna Yusupova (b. April 27, 1743–d. August 29, 1770). He served in the army as major general. His three sons were Mikhail Andreevich (1765–1812), Boris (1766–1822), and Aleksei (1767–1800).

3. Catherine II (the Great).

4. Alexander Mikhailovich Golitsyn (b. November 17, 1718–d. October 8, 1783) was married to Daria Alekseevna Gagarina (1724–98); the couple had no children. A. M. Golitsyn was a famous field marshal who fought against the Turks and was later a favorite of Catherine.

5. Ivan Mikhailovich Izmailov (d. 1787), member of the Section of Secret Affairs [*Prikaz Tainykh Del*], an important administrative unit answerable only to the tsar. He was married to Aleksandra Borisovna Yusupova (sister of Elisaveta).

6. Dmitri Vasilievich Golitsyn (1708–78).

I was raised in my father's house, and with his own funds he paid for my education in various sciences. At first I was educated in Russian grammar and spelling, and afterward was brought into the home of my teacher and taught the basic rudiments of the French and Italian languages. Later I concluded my study of these languages, with decent grades, at Moscow University, which I attended privately with the permission of the general director. Not having been manumitted by our masters, I could not register there formally.

At the university, apart from the two languages already mentioned, I finished studying Russian grammar and began learning Russian rhetoric, English, history, geography, mythology, iconology, and the rudiments of physics and chemistry. During my free time and with various teachers I studied draftsmanship, painting, architecture, geodesics, and the fundamentals of mathematics. I continued these studies for about eight months, after which time I had to leave off and remain idle for several months due to an illness I contracted. After my recovery, my father needed me to do the master's business and kept me by his side, thereby terminating my entire course of study.

But after a time and as a consequence of my own importunate requests, he allowed me to resume my studies at home. He arranged for Mr. Desnitskii, professor at Moscow University, to come over to teach me English, a subject for which I had a great predilection.[7] I continued to study architecture and drawing in the drafting office of Mr. Blank, state advisor and architect, under Mr. Blank's own supervision.[8] I went on studying other subjects as best I could, including French, Italian, history, geography, mythology,

7. Semyon Efimovich Desnitskii (1740?–89), professor of jurisprudence at Moscow University, often regarded as the founder of modern Russian legal theory and a critic, in such works as "Predstavleniia o uchrezhdenii zakonodatel'noi, suditel'noi i nakazatel'noi vlasti v Rossiskoi imperii" ("Ideas on institutions of legal, judicial and punitive power in the Russian empire," 1768), of the institution of serfdom. He was sent, along with Ivan Tretyakov, by I. I. Shuvalov to study in Scotland; he studied at Glasgow University from 1761 to 1767. There he heard Adam Smith's lectures on moral philosophy and may have been personally acquainted with Smith. (He also translated a work by one Thomas Borden, "Nastavnik zemledel'cheskii" ("The agricultural preceptor"). See Pavel S. Gratsianskii, *Desnitskii* (Moscow: Iuridicheskaia Literatura, 1978).

8. This may well be the architect Karl Blank, who worked under the famous M. F. Kazakov. Blank was involved in designing the connection of the houses of the Golitsyns and Dolgorukovs in 1774 (see T. F. Savarenskaia, ed., *Arkhitekturnye ansambli Moskvy: XV-nachala XX vekov* [Moscow: Stroiizdat, 1997], 228). There was also an I. Blank who worked in architecture.

G. V. Soroka, "The Office at Ostrovki." Soroka (born in 1823, died by his own hand in 1864), the son of serfs, painted this image of the estate office of his master, N. P. Miliukov, in 1844.

and iconology, but had to drop chemistry and physics, not being able to continue them without a teacher.

I persevered in this regime of learning for a year or more, despite the fact that my studies were interrupted almost daily by various matters pertaining to the estate and the house. I would have gone on even longer if I had not been compelled to go to the master's village to help carry out various plans having to do with wastelands and settlements. With this I was busy all summer until the end of autumn.

Then, after returning to my father's house, I was occupied for several months with the government census. The result was that, for almost a year, I left my studies untouched and forgot the better part of what I had begun to learn.

This unsettled life distressed me greatly. In spite of my bad health I tried with all my strength to renew my now-lapsed studies. My efforts were fruitless, however, for every day I was compelled to write and copy orders and expense sheets for the village, to work on the account books, and to do many others things concerning the house and the estate. For these things I had not the slightest ability or inclination.

These ongoing vexations and the barriers continually placed in the way of my desires made my life at that time utterly hateful to me. The degrading name of slave [*kholóp*] continually presented me with the fact that I was in bondage, on a heavy and oppressing chain. Thus I was driven to ask my father in the strongest possible terms if he might petition the masters and guardians for my emancipation. This he did, despite the fact that he had already gone to them with this request and had received no satisfaction whatsoever. Just as before, his request was denied, and I was left without the slightest hope of ever enjoying that which seemed more precious than anything: freedom.

This failure, together with the misery and grief I very often faced, deepened my detestation of bondage. Being unfortunately of a weak, highly sensitive, and passionate constitution, I could not tolerate this tormenting unease for long. After taking away what remained of my health, the pitiless disease that had manifested itself in me the previous spring soon brought me to the very portal of the grave. Not only did my family lose all hope for my recovery, they were, in addition, unable to find any remedy, knowing as they did the reason for my grief. The end of my unhappy life seemed very near indeed; but my youth, the efforts of doctors, and also perhaps the will of fate—as though preparing me for incomparably greater trouble to come—wrested me out of the greedy jaws of death. Nonetheless, for a long time I was still unable to recover—or rather, I did not bother to tend to my own recovery, consumed as I was by despair.

Finally I recovered my former health, and with it all the despondency and melancholy that had so gnawed at me. After miserably languishing more than three months, and observing that my health was again growing weaker by the hour, I took up the bold intention of once more asking our lords and guardians for the gift of freedom. I gave them a letter of petition I had written myself, in which I explained the reasons that had induced me to take such a step, and revealed my total detestation of and incapacity for slavery. I proposed that either I be made free in perpetuity, with the proviso that my maternal uncle, the nobleman Seniavin,[9] should in this case compensate for the great loss thereby incurred by my masters by offering up two of his own men suitable for recruitment in exchange, or that I should be sent into the army myself. But this tearful request was also scorned. With it I effected no change whatsoever in my life, apart from incurring the wrath and disdain of my masters and the displeasure of my father.

This blow was decisive! I offer my most heartfelt admission, to my eternal shame and vilification, that my blindness then exceeded all measure: I held the voice of reason in contempt and swore in my innermost soul that I would either succeed in obtaining my freedom or perish. I merely waited for a time suitable for the fulfillment of my contemptible intention, not thinking at all about what destructive consequences might come of this.

Soon after this I learned from a governor who had returned over the past winter from the home of my masters that they were to begin their voyage through Europe at the beginning of summer. In my blindness, I regarded this circumstance as auspicious indeed, promising recompense for all the persecutions I had suffered at the hands of pitiless fate. I adopted the intention, detestable and ruinous to me forevermore, of secretly leaving my homeland and my father's house, secreting away from him a sum of money sufficient for travel and shelter. I would then travel directly to my young lords and, appearing before them, beg of them both forgiveness for my (as I thought) involuntary crime and for my liberty. In addition I hoped to take advantage of their journey to satisfy a desire in which my soul had long since pined, namely, to visit foreign lands together with them. Upon receiving from them a letter of discharge, I hoped to remain for a time in Europe to renew, in some university or academy, those studies I had already begun. My greatest desire was to perfect my knowledge of Italian (in which I had already had a good amount of success), architecture, and painting, and I continued to dream of studying these subjects in Rome or Naples. I intended to return to my fatherland afterward and register in the civil service.[10]

9. Some members of the Seniavin family were famous naval commanders; however, I have been unable to find out more about Smirnov's "uncle."

10. On the practice of educating serfs as musicians, painters, and actors, see Richard Stites, *Serfdom, Society, and the Arts in Imperial Russia: The Pleasure and the Power* (New Haven, CT, and London: Yale University Press, 2005), 71–84, 238–243, 288–291, 332–343.

I revealed all of this to Matvei Kurbatov, a serf who had belonged to the dead General Lieutenant Prince Peter Mikhailovich Golitsyn, and who had also studied architecture with me. Kurbatov had more than once complained to me about his wretched condition and expressed his intention of being rid of it, in spite of the fact that this would involve subjecting himself to the greatest danger. He listened to my proposal with joy and vowed to share with me all that might befall us.

Through an officer with whom I was acquainted, Schliepenbach by name, I secured two orders for fresh post-horses, one in the name of the Lieutenant Miloslavtsov warranting passage through Pskov to Riga and the second bearing the name of the Italian merchant Camporesi[11] and allowing for travel to Saint Petersburg. I told the officer that I had been asked by acquaintances to obtain the orders on their behalf; believing this, he tendered them to me.

Finally, forgetting honor, the sacred duty of family, the laws of God and state, and turning my ear away from the wailings of conscience, I stole 3,500 rubles from my father. Together with this money and my comrade Kurbatov, I left Moscow on February 6, [1785], under the name of an Italian merchant, for Novgorod. I intended to leave Novgorod and travel leftward [i.e., west] through Pskov to Riga, as prescribed in my first pass; there I would look for an opportune time to cross the border.

At first this exploit, the first step I had ever taken toward crime, succeeded in accord with God's will, and satisfied my desires in every particular; until I reached Pskov, I encountered no obstacles to my unhappy enterprise. But in that city, righteous God, who takes vengeance against the dishonest and those who transgress his commandments, put a stumbling block in my unlawful path. I stopped at an inn to rest a little from the (for me) unusually fast trip. There I had the misfortune of encountering one of those cunning and artful people who, gifted from birth with all intellectual and physical qualities except honesty and wealth, live at the expense of their neighbors and in the shrewdest way transfer into their own pockets the wealth of all those simpletons who happen to fall into their hands.

---

11. It is poignant that Smirnov, who wanted to become an architect, seems to have taken his pseudonym from the Italian architect Francesco Camporesi (1747–1831), who worked in Moscow from the 1780s to the 1820s. From 1784 to 1796 Camporesi worked under Karl Blank (see note 8).

Such a person was the land surveyor Paul.[12] As I learned after my misfortune had already occurred, he had been directly informed by Pushchin, the innkeeper—who apparently was himself involved in various comparable schemes—that a traveling officer, carrying with him a good deal of money, had arrived in the inn. Pushchin informed Paul of this in order that the latter should not squander the opportunity, but rather by any manner of means make my acquaintance and, if possible, secure my trust. Paul fulfilled this laudable directive to the letter. In a short time he was able to draw me into friendship with him, for I, being unfortunately of a sincere and open soul, trustingly believed his deceitful compliments. It was in this way that he tried to make himself look good to me.

Seeing with what zeal he sought my friendship, I hastened to respond to his entreaties with equal kindness and goodwill. The difference was that his falsehearted amity was but a mask, concealing the perfidious intention of transferring that money, which I had secured through dishonest means myself, into his own pocket. My responsiveness was, by contrast, a consequence of my simpleheartedness and sincerity, as well as of the acquiescence of God, who had thus determined to lead me to the edge of that dreadful and bottomless abyss into which my unreflecting youth and haste had plunged me.

In short, Paul, in accord with the will of Pushchin, began by tricking me into staying several days in Pskov. During this time he went with me on several occasions to see Pushchin, to whom he referred as his sincere friend—an appellation that, as far as their identical proclivities were concerned, was truthful. In Pushchin's house, having made my head heavy with strong drink (to which I was not in the least accustomed), they drew me into a card game and, using a counterfeit deck, as Paul later admitted to me, played me out of 300 rubles. After this, seeing that I wouldn't play cards anymore and had no great liking for cards in any case, my sly mentor Paul took another route to the full depletion of my wallet. He convinced me to go with him to celebrate the upcoming Shrovetide in Saint Petersburg. Both his strong entreaties and my friendliness toward him led me to agree to this. I must make the admission, thereby exposing myself to derision, that Paul was so able through his hypocrisy to make his way into my trust that I regarded all his advice as not merely useful, but as necessary.

12. In Russian, *Pol'*. That the land surveyor's name is "Paul" (rather than the Russian "Pavel") suggests that he might be of French origin.

We traveled together soon [from] Pskov, and after stopping for three days in Gdov, where he had his own lodgings, arrived in Saint Petersburg and began living in a single apartment. We lived in the greatest harmony until he, not heeding moderation in the least, robbed me blind, as they say. Not only did he conduct me into sundry dissipations and offer me unavoidable opportunities to expend enormous sums of money (of which he always faithfully received half), he begged still more money of me for some [unnamed] acquaintance of his, using a false signet ring.[13] In one week alone, this acquaintance laid down 350 rubles, a horse, and a tombac watch[14] to me in pawn, in exchange for a gold watch. Paul further cheated me unworthily out of a sum of something less than 200 rubles, and finally, when I was settling accounts with him, swindled me out of more than 200 rubles.

I perceived that all of this was happening and denounced him for it. Doubtless I would have been able to sue him for this money. As I was one hundred times guiltier and more criminal than he was, however, not only did I not attempt to do this, but feared even entering into a dispute with him about the money, anxious that he, learning of my true condition, would turn me in to the authorities.

Thus I resolved that it was better to sacrifice a part of my own ill-gotten property than to risk certain disaster. For among other things, I was then, in opposition to all law, calling myself an "officer" and wore a full-dress uniform in accord with that rank, not having the slightest right to wear it, although at the time (in my stupidity and unreason) I regarded this deception as unimportant. Nonetheless, I did fear that I might face punishment because of my flight from my master and theft of money from my father. I decided to cancel all my accounts with that unconscionable dissembler and part ways with him after having broken off our acquaintance. This I did, and on March 6, having placed my possessions on a cart, sent it off together with my friend Kurbatov to Riga, whither I was planning to travel soon myself. For the trip I gave Kurbatov a travelling pass in my own name, where I dared to call myself a second major, in my inexperience and ignorance realizing neither the terrible punishment I was thereby exposing myself to nor how serious a crime I was committing. The onset of an illness

13. The insignia of a signet ring, used to mark official documents.
14. A watch made of tombac, an alloy of copper and zinc.

obliged me, however, to stay for a few days in Saint Petersburg, and I took lodgings in the London Inn under the assumed name of the Italian merchant. I had told Paul that I was going to Moscow, and this news gladdened him beyond all measure; he was happy that he was so successfully able to fill his pockets with my money.

Our almighty Creator, punishing me for my innumerable crimes, exacerbated my illness to such a degree that it became impossible for me even to leave my room, much less set off on such a long trip. Only the student Gerasimov, who had studied together with me in the university, knew of my stay in Saint Petersburg. He was the only person who came to see me in my new lodgings, which I never left, both because of my illness and from fear of meeting anyone I knew.

Meanwhile head chamberlain Prince Golitsyn, the guardian of our masters, had written to Princess Daria Alekseevna, wife of the deceased Alexander Mikhailovich Golitsyn, asking that she make an effort to find Kurbatov and me however possible. My father, who knew of my long-standing desire to travel to foreign countries, thought that I might be in Saint Petersburg, for it is in that city from whence one can most easily find opportunities to travel to foreign lands. The men entrusted with the task of finding me ascertained that the student Gerasimov knew of my whereabouts. With threats, they drove him into revealing in which room of the London Inn I was living.

Thus nine days after arriving in the city I was arrested by a noncommissioned officer and placed under guard. I was transferred first to the house of Princess Golitsyna,[15] and from thence to the Court of Assembly, where my [initial] deposition was taken. Following that interrogation I was sent to police headquarters, then after a short time in the lower court I was transferred the same day to the city prison.

Before this time I had attributed all the failures of my shameful undertaking to bad luck alone; little by little, however, I began to see just what a terrible labyrinth my unreasonable temper and youthful inexperience had led me into. Nevertheless I was very far from being able to predict even the smallest part of that terrible and painful punishment that I deserved in accord with the full justice of the law. Instead, I comforted myself with the

---

15. The princess Daria Alekseevna (see preceding paragraph).

thought that my adventures would conclude with my being delivered to my master. The only punishment I anticipated from him was conscription in the army, a fate that, not only then in my beleaguered state, but earlier also, I had regarded as the greatest happiness. But the almighty Creator deemed that I would endure incomparably greater grief and unhappiness for my transgressions![16]

On April 11 I was ordered to appear in the criminal court for the pronouncing of the court's resolution. Although I was still enervated by my ongoing illness, I took comfort in the vain hope that there I would soon reach the end of my troubles, and thus succeeded through great effort in arriving at the court. Upon hearing the sentence, dooming me to the most painful and dishonorable death, I felt as though stunned by a death-dealing stroke of thunder. I was still more forcefully smitten by the thought of my impending execution, having so little expected to meet with such a death. In a delirium and barely able to stir, I made it back to my pitiable shelter.

I dispatched a message to the home of my mistress and requested of my former acquaintances there that some one of them might come to see me, again solacing myself with the thought that it might be possible to fend off, if even for a short time, the death-dealing blow. To my total despair, however, I then experienced the rightness of the old saying: "a person has friends in good times, but when bad times come, those friends walk away and despise him." For in response it was told to me that those living in the house already knew of my sentence; since there was no chance of averting it, they dispassionately advised me patiently and nobly to endure the fate that had been assigned to me.

Tormented by woe and regret, forgotten by all, abandoned by the whole world at the end of my calamity-ridden life, I could see greedy death approaching with swift steps. This was a death that would certainly wrest me from out of the number of the living with the most painful torments, abandon my name to eternal disgrace and dishonor, and cover my innocent and unhappy family with shame. I then perceived the full breadth of my crimes and the heaviness of the punishment assigned to me with the full justice of the law. A thousand times I cursed my empty-headed lack of foresight and my straying down the wrong path; with the greatest fervor I

16. Smirnov has in mind the punishments to which he was condemned; see introductory remarks to this narrative.

sent prayers to almighty God, asking for His generous help in my so pitiful and desperate situation. From within the depths of my soul I gave birth to heartfelt regret for all of my transgressions. Finally, seeing that no hope whatsoever remained for my eventual deliverance, I resolved to bear the blow dealt to me by fate, steeling myself as much as possible. Humanity then began to quaver, however; a strong fever accompanied by frequent convulsions nearly succeeded in transporting me earlier than arranged into the dark abode of eternity.

That most terrible hour arrived, when I, standing in the place of execution, had to make amends for my crimes against the laws of God and country with the most ignominious and painful death. I had not the slightest hope of actually being able to survive the punishment assigned to me. The weakness of my constitution, my extreme sensitivity, my health (weakened by long and heavy illness), and my youth—all assured me that the hour of the fulfillment of the execution would be my last hour on earth.

The requisite number of guards had already gathered to accompany me and a priest had been sent to provide a dispensation for my sins and to administer the last rites. . . .

But then our almighty Creator looked with an eye of mercy on my sincere and clean-hearted regret and accepted my ardent prayers, sent up to Him from the depths of my soul. He instilled pity into the heart of the officer on duty there at the city prison. The officer observed that I was already barely breathing and postponed my transfer for a short time. He took it upon himself to report to the lord governor that not only was I unable to be conveyed to the place of execution, but that I would probably live only a few hours as it was. Soon a doctor was sent from the police headquarters to observe me. He found me in the most extreme state and reported this to the lord governor; for this reason, an order was sent that I be left in the infirmary of the prison until I recovered, and that a report on my condition be sent to the police headquarters every day.

This unquestionable sign of God's mercy, entirely unexpected by me, I accepted with the most heartfelt gratitude. As soon as my weakness allowed me to write, I composed a letter to her highness Daria Alekseevna, tearfully asking her to intervene into my woeful and desperate situation, and by her intercession preserve me from a most unspeakable death and my family from eternal dishonor and unhappiness. Wavering between fear and hope, I spent two days waiting for the decision as to my fate. On the third day I was taken by carriage to the home of his highness Prince Aleksandr

Alekseevich Vyazemskii, from whence, because of my illness, I was transferred the next day to the city hospital to recover. There I spent three months, during which time, through the efforts of doctors, I nearly succeeded in reviving the remains of my weak health, undermined as it was by great calamities. After my recovery, I was sent back to his highness on the 14th of that month.

This is the sincere and authentic explanation of all those circumstances that caused me to fall, by my own lack of circumspection, into such terrible troubles. My sole intention was to use the voyage already begun by my lords to see foreign lands along with them and then to petition my freedom from them, a request in which they, of course, would not deny me. Staying for a time in Italy to complete the studies I had begun, I intended to return to my fatherland to enlist in the [state] service.

In regard to my first interrogation: because of countless obstructions and the confusion of my own ideas, I departed from the truth in several places on that occasion and in some places wrote of things that never happened. For example, in the deposition taken from me during my illness by Lord Vyazinin, a member of the lower court, it is written that I had been in the court of her royal empress on more than one occasion before the hour of one in the afternoon. This is untrue; I was there only once, and not inside the inner chambers and only for the shortest time, hoping to inquire about a servant at the court whom I happened to know.

Now, sending the most heartfelt prayers to almighty God for the forgiveness of my heavy sins, I submissively await the decision as to my fate, feeling quite certain that for my crimes I deserve not only the punishment prescribed by law, but even greater chastisement. All my hope and faith I place upon the infinite mercy of God, upon His goodness toward a contrite sinner, and upon the boundless mercy and compassion of our humane and most merciful monarchy.

With that, Smirnov's text ends. His life, however, had a continuation. After a reconsideration of the case in the Secret Investigation Office and a report to Catherine the Great, Smirnov was sentenced by Catherine's order to be sent "as a soldier to the military troops stationed at Tobol'sk." (Tobol'sk was the city to which many of the Decembrists were exiled after their abortive 1825 revolt; see map on page 2.) Smirnov apparently accepted this sentence as a manifestation of the "inexpressible charity of her imperial greatness."[17]

About the later fate of Nikolai Smirnov, the documents of the Secret Investigation Office contain no information. However, there are other sources that make reference to him.

In 1797, Aleksandr Nikolaevich Radishchev (1749–1802) was in Tobol'sk during the last stretch of his period of exile in Siberia, where he had been sent in 1790 for publishing his subversive, anti-serfdom *Journey from St. Petersburg to Moscow*. Both of Radishchev's sons, Nikolai Aleksandrovich and Pavel Aleksandrovich, wrote brief biographies of their father;[18] Pavel's biography of Radishchev contains the following passage: "In 1797 there was a certain Smirnov living in Tobol'sk—a functionary who had been exiled there during Catherine's time for forging a promissory note for 20,000 rubles.[19] He was a freedman formerly belonging to Prince Golitsyn and had been educated with Golitsyn's son. He knew French splendidly well, was involved in literary writing, and sent articles to the journal run by Sokhatskii and Podishvalov, *Pleasant and Useful Ways to Pass the Time*,[20] writing under the pseudonym 'Daurets Nomokhon.'"[21] P. A. Radishchev identified one of Smirnov's articles, entitled "To Death" (1795), which began with the words: "Come, my beloved, and in your embraces I shall find the peace that has hitherto eluded me."[22]

---

17. See Sivkov, "Avtobiografiia krespostnogo intelligenta kontsa 18-ogo veka," 299.

18. D. S. Babkin, ed., *Biografiia A. N. Radishchev, napisannaia ego synov'iami* (Moscow: Akademiia Nauk, 1959). For more on the Smirnov/Radishchev connection, see also L. A. Kogan, *Krepostnye Vol'nodumtsy: XIX vek* (Moscow: Nauka, 1966), 69–70; and M. D. Kurmacheva, *Krepostnaia Intelligentsiia Rossii: Vtoraia polovina XVIII-nachalo XIX veka* (Moscow: Nauka, 1983), 259.

19. This last detail seems to be inaccurate.

20. *Priiatnoe i poleznoe preprovozhdenie vremeni,* published in Moscow from 1794 to 1798.

21. The first half of this pseudonym referred to one of Smirnov's places of exile, namely the Siberian province of Dauria; the second is evidently a calque of his last name into Mongolian. See P. A. Orlov, ed., *Russkaia Sentimental'naia Povest'* (Moscow: Izdatel'stvo Moskovskogo Universiteta, 1979), 142. One of Smirnov's prose works, a short story entitled "Zara" and adapted from Abbé Raynal's *Histoire des deux Indes* (1770), is included in this 1979 volume.

22. *Priiatnoe i poleznoe preprovozhdenie vremeni* 11 (1796): 279.

Smirnov published eleven compositions, some original works and some translations, in *Pleasant and Useful Ways to Pass the Time* between 1794 and 1796.[23]

Apparently Smirnov had extraordinary scribal abilities, being able, according to Pavel Radishchev, to write backward, beginning "with the last letter of the last line and going right to the beginning, without making a single mistake." Radishchev added that when Catherine exiled Smirnov to Siberia, she sent along a note for the governor of Tobol'sk, Denis Ivanovich Chicherin: "I'm sending you a bird—rule it with an iron rod."[24]

In Tobol'sk, Smirnov was employed as a teacher in military institutes and worked in some capacity in mining and factory concerns as well. He died in 1800, three years after having been transferred to work (probably as a scribe or accountant) in a cloth-making factory in Irkutsk, on Lake Baikal.[25]

23. He also published in the journal *Irtysh, prevrashchaiushchiisia v Ippokrenu.* See "N. S. Smirnov" in M. G. Al'tshuller and Iu. M. Lotman, eds., *Poety 1790–1810-x Godov* [*Biblioteka Poeta,* 2nd ed.] (Leningrad: Sovetskii Pisatel', 1971), 195–196. Six of Smirnov's poems were published in this 1971 volume (pp. 196–204).

24. Babkin, *Biografiia A. N. Radishchev,* 72.

25. Al'tshuller and Lotman, *Poety 1790–1810-x Godov,* 196.

P. (Petr O.)

News about Russia

In August of 1849, a thick packet was given to the main post office in Saint Petersburg, addressed to Prince Petr Georgievich Ol'denburgskii, a liberal-thinking aristocrat and relative of the tsar whose family estate was in the district of Iaroslavl', northeast of Moscow. The half-literate scribblings on the packet, the cheap paper of which the envelope was made, and the absence of the name of the sender, all struck the prince's subordinate officials as suspicious, and the packet was not accepted.

The packet was kept at the post office for seven months, in the expectation that the sender would return for it. In March of 1850, the packet was to be destroyed by the "dead letter" office. Before burning unclaimed mail, however, the usual practice was to open the letters and see what was inside. On this occasion, the postal officials found a notebook inside a covering of canvas, filled with verses.

On the cover of the notebook were the following words: "This book, called *News about Russia,* is taken from the life of the *mir* [peasant community], from the deeds and words of the people, with an appendix in verse, by Petr O.... I would now like to dedicate my verse to the sovereign Emperor Nikolai under the following conditions: (1) that he read everything contained in the manuscript; and (2) that after reading it, he not prosecute the writer. Without prior agreement to these conditions, the manuscript is not be read by the sovereign emperor Nikolai I and his exalted royal family, but consigned to the flames. The writer of the manuscript is a half-literate serf, belonging in body to a lord but in soul to Christ, Petr."

After reading the verses and finding their contents "blameworthy," postal officials sent the packet to the Third Department (the political investigation and surveillance service) of the tsar's chancellery.[1] Count Aleksei Fyodorovich Orlov, the boss of the Third Department from 1844–56, looked at the verses and informed Prince Ol'denburgskii of them. Orlov ordered his subordinates to look at other suspicious texts to see if "they could not find a similar hand or comparable forms of expression." But they failed to find the author of the verses, and the notebook was put into a file in the archive of the Third Department, where it was kept until the twentieth century. *News about Russia* was published only once, in 1961 (the centenary of the emancipation of the serfs), under the editorship of T. G. Snytko, who apparently rediscovered the manuscript.[2]

News about Russia was not the only piece of verse protest sent to the tsar, but it was, it seems, by far the longest and most ambitious.[3] The basic text is divided into three parts: a short preface "On the Life of the Author, P."; the long central section, "News and Prophecy about Russia," of which the central event is the serf narrator's failed attempt to marry a free peasant girl; and "News about Russia" proper, devoted to the recollections of the matchmaker Solomónida about how her serf parents sold her as a child to a free, childless peasant couple.

The simple frame structure of the poem is richly complicated by the generous insertion of dream visions, songs, and especially "side" narratives told in what appear to be semi-fictionalized voices other than the narrator's. Thus, within a tale told by the matchmaker Solomónida, a

---

1. For more on this organization, see P. S. Squire, *The Third Department: The Establishment and Practices of the Political Police in the Russia of Nicholas I* (Cambridge: Cambridge University Press, 1968).

2. T. G. Snytko, ed., *Vesti o Rossii: Povest' v stikhakh krepostnogo kres'ianina* (Iaroslavl': Iaroslavskoe knizhnoe izdatel'stvo, 1961). I have included a number of Snytko's explanatory notes here. The manuscript is in the State Archive of the Russian Federation (GARF), archive 109, file 100, from the year 1850. The poem was clearly thought to be authentic by the original investigators and has been treated as such by later historians, including Daniel Field in his *Rebels in the Name of the Tsar* (Boston: Unwin Hyman, 1989) and Peter Kolchin in his *Unfree Labor: American Slavery and Russian Serfdom* (Cambridge, MA, and London: Belknap Press of Harvard University Press, 1987).

3. Others included the "Historical Tale" by one Semyon Oleinichuk, and the anonymous "Voice of a Russian to the Tsar."

character will begin to tell a tale about someone else, who will also in turn begin his or her own independent narrative, until the reader finds himself at several removes from the main narrator, "P." I have attempted to reduce the confusion created by this technique through the insertion of some additional headings and parentheses, in order to indicate exactly who is speaking at a given point.

The language of the poem shows at once the author's literary pretensions (the use of poetic diction like "zephyrs," "ether," "halls of glory"; quotations from the verse fabulist Ivan Krylov), his semi-literacy (as registered in his grammatical inventiveness and rather restricted vocabulary), and his Iaroslavl' pedigree (especially as displayed in the rhymes, as when normally pronounced as "yo" [ë] are clearly intended to rhyme with the vowel "ye" [e], or the conflation of the instrumental into the dative plural—both of these features were characteristic of Iaroslavl' dialect). The end result is an astonishing syncretism: a mix of autobiography, natural description, dream vision, polemic, and verse drama that invites at least formal comparison with the great long poems of Pushkin and (later) Nikolai Nekrasov.

The translation here includes only the first and second parts of the poem and is based on the original manuscript. With few exceptions, stanza breaks reflect those in the manuscript. I have translated *News about Russia* into lines rather than paragraphs—it is a poem, after all—and have attempted to give some sense of its rhythmic feel (though not the music of its rhyme), and the alternating awkwardness, eloquence, and direct forcefulness of its diction.

Gathered from the life of the *mir*[4]
From the deeds and words of the people
Set in verses
By the half-literate peasant P.,
Belonging in body to a landlord,
But in soul, to Christ.

4. Pronounced like "mere": the peasant community; see the introduction.

Preface: On the Life of the Author, P.

It was in the village that I entered
Into childhood memory, and in the village
I grew until I had attained fifteen years,
With my family conjoined in one unit,
Among their labors, needs, and troubles.

My father, a man of ambition,
Went off in search of arts and trades.
Not finding them, he abandoned himself
To dissipation, drunkenness,
And lost the respect of his family.

Mother often reminded us
Of those earlier, happy years:
Their lives had passed in prosperity,
In the profitable business of trade.
She endured hardship later, as our condition
Declined, approached the extremes.
Often she'd release a stream of tears
When looking upon the poverty
Of her children, her very own.
With diligence she taught us
To pray to God, to labor always.
"Perhaps," she would say to neighbors,
"We will find happiness in our children."

I tried to help my mother
Always, and in everything.
Actively I engaged in work,
Women's work and men's work.
I learned to read and write, too,
And earlier than all my friends.

But then my parents obtained leave
For me to live and work in the city.
I recall how the carter brought us
Into that populous throng, like a forest.

P. (Petr O.)

For seven years I lived in the city,
(But often sought to visit the village!),
And there I came to know
Different people, another world,
And resolved to write these "News."
I set no store by them, regardless
Of the effort spent: I'm satisfied
That our Creator incited me
To take up writing in the first place,
And that he helped me finish
The middle and the end.

First Part: News and Prophecy about Russia

One spring I set out from the city
To visit our village, where I hoped to see
My relatives and my neighbors.
I was carried away by such a joy
That all my cares were cleaned away
Within my heart, and in my soul.
Leaving behind toil and trade, I rushed off
To see the radiance of spring days.
All the things my eyes remembered
Suddenly returned to me from far away:
Our village, so large, and the sight
Of green fields! And the clear stream
With its pools, where in childhood we swam.

Our hearts knew no afflictions:
We delighted in carefree summers,
Abandoned our huts for the fine weather,
Caught butterflies in the meadows,
Chased bees away from flowers,
Feasted our eyes on the forest birds.
And I could envision the cattle trail
Where the herdsmen would drive the stock;
I could hear the sound of horns and pipes,
And my heart was captured by that sound.
I felt as though I were already entering

The village, seated next to the coachman,
Driving a pair of horses; as though the neighbors
Were running from their houses,
Hurrying after me to wish me well.
Thus I soared upon my thoughts,
Hastening toward the embrace of my family.

Suddenly the images grew dim:
What do my weary eyes see?—
Along the Nevá,[5] a boat with a carrier
And bearing Iaroslávtsy![6]
Noisily we got into the boat,
And quickly put up sail;
The waters flowed with the zephyrs—
A favorable wind carried us along.

Here's how we took leave of the city:[7]

Some in the boat were weeping, some singing,
All heads dizzy with departure—
Wine gained the upper hand over us,
Scratching up sadness with joy,
Sparing neither mind nor heart,
Ruling over reason,
And forbidding thoughtful reverie.

First, the strong and cheerful wine
Lulled everyone in the boat to sleep,
Then gradually departed from everyone's head,
Though not without noise and boasting!
Upon their bags the Iaroslávtsy numbly slept,
Bound by a single wandering thought:
That they'd already finished work
And were hurrying home to rest.

---

5. River, at the mouth of which is situated Saint Petersburg.
6. People of the Iaroslavl' area: the author's fellow countrymen.
7. Saint Petersburg.

P. (Petr O.)

Nine o'clock had struck; by afternoon,
Already worn out by all the company,
I, too, had been won over
By deep and dreamless sleep.
But suddenly a voice was heard again:

—"Ho, people of Iaroslavl'! We've hit some rapids,
And you've got to get to shore!"

I looked—it was already morning,
And on our river road
The water rustled before us.
The earth was already freshened with dew,
The beautiful sun already shining.
How joyous it was! Along the riverbanks
Small flowers caught the eye,
Tiny brooks fell in the Nevá,
Groves and valleys grew green,
And zephyrs played in the branches;
Amid the noisy splendor of trees
Birds were singing everywhere,
Next to the earth and next to the sky.

Here the pilot moored our boat
And had most of us get out.
All the travelers drank their fill
Of brook water, bending to the pebbles;
Their hungover faces were so wrinkled
They seemed to have been shaken
Out of a bag. Paying no heed to nature's
Magnificence, they went along the shore,
And in one voice all denounced
The lazy tax farmer for not opening
An inn for them, on that very spot.[8]

8. Snytko's note: "'Tax-farmers' (in Russian, *otkúpshchiki*) were merchants who had purchased (from the government) the right to sell alcoholic beverages within a specific area. The state monopoly on the sale of alcohol, which had been established in Russia

Worn down with dismal sickness,
They ordered a mooring to the shore.
We sat in down the boat, having just eaten,
And betook ourselves again to sleep.

Meanwhile we heard voices once again:
The pilot and his boy called us
To help let down the sails,
And all the passengers came aboard.
We stepped onto the deck, and soon
Schliesselburg stood before us.[9]
From there our boat descended easily,
Smoothly, from the Nevá into the canals.

Praying to God for great Peter's glory,[10]
Upon that canal I gazed and thought:
"It is a long time since the wise one left,
But his light was bestowed upon the ages.
His kingly life flowed away in cares,
And only death could end his labors.
But in Russia, eternally,
His good deeds will never die.
He was a father to his children,
Worked miracles until he reached the grave,
Saw everything with his luminous eyes.
Now he's taken into the skies, like a god. . . ."

Suddenly a bustling broke off my thought—
Having sailed up to the locks, we stopped,
And each one stepped ashore. Through Schliesselburg
The travelers went their various ways—

------

already in the sixteenth century, took two forms—the sale of 'drink' in state-run taverns, or the transfer of this right of sale to tax-farmers. The two systems were in effect alternately and at several times. From 1819 to 1827, the government controlled the sale of alcohol itself, but the period of 1827 to 1863 saw a revival of the 'tax-farming' system. From this it follows that *News about Russia* was written after 1827."

    9. Town near Saint Petersburg, entry point into canal system.

    10. Peter the Great (1672–1725).

P. (Petr O.)

In eating houses we drank awhile,
Celebrated with feasting,
Till we returned again to shore and sail,
In a boat pulled by a tow horse
Ridden by a boy who drove him on.
Next to the main riverbank road we sailed
With an escort pilot at the wheel.

Thus we sailed through the canal,
And from it into the river,
Amusing ourselves in various ways
As we continued down our long path.
But soon we left the boat, and placed
A throng of bags upon the shore.
Hiring horses in the villages,
We hastened home.

The fields and meadows shone before us,
And choirs of little birds sang in the groves,
As though to me they were proclaiming:
"Look at everything with more perception!
See how the Almighty in heaven
Watches over nature's kingdom!
He, our steward,[11] sends rain
And good weather down to earth.
Then look at the decrepit settlements,
At the life of the ill-fated muzhíks,[12]
Observe the dominance of earthly powers
And the false splendor of their homes.
Then you will see that nature
Has bloomed indeed, has come alive
For humans; but it is a pity that,
From among our people,
None feast their eyes upon her.
The poor slaves in the villages live lives
Half-senseless, superstitious, and crude,

11. *Upravitel',* which also means "steward," "bailiff."
12. Pronounced "moo-ZHEEK": a standard, familiar word for "[male] peasant."

As though in expectance of destruction.
In squalid and filthy clothing
Are men, are women, like shadows."

Shuddering I often thought:
"Are their lives of poverty due to sloth?"
With pity I looked upon them,
Marveled at those who remained vital,
And wished to find among them
Someone more experienced, a person
Who might reveal all things to me clearly.

Well, once we stopped in a village
To change our horses. Muzhíks were bustling,
Loading carts and harnessing horses.
I looked, and out from the backyard rode
An old man, bedecked in gray hairs,
Bent already downward, but no lout.
With a pair of horses he rode along with us.

Cannily could this old man govern
A pair of lines, and well he knew
How to chasten horses without the whip.
He knew how to amuse the travelers
While keeping the cart away from potholes.
He taught the village lads how to drive
With passengers aboard, and with wise words
Subdued their discord and their rowdiness.
One could clearly see that those wild lads
Feared the old man, held his expertise
In high regard; they tempered,
Therefore, their pranks while on the road.

Once by and by, during an uphill stroll,
I spoke with the old man abóut this and that,
And, as part of the conversation,
Inquired about the villagers' lives in general:

"Tell me, old man, the truth about the people,
About their poverty and their blindness.

47

P. (Petr O.)

They're in ruinous shape in these parts—
They live without knowing what day it is. . . ."

The old man seemed to grow angry,
Nodded his head without a word,
And sought in this way to make reply:

    "Yes, we're fated to be unhappy;
    We're born into the world in chains,
    And are bound to live in them unto the grave.
    But you should know, traveler,
    The source of all our poverty:
    It's billeted to our homes (like soldiers!)
    By the custom of the nobles.
    And just as the place is governed stupidly,
    So the vices of the governors
    Have waxed beyond control.
    Let them gather obrók[13] from muzhíks—
    That's business, fine and dandy—
    But they're taking it from girls and from women![14]
    Or take me: already seventy years old,
    And taxed just the same as before.
    They order me to work alongside young men
    (The sweat pouring down my face like a river),
    To struggle and quarrel with fate,
    And beg the Creator to end my life.
    Plagued by torments, I work and work
    But nothing I have, and at all the trouble
    And the ruin, my eyes can hardly bear to look.
    Enlightenment will not pierce through to us
    While within this terrible bondage.

13. Pronounced "ahb-ROHK": "quit-rent," dues paid to the landowner in money or in kind. It contrasted (though sometimes coexisted) with *bárshchina* ("BAR-shcheenah"), the other main form of surplus extraction, where dues were paid in labor (usually three days a week devoted to work for the landlord). Bárshchina is generally translated with the technical term "corvée."

14. Implying, perhaps, sexual "quit-rent."

All of us weaken and fail, enchained in dues,
In thralldom, in ignorance—
Our fathers never taught us how to live
In this wide world; nor we our children.
. . . .[15]
Look, traveler: you see I'm already gray.
But I remember how, when I was still a child,
Standing in the plowed fields, my late grandpa
Spoke out loud in public on this theme:
'We laymen have to work, it's true,
And labor is useful to everyone on earth.
But what a pity: the nobles' robbery
And waste take everything from us!'
And so, you see—we knew long ago
That our lords are the cause of our poverty
And stupidity. So we set our hopes upon
Our Sovereign—and beyond the grave,
The Lord will enlighten the poor."

When the old man finished his speech,
I, now grown afraid, went on:

"Oh my good, my kind old man—
From now on I'll always be surprised
At how easily our minds grow envious,
And with what audacity they succumb
To the temptation of greed."

The Old Man's Speech

Don't be surprised by that, traveler:
The people are stupid in many ways.
See that worldly pile down there—[16]
All the passions in all their forms!

---

15. These and the following ellipses appear in the original manuscript.
16. They are looking down from a hill, presumably at a manor house.

Consider great King Solomon—[17]
The world's luxury seduced him, too,
And he bent his knees before that idol,
And often lost himself in his desires.
They say, however, that he was very wise,
And had enough of every treasure,
And lived in great contentment—
But still everything could not suffice.
So what's there to marvel at here, today?
The people's minds, like some ragged weather vane,
Spin round in lies like foul weather,
And they wander further into the darkness.
Already long ago, we should have made it known
That the people here are suffering
Under slavery; that they pray for their masters,
But only that their own kin might not be punished.
[*End of old man's speech.*]

We reached the top of the hill,
And hurriedly returned to our places
In the cart. The horses rushed along.
Soon we reached a *sloboda,*[18] and there
I took my leave of the good old man.

That respectable sloboda is there regarded
As a town. Water can be seen all round it,
And from its lakes a stream flows into the river.
The Iaroslávtsy gathered in the sloboda
And united into three artels.[19]
But the foremost artel was ours,
And appeared on the jetty like a crowd.
It's as though I can clearly see them now,
Those people, so young and gallant. . . .

17. On Solomon's wealth, see 1 Kings 4:20–25, 9:10–14, 11:4; Matthew 6:29; Luke 12:27.
18. Pronounced "sluh-bah-DA": a settlement exempted from normal state tax obligations. The community referred to by P. was doubtless a sloboda in name only, as this special status had been abolished in the eighteenth century.
19. Cooperative association of workmen or peasants, like a guild.

Photograph by M. P. Nastiukov, "The Banks of the Volga at Rybinsk," 1867.

There, by the water, we purchased a boat,
And they agreed to provide us with a guide.
Shifts at the rows we arranged among ourselves,
And the pilot commanded with his stroke.
We went first by lake, then by rivers,
Laboring day and night at the oars
Until, lo and behold: we found ourselves
In the Volga!
O mother, o holy river—
You revived joy within us.

From far away, the bright morning star
Lit up the city of Rybinsk for us.
Along the Volga, like a forest
Within the circle of the city,
Stood caravans filled with grain.
I could not look at the boats and mokshans[20]

20. A dialectal term for a riverboat used for hauling grain.

P. (Petr O.)

Without tears of joy, so hard it was to believe
That Russia had been so long under threat
Of famine. There's lots of grain in Russia,
And grain fortifies this world for life
Better than gold. So happiness turned
The weather on my face from foul to fair.
Sadness, a dangerous sickness in my heart,
Was lulled to dozy sleep.

Meanwhile my companions were having a romp
With the oars, and the boat flew along like an arrow.
Having reached shore, we stopped at the jetty,
And sold our light little boat. Together we made
Our reckonings, and hurried off to an inn,
Where inexpensively we dined.

When our feast was over, we left as a crowd,
Took our leave of many friends, and like tiny flies
Flew away by paths broad and diverse.

With six fellow passengers we left the city,
But not by water—for now our route was dry,
And we rushed along in two carts
Pulled by two horses. Soon upon our native place
We feasted our eyes: the meadows, knolls
And hills, and the green groves
Between them, and fast-flowing brooks.

Spring blossoms more splendidly in one's native place:
More delicately do the flowers put on their colors;
The nightingale, beside the stream, sings more loudly;
The zephyrs blow more coolingly. I felt
Enchanted in my native region, and everything
Before my eyes seemed to come alive:
As though in heaven, I savored every blessing.

But soon everything changed, as we rode
Into the first village. There, in dwellings
Like the huts of fishermen, lived the people.
Herders of cattle they were, living in a remote area,

Living together in a wasteland, in homes half-ruined.
The residents, like phantoms from the grave,
Or poor people struck with senility, dragged their feet
As though barely alive. And on their lips
One noticed a murmuring against poverty,
Expressed to the world. But the world did not perceive
Their half-mute whispers. For them there was no joy.

As we passed through the village
I was in sadness for my countrymen,
And, looking for a sympathetic response,
I asked the driver, "tell me—how has misery
Become so great, that people here seem inured to it?
Poverty surrounds this village, like a fire."

Forthwith the driver answered me:
          "Look over there, to your left—you'll see
          The manorial estate, beyond the bushes.
          That's what scorches the peasants here
          With heavy labor. Yes indeed, in our parts
          All the serfs suffer because of their masters,
          Who cruelly degrade their bondsmen
          And don't regard such treatment as a sin.
          Godliness is disappearing everywhere!
          That obrók, huge and strictly due
          The nobles, has inculcated the world
          With knavery and ignorance—
          Here, everything goes along a crooked path!
          Perilous for our fellow countrymen
          Is this holy native land of ours.
          The evil fate of horrible slavery
          Has scattered them in all directions.
          Leaving behind homes, wives, children,
          They dwell in foreign lands,
          Always at work, never a bright day,
          And tolerating much sadness.[21]

21. This is a reference to the peasant practice of finding temporary nonagricultural work away from home, and perhaps to the lives led by escaped serfs as well.

We've heard that our fellow landsmen
Sell merchandise in Russian cities.
No fools, these salesmen with their customers!—
Invisibly, they swindle them before their eyes.
They figure ways to pay their dues,
Sending money home to the village
For the 'kitty,'[22] to pay for grub and obrók.
But there are those who go still further,
And become involved in trade, so that
Their liberty they might purchase
(Though old age for them might be only five years
Down the road, or six). So these wise men,
With trade on the brain, do their business
Far and wide—many pass for merchants
And disperse amid the towns and cities.
But sooner or later, our traders' hands
And minds are bound by fate.
For although they might live like merchants,
It's all a fraud, a foolish show.
You see, traveler, what a fortress this is![23]

"It knows the way to sully anyone
And everyone. Rare's the one who emerges from it
With his sight intact, who grows up capable
Of avoiding vice. Look at how these serfs
Wander 'round the world at all hours,
Break into storerooms at night
And lead horses away from the fields.
It's no wonder things end up this way:
Without a voice, you can't complain
About your fate. But all the same, it's hard
To end one's days without some bread.
Look at how the wolf roves in winter,
How hunger drives him on like a whirlwind—

22. The word here is *skladka:* money collected from village peasants, either voluntarily or not, and set aside by village elders for some particular purpose.
23. "Fortress" (*krepost'*) is a substitution for "serfdom" (*krepostnoe pravo*).

In towns and villages he looks for food,
And often carries off dogs, unthinkingly.
He finds a way of living on this earth.
But a person isn't a wolf, see. . . ."

Having heard the driver's speech
I thought, "So that's how it is, it's gotten so bad. . . ."
Then, knowing that he knew, I asked:
"Tell me briefly, friend—
What do the people here require?"

Swiftly he replied:
 "Freedom,
 For tsar and Christian alike a single law!"

The kingly driver broke into a whistle,
And the horses rushed on down the road;
A Iaroslávets,[24] used to letting
His native passions blaze, he consoled himself
With plenty of galloping and racing.
But I sat there in my chains,
An innocent condemned to the fortress,[25]
And continued on toward my own dark lot,
Gazing the while at the world, in sorrow.

After this, three shifts of horses remained
Before I would reach my home.
Closely I observed, but saw no change
In the poor inhabitants encountered
Along the way. Everywhere the villages
Were wretched, with emptiness inside
The smoke-filled houses, people dressed
In filthy clothes, and darkness covering
Their minds. And everywhere, on fields
Of unplowed earth, lands deserted

24. That is, from the Iaroslavl' area.
25. See note 23.

P. (Petr O.)

Were to be seen—deserted in failure's wake
By bondsmen. O, bitter lot of the peasants!
Their days vanish into a mist.

I feel pity, for self and fellow man.
All our talents perish with us.
Slave labor is our inheritance
In this wide world in which we live,
And not one ray of enlightenment
Penetrates that burden through to us.
Here I recalled the old man's words,
Words which frightened me, and again
Sadness, anguish entered my heart
Like rust infecting iron. And if upon the cart
I chanced to fall asleep, woeful daydreams
Tormented me all the same. . . .

But the horses, as it happened, wiped away
My last tears with their swift running.
Soon I was so clenched in melancholy
That atop the cart I sat, just like
A haughty landowner or rich merchant,
Too lazy to help the ones who suffer.
Within my eyes, the source of tears dried up;
Sadness wore out all my feelings
And even my mind; it burdened all my thoughts.
Yet I heard how my friends were saying:
"We've got just thirty versts to go!"[26]
And they ordered the driver to hurry
To our native refuge.

The bright day declined, and evening twilight
Burned down like a candle; nocturnal shadows
Slowly covered all of nature's brilliance.
The fields vanished from our sight;

26. One verst (in Russian, *versta* ["vyair-STAH"]) is equivalent to about 1.06 kilometers.

Valleys and mountains concealed themselves,
And the choirs of gentle birds fell silent
In forests that had lost their rays of sun.
The time was already midnight,
And my companions fell mutely into sleep
While the horses rushed along, full speed.

One could tell where the nightingales sang,
Hearing their song. Loudly their voices rang out
In the green groves next to the brooks,
And flowed together with streams of pure water,
And with the breeze that played amid the leaves.

"Ah, deaf midnight guardians!
O native streams and groves,
Are you near my village?"

A nightingale warbled in response, and through
The fragrant languor of the trees
A breeze blew upon my face—
This breath of wind laid me to the soundest sleep
Of all the passengers upon the cart.

But my immortal soul slept not:
Dejected inside the dark body, from which
It seemed already to await separation,
My soul imagined things as in a daydream.
It wandered, it seemed, upon a high mountain
In dark autumn, above a deep and rapid river
In a gully far below, opening before my eyes
Like an abyss. In the distance, beyond the span
Of water, flowers in the meadows released
Their scents, and there were gardens on green hillocks
Where little birds were sweetly singing.
The ceaseless light of the sun shone through
These halls of glory, and people clothed in splendor
Took joy in blessings everlasting. My soul
Overheard no meek conversations,
Saw only hands ceaselessly clapping.

P. (Petr O.)

They paid no attention to me, a fact
Which only increased my suffering—
Ever more fiercely they tormented me,
A hopeless soul on the steep slope of sorrow
And of fear, and I asked merciful God
Not to leave me in that place. I stopped
In horror, frozen at the edge of the abyss,
But soon I seemed to topple over,
And fell down, all atremble, before a hut. . . .
A gate opened with a tap; the driver said:
      "Here's your house!"

I heard the family bustling inside,
Then—a-running, with a clatter!—at once
Before me stood my mother and my father.
With lighted torches in their hands, and hearts
Burning hot with love, they hurried
To meet their near and dear one. And from
Their mouths came tendernesses, pleasing to my soul.

"It was hard, but we waited up for you,
Dear son," they said, "until the breaking
Of the nighttime silence." Pulling me into
Their embrace, they kissed me on the lips
And cheeks, and watered my light-brown curls
With tears of joy. Then three young girls
Ran in with greetings for me—my own sisters,
Entwining me round with their endearments.
Oh, with what a happy result I plunged
In my dream from that untold height!
Waking, I found myself with family,
And feelings of joy grew lively again.
My happiness made me forget
The fate of the people I had seen:
For one arriving home, home conceals
All poverty, and it becomes an object of delight
For heart and soul. I even forgot about those friends
With whom I'd taken leave when I arrived—

They left to neighboring villages
To join with kin, as we had done.

Stepping into the *izbá*,[27] I bumped my head
Against the low shelves inside, and sat upon
The white bench, surrounded again by a crowd
Of relatives. Conversations began among us:
I went on about city things, while they sought
To tell me all the village news. And so
From sundown until daybreak we sat
In conversation. Feasting their eyes upon me,
They observed me with a steady gaze.

Some peasants interrupted us that morning
When they stopped by to greet me—
Poor men they were, dressed in meager clothing.
Bowing down, this is what they said:

    "Dear neighbor . . .
    We've been waiting for you for a long time.
    Have you heard anything about our sons?"
And they received accurate news.

Meanwhile father had invited them
To sit at our uncovered table. A *shtof*[28]
Of simple wine[29] was brought, that guests
Might be provided for, as ceremony requires.
They congratulated me on my arrival
And passed the wineglasses round and round.
This mirth, purchased with money, quickly
Raised their spirits. O, how many Russians

---

27. Pronounced "eez-BAH": a peasant hut.

28. A shtof was an old Russian unit of liquid measure, equivalent to 1.23 liters; the word could also refer to a bottle of this measure.

29. "Wine" is probably a poeticism here; vodka or some kind of ale would be the more likely beverage.

Trade their health for that purchase!
Many, many come to ruin for its sake;
They end their days before their time.

The neighbors, in their drunken condition,
Expatiated on all topics. Loudly they went on and on
About offences and violations of order,
About the envy of treacherous elders,
About the depredations of base lackeys,
About the weakness and infant cowardice
Of our cruel lords. One of the neighbors,
Ermil, spoke with a goblet of wine in his hand:

> "Let's drink to the court of Shemiaka,[30]
> And to our brave voevódes![31]
> And to the blossoming of Asiatic customs,
> And to the income taken from us by force!"

And he drank.

At this Maksim, the other neighbor,
Looked at Ermil and said:

> "But more proprietors than before have lost
> Themselves in voluptuous living,
> And the payments they oblige are more ruinous

30. "The court of Shemiaka" is an idiom meaning "an unfair trial" or "kangaroo court." The expression derives "apparently from [Shemiaka], the name of an arbitrary and casuistic judge in a satirical old Russian tale" (Sophia Lubensky, *Russian-English Dictionary of Idioms* [New York: Random House, 1995]). See M. I. Sukhomlinov, "Povest' o sude Shemiaki," *Issledovaniia po drevnei russkoi literature* [*Sbornik otdeleniia russkogo iazyka i slovestnosti Imperatorskoi Akademii Nauk,* vol. 85, no. 1] (Saint Petersburg: Tipografiia Imperatorskoi Akademii Nauk, 1908 [reprinted Nendeln, Liechtenstein: Kraus Reprint Ltd., 1966]), 637–671.

31. A voevóde ("voy-uh-VODE") was either (1) a commander of an army in medieval Russia or (2) the governor of a town or province in the Muscovite period. Here it is a sarcastic reference to the landowners.

To peasant farmers than they were. For the poor,
A terrible time has arrived; it's as though
The time had come for all of us to die . . .
Only the rich have the means to live,
And they can buy and sell besides!"

Finally I heard how my father spoke to them:

The Father's Speech[32]

Now listen, friends, and I'll deliver my reproach
Against our "law." As far as I can tell,
It's just not possible that one person be
Serf to another. Whoever wishes to have a serf
Is neither wholly good nor bad, but a fool—
As though he thought he had the power
To be the father of another's children.
But this is just the folly whereby these fathers,
These slipshod fathers, have sunk into luxury
Over all these years. Because of them, their slaves
Inclined to vice from birth, like bastard children.
We see how the noblemen regard the peasant
As a fool, use "peasant" as a term of abuse—
They use the same word to revile their enemies.
Through us they are rich, and at us they rage,
Us they tyrannize, trample underfoot,
Not fearing the law of God, their minds
Soaring proudly overhead and high.
But what do they have that we don't have?
Look, and you'll see that in feeling and desire
They're exactly the same as we are—
"Their clothes are cleaner," that's all.[33]

32. This subtitle does not appear in the original but was added to clarify the shifts in narrative voice in the poem. Unless otherwise noted, all other subtitles appeared in the original.
33. P.'s note: "'Cleaner clothes' [*pochishche odeian'em*] names the art of beautiful speech, through the help of which one more learnedly expresses one's wishes, many of

P. (Petr O.)

And so, without experience, untutored
By hard work, they gleam like the scale
Of a snake, with a well-schooled look,
And poison seeps into the world
From their violent hearts.

Ah, how terrible it is to think of Russia.
It's impossible to number her calamities.
From my youth, both day and night,
I've been mourning for the world and myself.
Cruelly, fate corrects the slave—and yet
We should have been taught in childhood,
Set early on the proper path for life!
But how much can we put up with,
And what must we put up with now?
God gave us minds and fields of earth,
But there's no exit out the fortress door[34]
From this bondage into a proper life.

O plow, good friend of the people,
I pity you, for you are greatly neglected
Among us—you, solid root of the kingdom.

Listen, neighbors, and let me tell you
Of a nighttime dream I had about these things.
Don't think I'm joking: I really dreamed it.

It was as though I was near a big village,
Dressed up in holiday garb. I walked
Upon and across the land, then up I rose
Into a spacious garden. It appeared to be
In full spring color, for the tips of trees
Were clothed in green. But there was no hope

---

which (for this reason) are generated uselessly, out of not knowing how difficult it is to actually fulfill any of those wishes." The duality of the figure is clear: nobles both dress and speak more "cleanly," that is, "respectably."

34. See note 23.

Of buds—the place had long since been
In wretched shape. Among the trees,
The branches were but few, although
The tips grow green indeed; the roots
Rot and molder in the frost, deprived
Of even a single pleasant day of weather.
Taking fright on seeing this, I lost
The joy I had in life.
                              Distressed in body
And in soul, I repented having clambered up
Into that garden. Forthwith I would have run
Away from it, but suddenly the gardener
Caught up with me and said:
"From whom are you running?"
"Instead of joys, delights," I said to him,
"Here I saw great harm, great woe:
The garden is withering, not blossoming!"

Looking me in the face, the gardener,
As though taking pity on me, began to speak:

> "Muzhík, our lord knew what was happening here
> Long ago, and without your help. And soon
> He'll order us back into the garden (or so
> We suppose), to establish everything anew;
> That we might uproot all the evil and the woe
> Apparent here. A high fence all around here
> Chokes out many plants; neither rays of sun
> Nor cooling breeze flow through it when
> Most needed. We'll break it down, and clear
> The place of rubbish, and afterward
> We'll dig a ditch around it, and enclose it
> With a palisade. It's our good fortune
> That there's a river here, flowing with
> Clear streams, a river we call Knowledge—
> Near it grows a tree, all by itself.
> We'll hasten to make something of our lives here,
> While we live. Fountains we will build
> In the garden, and cultivate every kind

Of fruit. You, humble muzhík, my friend,
Take comfort in this, and return to your home.
Fate might oppress you, but God
And tsar are always with you!"

Hurriedly I got away from there,
And my slumber was broken of a sudden
By the morning light. I rose and went to the fields,
Spending the day with dejection in my heart.
That evening I rode home, ate supper, laid down
To sleep, and thought to myself of how
Our son had promised to return just then.
And I sighed for him with all my soul.
My heart pounded with impatience,
But was eventually subdued into
The deepest sleep. I never dreamt a single dream
The entire night, and only at dawn I finally
Budged, when my eldest daughter
Woke us up—out of bed I leapt, headlong
I ran, to meet my son—may God be praised.

[End of father's speech. P. resumes his narration.]
Our peasant men were visited in the meantime
By their wives, who angrily called them home,
Saying they'd forgotten all the work they had to do.
Their husbands didn't heed them right away,
But soon they stepped outside, and standing on
The road, they looked upon our house and said:
"Vasilei's[35] home has changed for the better
Now that his son has returned to him;
He's come up renewed out of all the rot,
And returned to himself a happy man."
They marveled at the change, and gazed
Upon our windows with admiration. Then off
They went to plow the fields, one by one.

35. Vasilei is the father's first name.

But my father did not work that day at all.
He celebrated—but sudden cares found lodging
Once again inside my feeble heart. He brought
A letter of assessment, and read it aloud to me.
Shame, surprise! To him my employer
Had written, and roundly discredited me.

Letter from a Saint Petersburg Merchant
to My Father

Vasilei, old friend, hello! Do you remember
Who I am? I was your dear friend and your neighbor,
Your beloved Eremei, your comrade in the days
Of careless youth. Ah, how we'd run about with girls,
In splendid days of spring; how they'd sing
Their cheerful songs to us, dancing all the while
In rings! It seems that fate disposed of those good things,
And separated me from you as well. Of your fair share
Of fortune, fortune did you out, while I received
A handful of gold from her. Yet let me say this to you
Alone: the fact is, that I'm miserably wasting away,
Having used up my mind on trade. I can hardly
Even sleep—oh, what thoughts run through my head
At night! Sometimes I imagine that I paid too much
For something; sometimes I'm not happy
With my profits; sometimes things don't go well
With my workers, strictly though I manage them.
You could get buried under all the workers,
There's so many: a regular drove of shop assistants.
And virtually for free they work for us!
As worse than cattle we regard them, with words
Abuse them, continually vowing to fire them—
But would you think of them any differently?
These beggars put up with their vexations,
But that doesn't stop them from stealing money, just
As mercilessly as moles pilfer our winter corn.
That's why you often hear those hateful rumors
Flying around, of how a merchant has suddenly become

P. (Petr O.)

A shepherd, and dragged off to prison for his debts.
But let's not talk any more about that. . . .

Listen, friend, to just a few more words:
I won't say that *your* son is a thief,
But an empty-headed fool he certainly is.
With me he's lived (of course you know)
From the age of fifteen years till twenty-three.
I taught him all I knew about the business—
But do you think he had the slightest talent for it?
He was ashamed to ask questions, timid when asked
To cheat the customers, too lazy to pawn bad goods off
On them—he wouldn't even give them short measure!
When someone's shy like that, quiet like a child,
Thoughtful, calm, and even-tempered—
You can see for yourself, I'm not writing this in jest—
He's not fit for trade at all! At other times,
However, he'd be as fiery as powder, violent
And fearless with his enemies, terribly wrathful
And harsh with them, as though he were a beast
Or some mysterious foe. Sometimes he would talk
To friends, and spoke like one who knew all things
About all things. Secretly I'd listen, and more than once
I marveled at his mind and character.
Judging from his words, I hoped to find in him
A tradesman of the boldest sort. But all that time,
I found no entryway into his brainless mind,
And so came to regard him as utterly void.
I denied him any post or responsibilities,
Though as you'll see, my treatment of him wasn't
Inhumane: I even sent him off with money
In his pocket. But I'll never have him work for me
Again! I cared for him as best I could,
Watched him as a wet nurse does a child—
Now may God our Father protect him,
And let fate be a mommy to him! I advise you,
My friend, to let him suffer at summertime labor;
Train him yourself in plowing, and in time

He'll come to like it. Let him check out all the avenues
And let him select some kind of work whereby
He'll make his daily bread—one's got to keep busy,
Whether with his body or with his head
And there's no harm in working for another.
One can't in good conscience just contentedly sit
And gaze upon the world. They oppress the poor
Whose work does harm, who work for glory
And for luxury; they go bad, sunk in boredom
And viciousness, and live for destruction's sake.
How I fear that ruination, to fall into that abyss:
The whole world is beginning to bend away
From the old law. But I won't speak of where
Our law is weak, where it's unsatisfying to me,
Because you and your son—are slaves,
And I've been free a long, long time.

Well, my friend, I'm in not in the mood to write
Any more than's necessary. Please don't
Call me to account for my words, and do
Forgive my lack of time and leisure.

"So, dear son," my father said, "your employer
Is displeased with you, it seems. In the city
He's my only friend, so there you've lost your place
For good. I suppose you think that you can look
To others for a place to work, and that
They'll take you just because of how you look?
Again you'll fail to set your mind to business,
And again they'll send you packing to the village.
Again you'll pace around with naught to do,
And contemplate returning home. 'This means
That fate has ordered me to take to laboring on
The land,' you'll think. But let's suppose you do
Start plowing in the village, and that you come
To understand that art, and make enough to earn
Your daily bread. But do you think you'll have
Enough to pay obrók? Our master has some land,

And at a decent price: 20 rubles
Per desyátin,[36] and taxes aren't too high.
But the harvest's getting worse and worse
From year to year, and our supply of grain
Is running out; we're milling and seeding new rye,
It's true—but next to the old stuff, the young rye
Won't sprout. It's scared off by the drought
And cold, and rots quite away, not setting seed.
Besides, our poverty means the land is poorly
Fertilized; no one gets much dung to spread,
And what we get won't cover half a field.
We don't have many cattle, either . . . it seems
We suffer from all sorts of not-enough.

"It's grown difficult to live on earth, it has—
It appears as though we've sinned 'fore God.
We've got a family here: my daughters three,
And you, my son. Your mother's miserable, however,
And so am I—our master just won't let us live
In peace! The girls are angry (though all in vain),
For a woeful piece of news they've just been given:
They'll be seized and married off by force!
And you—you're also to be married now.[37]

"Our unjust rulers rule us cruelly; they form
Unions of marriage by force, and lead us thus
To trouble and disaster. For you, my son
(I'll say it again), the first of your troubles
Is already here. There'll be no: 'have you thought
Of getting married?' 'Here's your wife!' is what

36. An old Russian land measure, equivalent to 2.7 acres or 1.09 hectares (*Oxford Russian Dictionary* [Oxford and New York: Oxford University Press, 1993]).

37. The ability of serfowners to compel or prevent marriage is crucial to the narrative of *News about Russia*, as will be seen. However, it is far from clear that masters generally closely regulated serf marriage, at least after the late eighteenth century. See John Bushnell, "Did Serf Owners Control Serf Marriage? Orlov Serfs and Their Neighbors, 1773–1861," *Slavic Review* 52:3 (1993): 419–445.

They'll say. But see the suffering brought upon
A man who doesn't like the woman with whom
He lives! It also happens that a wife
Is given a husband, without a thought of what
She thinks; her life with him is like a life
In fire, and sad she'll be unto the grave.

"It's awful, talking about the life of slaves,
About the ones inside the fortress, dragged
Around by monstrous fate, despite the rule
Of nature and the world. You'll find rules
In place on each estate, just as courtiers
Have their throne rooms ready for receptions,
With guards on duty in the anterooms.
On this estate the judgment goes a certain way,
On that estate another, on a third—
Who knows? But everyone, everywhere,
Judges to suit himself. So if we want
To draw conclusions, the result we'll get
Is: lawlessness, no matter where we turn.
On the neighboring estate are lords
Whose serfs can marry whom they will.
But if you think about it: who would wish
Upon the *meshchanki* [38] such a bitter lot?
The maidens who are free are scared of you
And all the other handsome bachelors.
They know the lot of serfs, and proud they stand
Before us, proudly free. But young meshchanins
Flirt about with all the girls, just as they
See fit; they may be fools and freaks, and yet
They marry anyone they want. But what
Is there to do, dear son? It's not for us
To follow in their ways. Remember that
You're not alone on earth—that many, many
Souls are born in bondage, and the thought

---

38. *Meshchanka* (plural, *meshchanki*): feminine form of *meshchanin*—free townspeople, often involved in trade.

Of bondage makes them pound their heads, without
Exception.
       So just listen to my words,
And I'll tell you how to be a clever slave.

"Be able to control yourself; contend
Against caprice and sloth with reason's help;
Have the knowledge to distinguish bad
From good, and save your money for when trouble
Comes. Don't lose yourself on crooked paths,
And have the wit to live within a faithless world.
Learn to serve both kinds of people, bad
And good, but cling yourself to the path of truth.
When happy, never mingle pride into
Your joy; it's pride that turns us into madmen.
Deal gently with your fellow man;
Gentleness, for us, is wisdom's way.
Learn how to live in slavery, and how
To honor the *poméshchik*;[39] when you stand
Before him, learn to seem like an idiotic
Beggar, but hide from him your mind and actual
Condition. Hide everything each time you're asked
The reasons why we're living as we do—
Hide it till the day you die!—and be
Aware that even decent people can be
Spoiled by envy; even those who are smart
Can be consumed by hatred. Everything,
You must conceal from everyone of lower rank:
From elders, *sótskys*,[40] neighbors near—
From all the world's eyes, no less. I see
The poor, and how they judge a man who tries
To rectify his fate, through deeds or with
His mind. Suddenly, his fellows envy him.
They crush him. All around he hears abusive

---

39. Pronounced "pah-MYESHCH-chik": landowner.
40. Pronounced "SOHT-skee": literally a "hundredth," but designating a peasant assigned to keep order on a large estate.

Noise. They curse—and as a single crowd
They long to fall upon him. Yet they do not
Always find the strength to stamp the favored one
Back down into the mud. He's sometimes given
The blessings fate had promised him—and when
A new man's what he's become, he'll pay no heed
To this malicious world, and cast no glance
Toward the groaning poor, and will be prideful
All the same. This new proprietor will have
No sense that he's a sinner; of his desiccated virtue,
Scarce a single drop will fall upon his servants.
Now become a parsimonious manager
Of property, himself he suffers day and night;
He's clearly become oppressor of the poor himself,
Burning all the while alive, in torment.

"So all those Russian practices of ours—
You won't figure them out anytime soon!
The poor don't live correctly, that's for sure,
But neither will you find much good among
The rich. We're filled with envy, pride, stupidity,
Ecstatic in our own self-love. It's either
Luxury or stinginess—and never
Moderation! Everyone's infected
With the bane of slavery! The very air's
A-stink with falsities, indignities
Spread 'round by that poisonous disease;
We are each other's suffering, and each
Is tyrant to the other. Brotherly love
Has but weakly made its roots among us,
And of pagan blood (brought us by the yoke),[41]
We've hardly been purged at all, that's clear.
Nothing of the Gospel light shines down
To us, through the darkness of false deeds.
Whoever sees that light but dwells in darkness—
That person will meet torment after death.

41. A reference to the "Tatar yoke," the period of Mongol domination of the Rus' principalities (1240–1480).

P. (Petr O.)

"O, woe to all of those who spoil the work
Of those who have but little binding their minds,
Their talents, and their liberty, and give
No teaching to those who live in blindness.
Who do not *themselves* partake of education,
But indulge their weakness for vain leisure!
(Vain, and for whose sake so many are thrown
Into tormenting darkness!—and yet they are
The first who'll perish in that final blindness.)
Yet God forbid, my son, that you should e'er
Concern yourself with things so void and empty . . .

"But still I'll show you more—and see you don't forget!

"Don't brag about your money, and don't shine
With intellect—you show more cunning when
You keep yourself concealed from the masters.
Don't build a fine, a well-made home; don't sew
Yourself good clothes; just live as simply as
You can, in just the very way that all we
Ignorant people do. Silently
But firmly, the nobility sustains
That ignorance, sustains with its strong hand.

"Whether the gates that lead from darkness unto
Light will open soon for us, I cannot say—
But long ago the slaves should have been brought
From out of their serf prison; the chain
That had been fastened by their enemies torn
Away; little by little their minds enlightened.
May God assist the tsar with this!—
With that I end my rhythmical words."

"Thank you, father," I replied, "for all this
Useful teaching. But what a pity, that this
Enrichment for your son comes late, at last.
Why did my parent dawdle so long, and why
Wasn't he observant when the time
Was ripe? You missed the spring of childhood,

72

Thus diminishing your fruit, your seed.
You let bad habits grow, and failed to uproot
Ignorance. The peril's great if one
Lets reason grow along with ignorance;
The good fruit's smothered in benightedness.
Unillumined by the rays of sun,
An apple tree, standing in a darkened
Grove, I am pastured in a world
Where little light's been seen by those who live here.
Am I to live as fate has ordered, so that
My days pass restlessly away, sunk deep
Into this backwater; so that my mind
Declines and molders away untended,
Amid storms of uncertainty?

"Father, allow me to speak, and let me make
Of fate the following request."

The Son's Request[42]

Give me, fate, at least a couple days'
Respite from stormy weather, that I might hear
The moans of the unfortunate, and reveal
The vice residing at the root of Russian law.
Everything's gone worse and worse from year
To year, because of all those serf lords here,
For liberty's imprisoned, and living humans
Bought and sold. But what else do we see?
Utter ignorance is everywhere
Among the people; the man who's learned yields
A seed that's unproductive, choked by lies
And dissipation. Noxious is the order
The bosses' crooked ways have brought about.
Their rule's enserfed the world, divested it
Of freedom in all kinds of ways. In court,
The law's the judge's law, and whatever

42. Subtitle added.

P. (Petr O.)

They proclaim is hidden far from us.
Indeed, the law's in bondage to the nobles,
And everywhere obeys them blindly. Not
A one of all us working laymen knows
The law or how to find it. Merchants, freedmen,
Peasants—none of them have any voice
Before the law. But might we laymen reach
Unto our tsar, and scorning all corrupt
Deceit, make our request before him thus?—

"Our great tsar—let your new law
Rain down upon us!

"Blind warlords are leading us
Down a thorny path, into the darkness.
Proclaim to us your wise law,
That the judges read it,
That their judgments stand before it,
That their fidelity be impelled by it;
That the hand of every judge
Might write the sentences of the guilty
Equitably, from the prince to the peasant,
And give no encouragement to vice!
That the breed of judges might entirely lose
Their taste for collecting bribes,
And that what they pronounce might shame
The lying prince and lying peasant alike.
The poor see better than anyone else
The injustice of the court and persecution
By the strong. On serfs especially, all anger,
Woe, and torment are poured.
No one will lead truth into the world
Without the deliverance of these unhappy people—
Now it's as in winter, during a terrible storm,
And all paths are swept away, as though by evil lies."

Father, let me ask again:
Is it so impossible to find someone else
From among the people—that we might,

As a threesome, approach the tsar,
And advise him on how all might be free?

The Father's Response

Forget my words, forget them forever!
Forget what you saw of the world! Is it for you
To sing your dreams of freedom on a lyre?
You were born a peasant on this earth,
And must learn to bear that burden.
You were poorly brought up, never studied—
Is it for the likes of you, my son, to approach the tsar?
Is it for you to advise the great one
On such a matter as freedom for us all,
And go responding to his questions
In dull and colorless words?
He will listen, then command you to be silent,
And never ask you again about anything—
Or else he'll think to send you off
To a place where not even the ravens
Bother to carry off the bones.
Or he'll send you to be judged
By our unjust government.
What then, alas, will happen here?
What new misfortune will befall you?
Your noble undertaking will bring
Judges of the law to you,
And perhaps like scribes, like Pharisees,
They'll have you slaughtered in the square.

So why are you thinking to pour
Yet another bitter cup for yourself,
When you scorn even to begin
To drink from the cup we have?
How faint hearted you are now,
That you would presume to go down such a path!
Stop it! Hurl this stuff out of your head,
And never think of it again.
And remember: tomorrow we go together

P. (Petr O.)

Anonymous nineteenth-century drawing, "Peasant at Work."

To plow in the open field,
And things will go twice as well for you
Once you've become accustomed to innocent labor.
[*End of father's response.*]

That day passed, and the night as well. . . .
In the morning I joined my father,
Asked the Creator to help us,
And learned how to plow in the fields.

One could see that eternal God, in secret,
Had given me understanding enough to learn.
I worked as many days as I could,
And let my sorrow about everything slip my mind.
I began to eat more at this time,
And slept more soundly and pleasantly at night.
Soon I began to feel something different
In myself, in my new role.
Through working I strengthened a body
That had been weakened by care;
But the heavy, monotonous work
Much dulled my mind.
It seemed that a single Sunday
Lasted longer than all the workdays.

Then one day, when the sun's shadow
Had passed by two hours the point of noon,
Girls gathered in noisy groups about the houses
And suddenly fell silent—I saw then
How they dispersed back into their homes.
My little sisters returned home,
Wearing their finest outfits,
Washing their faces with water,
And giving me the news in these words:

> "Go get dressed like us for the party, brother.
> You're no worse looking than anyone else,
> And many will be attending
> Who are in the same condition as we are.
> Go look at the group of maidens,
> And likewise show yourself to them;
> Listen to the choir of village singers—
> They will bring you cheer.
> Many beauties will gather there
> With all kinds of faces—Who knows?
> From among them you might find
> Your own heart's love."

Gladly I agreed to pay a visit,
And, getting dressed, bustled along with them,
Hoping to find the object of my love.

I looked, and already gathered there before us
Were crowds of girls beneath the windowsill.
All clustered together, they suddenly
Took off like one great herd.
Along the way, they enjoyed themselves
With happy songs, to divvy up the time.

Before us, young fields rippled with
The cooling wind. Before we reached the end,
We went into the bushes, rustling all
Around us, and from them onto a meadow
Green, where ripe flowers shone,
Each one wearing its own costume.

P. (Petr O.)

The varied faces of the girls
Pierced through the hearts of the youths
With their tender smiles, sweet glances.
A fiery battle then took place
Right there, near the village:
A battle that has killed and injured many
Without bullets or heavy lead!
While all the while, the happy choir of singers
Released their magical sound.

Shyly I looked upon the girls, and then—
What else? I fell into the bonds of love.
Into bondage—and not into further exile:
Fate drew me into the round dance,
Where the noisy crowd came to feel
An enchantment all around.

A girl walked along with me, her hand
Gripped in my hand. And love flared up
Within us both, while the dance went on,
Unhurriedly. I was able courteously to ask
About her village, what it was called,
And an answer was quickly prepared.

Oh heart, do not forget about her!
Preserve this beauty as your object;
To accompany you during the sad days
In this poor and cheerless world of ours,
You'll not find anyone sweeter than she.
She shines with beauty like the clear days of May,
And her words, simple as a child's,
Are more pleasant than the harp or gusli,[43]
With her crimson cheeks, white face,
Her gaze tender and shy.
From her pink lips poured those words
Into my heart, into my soul.

43. A stringed musical instrument like a psaltery.

Her form, her legs and breast as white as snow—
They seized every thought within my mind!
How could one not sigh, on taking leave?
Without her, life will be left in a new darkness!

Leaving her, all was sour to me,
And at home I never slept a wink.
My father went to the stárosta[44]
And asked that I be allowed to marry as I wished.
In response the boss replied:

> "There's nothin' more you can do now.
> First you need to propose marriage,
> So I'll write a letter to the bárin,[45] with your help.
> I'll ask him to provide all the needed resources.
> Perhaps he'll allow it, somehow. . . .
> To make it happen, you, father
> Must pray to God both day and night,
> And go to see the authorities with shining eyes,
> So they'll bring happiness to a young man.
> But don't say much to them.
> You should know that every bárin
> Regards himself as tsar, fate, and God above us,
> And that each slave lives as his worshipper.
> It would seem as clear as can be
> That we're always offering prayers to them,
> That we're always standing in fear
> Before their proud faces, with our hats removed.
> And often, when they tax us despotically
> We diligently repair their homes,
> And pray on bended knee before them,
> Just as though it were a sacred rite.
> But it's in vain that we pray so assiduously.
> The idol makers don't hear our prayers,
> But spread violence around, and thoughtlessly

44. Pronounced "STAR-us-tuh": the village elder or chief peasant communal official.
45. Pronounced "BAHR-in": master, landowner.

Squander all the labors of the people.
Such dark dealings—how could the devil himself
Not be involved? He orders them to deify
Themselves, and us to pray 'alla, save us!'
We honor them as our divinities,
Fulfill their commandments,
And thereby ruin everything around,
Forgetting God's truth.
All right: you pay heed to my words;
Go, and do what you have to do."

My father came and explained the situation
And his words to his brooding son.

"Your sisters have sought out a matchmaker,
A smart and gentle old woman—
They sent her off to your girl's village
That she should do what must be done."

My matchmaker departed then,
And long it was before she returned.
I was tossed in fear 'twixt hot and cold,
Waiting for the unknown answer. Anxious,
I was ever on the point of saying,
"Will they really fail to give to me
The object of my love?" Then all of a sudden,
As though she had pursued my thoughts,
The matchmaker stood right there, by the door.

The Matchmaker Solomónida[46] with Her Answer

"I suffered and I strove, old woman that
I am—and yet I've brought rejection all the same."

46. The matchmaker Solomónida is the main figure in *News about Russia*'s somewhat
repetitive third section (not translated here). Her name is doubtlessly intended to resonate
with that of the biblical Solomon and to allude to her wisdom. It is with her that the complex embedded narration of the poem's second part begins here.

The Suitor

"But why? Ah, what a slap in the face
This is! And with what vigor you left to see them!"

The Matchmaker

"Well, settle accounts with me just as
You will, but do forgive me for this blow.
Your beloved is of one mind with you,
And she'd go with you to hell if needed.
But what good's that, if her family won't
Assent? Why would you fall in love
With a meshchanka,[47] when you're a master's slave
Yourself? We will be told to search and find for you
A peasant girl; her, they'll pass to a meshchanin."

The Suitor

"Old woman, are they truly rich, the father
And the mother of the one I love?"

The Matchmaker

"Oh, my child . . . and yet they fear the courts,
And boiars' taxes and arrests. These days,
It seems that people do not care about
Who's in love with whom. They turn squeamish,
Rather, when they learn that you were born
Into the world a serf. Just think about the facts:
Your freedom's been taken away from you!

"Oh, you people. . . .
I grieve for you, that yours is such a fate.
Peasants, poor peasants!—you're always in the claws

47. See note 38.

P. (Petr O.)

Of recreants. The proud nobles spin us round
Just as though we were obedient horses.
Your cup is bitter, bitter—your fate
Is in their power, and guiltlessly you may
Be punished, your property taken away from you.
Peasant minds have withered from all these
Duties and obróks, and the villages have gone
To ruin, trying to pay these terrible dues
On time. Your houses show how poor they are
Through the cracks and through the windows.
It's hard to find cakes in places where
There's often not a crumb of bread. Here
Among the slaves, the fearful plague of poverty
Rages. Oh, how this nakedness and hunger
Pains me nigh unto the heart!

"But what physician will help us heal
So many illnesses?—one, only one—
The one who can destroy the bonds of slavery.
Raise your hands up to the skies, and pray
With howling unto our sovereign! Then go,
Eyes filled with tears, and ask the tsar of Russia.

"Is this really pleasing to God?[48]
[. . . . .]

"Of a Monday, before the sun had risen,
A certain Stepan of ours went off to the village.
I saw how he returned on Saturday,
Looking pitiable, coming back that evening
From the village. 'When will he begin
His work,' I thought, 'his wretched, poor-man's
Labor?' I bowed down low before him;
He reined in his jade, and spoke to me about
Such things. . . . I understood him, but was stunned."

48. There is a blank after this line; perhaps several lines are missing here.

Here I Repeat My Conversation with Stepan
Word-for-Word[49]

'Today,' said Stepan, in a weary voice,
'We finished laying in the springtime crop. . . .
No one in the village shows the peasants
Hospitality; the patience we require is great—
For instance: we just finished plowing the master's
Field—a big one, too, it'd take you quite
A while to walk around it—and that's why all
Are late getting their crops in, and few
Of us have seed to plant, at that. They plowed
In rain last year, and haven't got the planting
Done on time for several years, and never
Seem to get the harvest in. And so
We live in poverty, no doubt of that.
Our lords' regime is bad—not worth a cent,
To tell the truth—and when the weather's good,
They wear the people down with bárshchina.[50]

'Sometimes, rain begins to fall at noon;
You look up—the butler's running to the field.
"You all get home, get home," he shouts, "and don't
You make another pass, you'll spoil the fields."
A jade can't just skip across a field like that,
And yet 'cross seven versts you've got to drag
Equipment back. Everything's all sodden,
See, with rain, and every step you take you sink
In mud. Success is pretty meager in this business!

'And so, last week for instance, the *desiátskii*[51]
With an order came to us, announcing,

49. "I" here refers to Solomónida.
50. See note 13.
51. Derived from the word for a "tenth," the word desiátskii designated a peasant assigned to keep order on a large estate.

Like a ringing bell, that on the morn
All were to appear with their equipment[52]
In the village. We slept that night, and went
Together in the morning to the master's field.
But who can foretell the will of God! Twice
We set out, and twice the rain and wind
Began to fly—and so they drove us home,
You see, in midst of storm back home to work.[53]
And all that you can do is weep, and go
A-begging. . . . Trouble, how do we avoid you?

'Back and forth you walk, you want to eat,
But what will you find at home on which to dine?
We used up all our grain last fall; it might
Be possible to buy, but where will you get
The money?
        I marvel, I marvel at our lords,
At how they spend their time at feasts, and see
Us laborers as naught but beasts. But isn't
A peasant a person too? Just look—we also
Want to eat; we need to put on clothes,
Miserable though they may be; we don't
Eat grass or hay, and we're ashamed of standing
Naked in front of people. If only those
Were our only worries—food and clothes
Enough we'd find, and through our labor find
Enlightenment. But how long will it take
For us to find an order that is good?'

52. In Russian, *pribor*. P.'s note: "'Pribor' is the name given to those peasant tools which, when needed, are brought along when doing village labor."

53. Snytko's note: "The poméshchik determined the bárshchina-days at his discretion, selecting, naturally, those times when it was easier/more convenient to perform agricultural labor. The days remaining to the peasants for work on their own land were unproductive for field labor. In order to increase the number of bárshchina-days, the landlords would have the peasants go back to their own fields if the weather turned bad in the middle of the day; the interrupted day would not count as a day of completed bárshchina. Stepan is telling Solomónida about precisely this form of predatory usage of peasant labor by the landlords."

"I grieved for him, and asked him thus
Of his unhappiness: '—Have you been long,
Stepanushko, in such a miserable state?'"

Stepan

"Ah, granny Solomónida,
My Stepanida's[54] forgotten much, but I,
Of course, remember more. I can recall
The month, the day, the very hour
When destitution settled in our midst.
In 18—, it was, the year they took the last
Of liberty away from us. Our former bárin
Was farming out the land, and lived himself
Off small-time trade in spirits. But then he fell
Into a trap, like some inexperienced
Wolf, and we ended up in mortgage to
The state. We were gladdened by the news
At first, for everyone imagined we'd
Enjoy the government's protection.[55]
But we ended up without our rapture—
The whole estate was sold by public sale.
Bezdoúshin[56] bought us at that time, and on us
Played a filthy trick: in just a year,
From us he seized exactly the amount
He'd paid for us. So we've been serving him
His profit many a moon already, but we
Can walk about stark nude for all he cares!"

Solomónida [57]

"I sat down next to Stepan and carried on
Our talk, and spoke as though it were a song.

54. Stepan's wife.
55. That is, Stepan had thought they would become state peasants, rather than sold again as serfs.
56. An invented surname deriving from the word for "soulless" or "heartless."
57. Subtitle added.

"'Muzhík, you've hit the point,' I said.
'A dainty morsel fell before the eyes
Of the poméshchik; he bought you for
A profit, then he squeezed you dry.
It's no surprise that all the power's in
The nobles' hands—they trade in people just
The way they do with rams! The difference is,
That cattle in the forests and the valleys
Have shepherds watching over them.
So why must people suffer at the hands
Of other people? Were the masters sent
By God Himself, to penalize the Russians
For their sins, to agonize them with
The lash? And could it be the work of God
That we've been handed to authorities
Who have the power to torment our bodies
Our entire lives, and lead our souls
To sin? Our souls, it's true, may well be made
In God's own image, and it's true that even those
In bondage might be saved; and yet the lot
Of mortals is a strict one still, our bodies
Sold for nothing to destruction.

"And here we see how much we differ from
The people who were first to dwell on earth—
Our Adam never lived a lordly life,
And nor did Noah with his sons. But swarms
Have multiplied upon the earth since then—
Yet God commands that we remember Nature,
That earthly power was distributed
By Him. All tsars are placed by God upon
Their thrones of power for as long as they
Shall live. And to the tsar we pledge our lives,
And give to our Creator praise!

"Yes, his right hand will bring us wisdom,[58]
And dropping from the skies, with speed as swift

58. In the Bible, God's right hand is represented as the hand of just and active

As thought, above the head of our king
Will shine a new dawn! And he'll abjure
The abusive ways of all the former tsars
Of Russia, and he will put a stop to all
The violence and vices of his children.
So much good the tsar would do, if only
He'd perform great deeds like these—he would
Be like the tsar of tsars in ancient times,[59]
And greater still than Peter was great.'

"I finished my words, then looked at Stepan's face;
Not yet dragged down by sleep, he thought of how
He might convey his thoughts to me.
I hearkened, and he began the talk.
The topic was again the nobles in
Their court—I can pass his words along,
Whether they be of profit to you or not.
He spoke of the deeds of our lords, and sought
To explain these things to me."

The Groom[60]

"Do go on—continue, matchmaker, do."

Stepan's Speech

"Granny, it seems I've heard the tale you tell
Already twice today—and though we'll all
Delight in that good news when it arrives,
I doubt I'll have the will to carry on
'Til then. We spoke of freedom, but the truth
Is that we're cramped in what we do
By bondage. Day by day the evil grows,
Dealing its blows to all the world,

---

intervention, and Christ sits at God's right hand (Acts 7:55, Colossians 3:1); for a few examples, see Exodus 15:6, Psalm 21:8, Psalm 48:10, Psalm 118:15–16, and Isaiah 41:10.

    59. Possibly a reference to Christ, referred to as "King of kings" in Revelation 17:14, 19:16.

    60. That is, P., the poem's main narrator.

And we see terrible conflagrations all
Around, like some enormous flood of fire.
But where do you go to leave this trouble behind?
Where do you go to evade the torment?
You can bustle here and bustle there,
But still you'll fall into the claws of evil!
Just watch the goings-on inside the village:
They defame us and they curse us—they say
We're black and sticky, just like tar, although
The person they're debasing might be made
Of gold. Just go there, and oh, the words you'll find—
Your tongue will laugh and weep at once.

    "Listen!—

"Yesterday, I came back early from
The fields. I put away the horse, and took
A seat among the housemaids, and there
I sat a spell—when of a sudden, Vaniushka,
The footman, appeared among us, running.
I saw he wanted to have some fun,
As he whirled around in front of me,
And sang a tune with simple words,
Nothing fancy. But I understood
His song, and though a little rough the tune
May be, just listen to the kind of song it is."

The Footman's Song

    "I heard the bárin's whistle, so
    I jumped forthwith to where he was.
    He called me over like a dog.
    I stood before him in a sec,
    And now you'll hear the order that
    I got from him:

        'Call the hefty guy, the one
        Who's on obrók, who lived awhile
        In Saint Petersburg. And also call

The fat one, Akulína,
Who Vetrov lost to me at cards.'

"'Yesterday,' I told him, 'bárin,
You won seven, but you only
Got Irinas, Feklas, and
Some skinny Akulínas . . .'[61]

"That very week it happened that
The bárin from a ball returned—
His mood was bad, he swore at us
For nothing—beat us too, without
Excuse. Behind his back they cursed
His name. The cook was so enraged
He ran away. And then the coachmen
Told us that the bárin had
Been playing cards and lost some money.

"Well, let's thank God, at least—
If his father-in-law hadn't pulled him
From the cards in time, in a moment
To terrible trouble he'd consign
The village, with its souls,[62]
Its fields, meadows, vacant places.

"Hatred flowed out far and wide
Through the village of Zarech'e on the hill.
And games of chance became the custom
In the tower of Obiraev.[63]
Day and night the nobles play
For money and for peasants.

"A time came when muzhíks
No longer could survive this loss.

61. These are all the names of (serf) women.
62. That is, the peasants.
63. Evidently a fictional, allegorical name for some local landlord, deriving from the verb *obirat'*, meaning (in one of its slang usages) "to rob, to clean out" (*Oxford Russian Dictionary*).

89

P. (Petr O.)

The little kings[64] have ruined Rus'[65]
With pillage and despotic luxury,
And for their profit they've been playing
'People'—just as they'd play gorodkí.[66]

"Near us lives a clever man—Razzórin.[67]
Doesn't play at cards, owns thirteen souls,
[. . . . .]
But here's the way he gets his money:
He racks some peasants with bárshchina,
Flogs them cruelly if they're lazy,
Collects taxes on the things they make.
In town live fifteen souls of his, from whom
He takes obrók three times a year,
And threatens them by letter, commanding them
To get the payment in on time.

"And so they worry and they fret,
And just like youthful hens, they lay
Enormous eggs—not normal eggs,
But golden ones. Razzórin thrives
On all his profit—lives the way
Not many can afford to live—
But when he dies, that voevóde,[68]
He'll be judged by God as well.

"And here my song comes to an end.
How do the bárins preserve their peasants?
Just the way a pack of wolves, who fall
Upon a flock of sheep, rip them
Hungrily apart. Or here's the simile

---

64. The landlords, with perhaps a punning reference to "kings" in cards.
65. Here, traditional name for the Russian lands.
66. A game similar to skittles.
67. This fictional family name derives from the verb *razorít'*: to destroy, to ruin.
68. See note 31.

I'd use in every peasant house:
'The lords protect their property
As fire protects the dry straw.'"
[*End of song.*]

"One ought to run and lend a kindly word
To that man, hefty, laden with obrók,"
Continued Vaniushka. "Oh, these engagements
Of unequal pairs—and that Akulína's the one
Who should be called for him . . ."

Stepan[69]

"I look, and there goes Vaniushka, who leads
A handsome lad along with Akulína.
Sad, despondent, the groom walks on
With head hanging low. I pressed my way
Into the village, and (as one already used
To our master's blows) laid down beside
His door, a tad ajar, and pressed my ear to it.

"They entered, and began to pray to God
Before the icon; then to the right they turned
And bowed before their master, as though he sat
Upon a throne. Seated at the table
The poméshchik was; in an armchair both
Expensive and fashionable he sat.
The table was decorously laden with crystal,
And many golden dishes, trays, and cups.
The cleanness of the rooms was visible
To me: the parquet floors all coated with wax,
Bright hue of vases on the windowsills,
And walls upholstered o'er with velvet. . . .

"Suddenly I hear a question from the bárin:

69. Here Stepan resumes telling the story in his own voice.

P. (Petr O.)

A. G. Venetsianov, "The Threshing Barn," 1822–23. Serf artist G. V. Soroka (see images on pages 26 and 119) was one of Venetsianov's students.

—'So why have you come?'
—'By your order.'
—'Eh?'
—'By your order.'
—'And so? . . . alright, let's get down to business now.
What's that there you've brought to me?'
—'We ask that you accept this sugar, tea, and almond.'[70]
—'Ah, that's nice, many thanks, many thanks.

'Well now, I can see you're still a bachelor,
But here I've got a girl for you: clever,
Comely, a good stout frame, though not,
Perhaps, a lass as young as you might choose.

70. P.'s note: "The peasant on obrók asks that the tea, sugar, and almond be accepted because of a practice common among many poméshchiki: anyone arriving with a request had to appear in the village with gifts, bowing down low. Such was the way things were on Bezdoúshin's estate."

Anyone would like to marry her, I'm sure,
But I'll give her to the one who knows
How to run things as they should be run.

'So just how much obrók do you pay per year?
And just how many days do you work for me?'

'In obrók, I pay 250, sir,
And 47 rubles for the *prisyólok*;[71]
A week I spend on cutting hay,
And twenty days at harvest and the plow.'

'And just how big a family do you have?'

'My father, who's an aged man already; I,
And a couple of my aunts, two old women. . . .'

'Ah yes, I know—a year it's been since you
Last paid so much as a poloúshka[72] for them.'

'Sir, my father's just as old as they are.
Mightn't you lessen the obrók a bit?'

'Shut up, fool! No more of your tricks!
That old man's got a gift for work.
Now don't you see, you fool, that I
Have set aside a bride for you?
You now may don the marriage wreath with her,
And afterward you'll live together in love.'

'Might I also take up some few words
With you? Before you I bow, on bended knee!

71. P.'s note: "What the peasants call 'prisyóloks' are cattle-yards built on land far from the village and near good soil for plowing or making hay. This soil is worked for the most part by peasants on obrók during those days of [obligatory] labor imposed upon them."

72. A quarter-kopeck piece.

[I'm not a cunning man myself, you know,]73
And everything I'm telling you is true.
The bride you've chosen doesn't look too bad;
Perhaps she'll even come to feel love
For me—but my heart and soul are saying
That this wedding will be the ruin of me!

'So please re . . .'—'Shut up!'—'. . . lease . . .'74
'Shhhhhhhuuuut UP!'
'. . . from this fa . . .'—'Stop, stop, stop!!!

'Hey, Fomka! Driver! Come, come, come!
. . . .
Grab his hair! Yes, that's the way!
Beat him, thrash him, flog him, tear him apart!
I see what's up: he's become a dandy, now!
He's even started monitoring "love"!
There, that's it, that's how, that it!!'"

Stepan [Continues in His Own Words]

"And so Bezdoúshin sinned away inside
The house, while Ivan75 and I were sitting in
The footmen's chambers. I was laughing at
Ivan, at how he rushed around, looking out
Of one window, then another, telling me:

"'Look, Stepan, at how our coachman, Andrian,
Is agonizing in the stable. What a scream!
There, he's busting the curry-comb against
The wall—a comedian, that's what he is!
. . . .
Look, now he's whipping the horses!
. . . .

73. Line only partially legible in original manuscript.
74. Written this way in the original manuscript.
75. That is, Vaniushka, the footman (mentioned previously).

Hahahahahahahaha! He's turning the carriage around,
. . . .
Now he's tearing the plates off the breech bands!
Oh, there he's played himself out; he's looking
Our way, it seems, but against the light.
. . . .
Again he's running in and out the stable gates.

"'Oh, poor Andriakha,
See how Okuliakha[76] tortures him! . . .
He's so upset about his change in fortune. . . . [77]
. . . .
Well, what do you know! He's coming over here,
Talking away to himself. We'll hear him curse
The bárin, that's sure—this guy'll be trouble!
. . . Here he is.

"'What did you come over here for, Andrian?'

'I want to see the bárin.'

'No way!'

'Be quiet, Ivan, please be quiet. I want
To quit this job of mine. You can see
Just what lot befalls each one inside
Our manor house. We live to be ruined,
As though in Sodom, abandoned alive to demons.
Perhaps inside the house you needn't do
Such heavy work, but there's no good life here.
Into the army willingly you'll go,
Wandering to and fro across the earth—

76. "Andriakha" and "Okuliakha" are slightly belittling variants of Andrian and Okulina.

77. That is, Andrian, the coachman, is bewailing the bárin's changed intentions; Andrian's beloved, Akulina (or Okulina), is to go to "the handsome lad" who has just been beaten in the bárin's chambers.

But not because you like it!
Beatings, hunger and trouble, a ragged cloak
And boots—no, we've got no wish to see
The world, not even if we left together with
The other servants.
                    Did I never serve
Inside the house? Didn't I help put things
In order? I never spared my health at work,
Wasn't conniving or deceitful—just rode
Along in fear beside the bárin. . . .

'Flogging peasants is my business—
You're always ordered to strike away
With a mighty swing—at times I'd just
About unscrew my arms from my shoulders.
I've been the object of wrath myself;
Six times they've tried to flog me, and no way
Will I escape that foul business a seventh time . . .
. . . .

'Ah, deeds, deeds . . . everyone protects himself,
And no one grieves for me—no one cares
That my bones ache, that they measure
Bad weather like a calendar . . .

'The bárin, as it happens, has given me
Okulina, as reward for all my work.
I fell in love, lived here and there with her,
But now I look—and I've been fooled!
So I'm going to flee, leaving everything behind!'

'Listen, Andrian!
Don't do it, brother mine! You're drunk!'

'No, I'm not one bit drunk. Of course,
I did drain a glass for boldness' sake,
So as not to quail, after I'd resolved
To have done with the bárin. I'm going now.'

'Go then—just don't frighten us!'

[*Stepan resumes in his own voice.*]
"And the coachman, with half-drunken eyes,
Suddenly grasped the words he'd thought about
So carefully, and for the first time in his life
Crossed the threshold of slavery.

"He went into the room, poor man,
And pressed himself against the wall.
Seeing him, the bárin cried: 'And what
Might you be doing here, Andriashka?!'

"Andrian answered him timidly:
'I came here, sir, to find the reason why. . . .
Not long ago in the servants',[78] I heard that you
Are planning to pass Okulina on to someone else.
So did you give her to me for a laugh, or what?!
I don't believe I'm thought of as a fool
Among the servants, sir! And everyone already knows
That I've been living with Okulina for a long time, sir.
And none of them pities me in the least, of course . . .
Give me Okulina, so they don't laugh at me!'

"Suddenly, we heard a new commotion:
The bárin in a fury stamps his feet
And threatens; Andrian says his piece as well,
And both of them speak together, at once:[79]

Bárin	*Andrian*
'What is this? Out of here!'	'Allow me to marry her!'
'What! I'll bury you up to your ears!'	'Am I really not worthy of her?'
'What is this? Out of here!'	'Allow me to marry her!'

78. That is, the servants' quarters.
79. The next section is written as indicated, in parallel (and in the original, rhyming) columns.

'Ho, a stick! I'll smash your head for   'I'm always serving you, it seems . . .'
   you!'
'Hurry, you bastards! Oh, what a   'You said yourself, "Andrian . . .
   rowdy!'
'I'll have your hide for a drum   . . . take anyone from these seven,
   skin!'   brother."'

"The bárin didn't wait for footmen to arrive,
And took to beating his coachman with a walking stick:
'Here's Okulina for you, here's your Okuliakha,
Okuliakha-a akha-akha-akha-kha-kha-kha-Okuliakha!'
250 blows in all.
     For the bride:[80]
'Here's Andrian for you, here's your Andrian!
Andriakha-akha-akha-akha-kha-kha-Andriakha!'
    95 times.

"The bárin was exhausted, having beaten them,
So drained, indeed, that he fell into a faint.
In the servants ran, and, trembling, locked
The three criminals securely in the anteroom;
An escort guarded them there. Upon a couch
The master was laid, but Andrian,
The miserable coachman, beaten, wept and cried.

"Later, when all was quiet, to the footmen
He recounted all the master's deeds—
Those deeds were not good in the least."

Andrian

"The nobility's blows will make you old. . . .
Unjustly did the bárin beat me so. . . .

[*Andrian speaks here of the past.*]
"They'd bring peasant maids into the house,

---

80. Apparently, the bárin has Okulina brought in and flogs her as well.

Although I never asked to see them once.
And though they often asked us to gather
And look over girls we might take for brides,
It was easy to put up with that deception,
Because we knew they were pressuring the girls
For redemption;[81] we knew the reason for
The gathering, and what the peasant men outside
Were feeling. Those girls fear a life with us
No less than poison—so once again,
Pity the poor muzhíks! Five hundred's the price
For a daughter, and so they sell their property
And cattle, and finally bring their homes to ruin,
Giving everything over to the nobles. . . .

"So there's no sweetness in the lives of peasants
Either—what could be more harsh and bitter?
God in heaven, forgive my transgressions!
Countless people I've flogged already,
And to fulfill what was of me commanded,
Took up the duties of an executioner.
I whipped unhappy people for the sake
Of obrók, to make them pay their dues,
To secure the landlord's mighty profit,
To seize what's levied by recruitment.[82]
The peasants call it all the same 'obrók,'
And hand over money in piles and piles;
The nobles look only at their losses,
And beat and whip if they're not paid.

"I recall how once I cruelly beat
Three peasants in a row who hadn't paid—

---

81. That is, according to Andrian, the landowner would threaten to simply give peasant girls over to his lackeys if their families didn't pay a redemption payment. The situation is one of extortion.

82. The implication here seems to be that the landlord would extort bribes from peasants who were trying to keep their sons out of the army. Serfholders were generally obliged to send a specific number of recruits into the Russian army.

P. (Petr O.)

And heard the bárin smoothly sing a song
About them, in a pleasing, cheerless voice.
Meanwhile he'd be casting nasty glances
On the crowd of peasants gathered there,
And proposed to teach them how to live, in song.

"It seems that once he wrote another song,
But lost it on the road (it must have dropped
From out his rolled-up cuffs, as he waved
His arms about)—why should he care
In any case? Well, he returned from his walk,
The bárin did, and spoke of his loss in just this way:

"'I lost a manuscript along the road. . . .
Rolled up it was, just like a tube or coil.'
'I didn't pick it up, sir,' I responded. He spat
In my face, and walked vexedly away.
But I really hadn't seen it . . . yet.
For one of the beaten peasants had tramped it
Into the dung with his feet. I retrieved it
Afterward, and today I've brought it
With me here, as consolation to myself. . . ."

[*Stepan resumes in his own voice.*]
"He passed the notebook to one of the coachmen,
Who took the book and read aloud to all."

Song in Time of Punishment, Sung as an Admonition to Peasants

"Listen here, rogue, to refrains
Sung by us educated Russians.
Beasts, goats, slackers—all of you
Must labor for the nobles!
For us, kingship you must secure—
That's the Russian medicine for you!
There's a big pile of birch rods—
Hey, Andriashka, bring them out!
Long ago the due date passed—
So now remember, rascal, keep it in mind!

"Kill yourself at work from childhood on,
And don't be just a thoughtless beast;
Forget about your weekly holidays,
And think of one thing only:
How you'll pay your debt to master.

"I'll not relieve you of your duties—
I'll flay you all down to your heels!
So you remember how to act
Where money is concerned;
So you remember our command
Never to carouse; and so
You'll know that, among ourselves,
We feast when you're not there.
There the champagne hisses like a snake,
And under its spray, we rejoice.
And soundly our conscience sleeps,
Because we've forgotten what conscience is,
And make no mention of it.

"It's your fault that we grab tribute from
The innocent—how to answer God for that?
We're selling souls,[83] it may be true,
Because of money—we need money!
Our large expenses, in every home,
Demand that we always fret
To keep it coming in. And with you folk
With you—it's not easy either. . . ."
[*End.*]

Andrian

"After this song, the boiárin[84] bid
That I flog another one. Angrily he said:
'Don't spare him!' All he did was wave his hand."

83. That is, serfs (perhaps with an implied reference to the landowner's "soul" as well).
84. The landlord.

P. (Petr O.)

Second Song of Secret Meditation

"Why is everyone scared of blowing money?
Let all things blossom, all things gleam!
My profits aren't spoiled by luxury,
And large profit bears fruit. My house
Is furnished through profit like a palace;
There's a garden before the house,
Ponds fed by rivers, and not least,
A staff of many persons
Who're always serving me.
They are all my serfs,
And look upon my face with fear,
Render me all earthly homage,
Regard their master as a god.
For what more could I wish?

"Work's in full swing on the fields:
Of cattle I've a herd that's grand;
The hunt with barking dogs goes well.
I've got a booroon[85] of peasants,
And a herd of the finest horses.
I've traveled over half the world,
And seen people of various kinds;
It's just a pity, that travel sours
The profits of many here,
Especially when gold here flows
Like a river, even during time of spring.

"I recall a story strange but true:
When I left for my voyage
Beyond our own Russian border,
My protector was the profit I had made.
How can we not love it passionately?
With profit, you can even make your way
To Paris! But there, however, as you
Carry on, there's danger it'll be swept

---

85. P.'s note: "Booroon—this word is used to signify that, of which one has a lot."

102

Away. There you'll shine in a sea of luxury,
Splashing against abundant obrók.
But the longer you stay there,
You'll see the shape you're income's in . . .
It's half-dead, quietly rattling,
Then grows entirely weak, languishes;
Life fades from money hour to hour,
And the cheer it brings is less and less.
And so we don't lose our funds abroad,
Home we go, to give our cash the cure!
We gather stárostas together in the village,
And give our income health again."
[*End of song.*]

Andrian

"And so I whip away, murmuring at times
About it: 'Sir, the muzhík is already silent . . .'
And he in his usual way replies: 'Strike,
And slash away! He's breathing, I can see!
That's the way! That's it, that's it! Alright, stop.'
And so you finish. There the flogged one lies.
You pick him up. The poor man shakes
And can hardly stand on his feet.
The bárin meanwhile reads to him about
Obrók and other dues, threatening
To punish in advance. Oh, how hard it is,
Fulfilling all these subtle lessons!"

Here Are the Words of the Coachman to the Peasant on Obrók[86]

"And so, my rival, did you hear
My songs and truthful tales?
You're young and handsome, but you'll
Be wrecked by how things go 'round here.

86. These words are presumably spoken by Andrian to the peasant who was beaten just before he was.

P. (Petr O.)

Suddenly in spring you'll fade, before
Summer arrives, because of weather that's cold
And bad. And sorrowful years you'll drag
Along, without the object of your love.
Don't dream of joyous arrivals
From far-off foreign lands to this,
Your native country. For us here, it is night;
The stars are covered over, and clouds
Of storm are hanging over you!

"You will see the bárin as a judge,
And the power given him by law.
He pours bitterness into a vessel
And orders us to drink it dry.
How difficult it is to find our joy,
When suffering at the hands of evil fate.
At the outset of our path in life,
Mind and knowledge are destroyed by bondage.
Hour by hour, the masters commit
Their villainies, and turn our hearts
Into a wasteland. Our bodies are open to
Their whims, and we live the same as beasts.
Nor science nor politics do we know,
Blind men that we are, from birth;
We do not plead to God for wisdom,
And so the educated think us fools.
This is why my dear departed dad
Told me not to speak too much.
He taught me to live with iron patience
As he felt his own life reach its end."

The Words of Stepan Regarding Andrian's Censures[87]

"Suddenly the bárin recovered consciousness,
And loudly called his footmen. He shouted, roared,
Commanded, and an order cruel was issued.

87. Again, the text returns to Stepan's own narrative voice.

"He gathered all of us muzhíks in a group
To flog, in the stable, the coachman Andrian.
There a 'bed' was prepared,[88] and switches too,
In many bunches. The young lads went,
A wide and single host, into the tower,
And let the sufferer know about
The fateful sorrows awaiting him.

"On hearing this, the criminal took fright,
And began to shake like leaves in the heat;
He prayed to the bárin, bending low,
And let flow bitter tears: 'Father, send me off
Instead to be a soldier—or even to
Siberia—just spare me from this retribution;
Master, I'm scared of lying beneath the switch . . .'

"But the coachman's supplication was in vain.
The poméshchik said: 'I do *not* forgive!
First I'll have your hide thrice over,
And then I'll lather your forehead for you!'[89]
The muzhíks had meanwhile come inside,
And Bezdoúshin ordered them to seize him.
Andrian went mute, as the order was received."

The Boiarin's[90] Command

"Bring that barrrrrrrrbarian into the stable!
How dare he be so rude to me?
Let the switches roll, and don't keep count
Of how many times you strike!
And watch: be sure you spare him not!
If not, you'll be in trouble, all of you!
Bring the girl here too; she needs a flogging

88. Presumably a kind of wooden horizontal surface onto which the person undergoing punishment was strapped.
89. An odd expression, apparently meaning "send off to the army."
90. Another term meaning (here) bárin, landlord.

Just as bad, so they'll *both* keep honest.
You, obróchnyi,[91] go away,
But appear again tomorrow morn."

Stepan[92]

"The crowd brought in the couple, as though into
A bedroom, splendidly decked out for bride
And groom. Not matchmaker, but poméshchik,
Scourge of unhappy slaves, led the ritual here.

"Seized by fear, the criminal walked along,
Like some guilty idol, dumb, to the abyss.
His face seemed coated by mysterious dust . . .
Andrian went into the stable, took off
His clothes, crossed himself and laid,
Already void of sorrow, upon the terrible bed.
We tied him tightly down, and others to the left
Placed the girl upon the stove bench;[93]
Four men held her down.

"Everything was silent, at the start.
On both sides, young men in pairs
Attentively awaited the command.
Then they heard it, and they began.

"A loud whistling of cudgels was heard,
Along with nobility's sung refrains;
In a pedagogic tenor, our master sang.
The descant was furnished by the mournful girl,
And the coachman roared the bass the while.
And so this choir of discord sang away,
And everyone was scared of what might lay
Ahead; the people, in their kitchens half asleep,
Shuddered as they heard the sounds.

---

91. A peasant on obrók; here, the peasant who was flogged first.
92. Subtitle added.
93. Traditional bench in peasant huts, running along the walls of the izbá.

"They sang there for a long, long time.
Then first the descant, and then the bass
Grew tired and fell silent. But the tenor sang
To us a long while after. And then our gentle bard
Grew tired of his vengeful malice too,
Fell silent, and went away at length into
The darkness and his home. We left the sufferers
Behind, and wandered home to rest ourselves.
The stable gates were locked, and how
They slept there, we don't know."

Stepan's Dream and Various Stories

"But I fell asleep, and a terrible dream vexed
My breast with sorrow. During the night, I moaned
A great moan; I'd not want to hear that moan
From you.
          Here is what I saw in my dream:
My wife and poor babies wasted away
In hunger, they did; they called me home,
And they weren't kidding either. How I rushed
And ran to them, thought of ways that I
Might help—but then I saw, and slept no more—
I was called to work in the fields. . . .

"I rose, and potent fear ran coldly through
My veins. Roughly I put a harness on a horse
And rode out the gates. I went with gloomy
Spirit, and heart as cold as ice. About
A single thing I thought, mournfully,
With bitter feeling. Of my dream, I'd grown
More terrified, thinking that my fate it was
To live this way—and riding in a barren field,
I lost my way. The dark gray horse brought me
To the forest, whirling around there with me.

"Then behold! I hear a noise rising on the fields,
For the people there had broken into laughter,
Crying—'look how Stepan has lost his way!'
I gathered myself together then, whipped

And cursed the horse as the little rascal
She was, and hurried away to plow—
The jade went off, twirling her tail. . . .

"Boldly I approached the people, explained
Myself before the desiátskii,[94] and had a laugh
With him. Then I went to work.
We worked like one artel, laboring hard
In our sweat, until we all fell tired
From our work, and sat to breakfast by
The river. We tasted blessed nourishment—
Stale bread and water—and declared
Among ourselves: 'Here the poor envy not
The viands of the rich!'
                          'Our life is hard,
Brothers, hard,' said Pakhom while at rest;
'The nobles are sated with every kind of meat,
But forget about us entirely.' 'Oh, the nobles don't
Forget us,' said Sidor in response; 'In summer they often
Beckon us to their wide fields: we don't demand
Their bread and salt,[95] but hurry to plow their land
For them, with bucketfuls of families cutting hay,
And, when the time comes, reaping their crops
As well. First we grind their corn and rye
(While dragging out our miserable existence),
And bring offerings to them of rams,
Of berries, mushrooms, and of birds.
Firewood and kindling we cut for them
In fall; and women weave sackcloth during
Winter, while we cart everything around—
And the boiars[96] carry on with their own thing!'

"Languidly, Klim added the following:
'Our bárin goes so far as to enter in a single book

94. See note 51.
95. Traditional symbol of hospitality.
96. Here, the landlords.

Peasants and cattle in one set of accounts.
The other day, the majordomo came by,
And grouped us with the beasts in his book;
A flock of chickens, pecking at their feed,
Likewise ended up archived with us!
(The rooster got jealous when he noticed this!)'

. . . .

"Well, we all had a good laugh over this,
And prayed together after finishing breakfast.
We set ourselves to work again,
And rushed to polish off that field.

"We went from one end to the other,
And, arriving at the other side,
Everyone stretched his legs along the road,
When there appeared a young man on obrók.
He was riding from the village to his home,
And had to wait for us; he sat there, head
Hung low, as though he'd been condemned
To death. How did we react? Same as everywhere:
Rank respects nothing else but—rank.
None made way for him without his asking first.

"I saw the desiátskii waving his hand at me
        And saying:
'Stepan, go and ask the little guy just how
The bárin dealt with him—did he give him
Akulína, or did he find him someone else?
Some peasant on obrók is taking her away, it seems,
And so it's likely that the coachman will go mad.'[97]
So I went over to this obróchnyi, and had
A civil converse with him, as follows here."

97. That is, Andrian.

P. (Petr O.)

The Conversations of Stepan
with the Peasant on Obrók

Stepan

"Hello, good young fellow!"

Peasant on Obrók

"Hello there, uncle!"[98]

Stepan

"Boast to me a little, stranger, about the things
Awarded you by the bárin—unless, of course,
He dumped half a cart of sorrow on you?"

Peasant on Obrók

"Ah, uncle!—just about a whole cart, in fact.
I sat there in the village, feeling that
It was a cave or den of thieves; I felt
That all that was left was to collapse,
After seeing all these ruined fates.
Today the bárin ruled that eight slaves more
Be flogged. Cruelly he demanded that I choose
One of two peasant girls. Two choices he gave
To me: in a week, either get married
Or buy freedom for myself.
I stood there without saying anything,
And the bárin demanded that I answer.
So I started speaking further:
'Freedom? Am I worth a lot to you?'
'7,000 assignats, and on top of that
All [your] land, grain, cattle, and house,
And your father, of course.'

"In response I said to him: 'My lord, ask of me
Only 3,000 rubles, no more. I then

---

98. A familiar title, not implying familial relationship.

Will work for you twelve years,
And afterward be freed.'"

The Bárin's Response

"3,000, I will not take.
Fool! Have you heard how families
In your village have been doing?
Per brother, they doled 10,000 out,
They'd also lived in cities—fine fellows,
Of course! But you, you're empty headed,
And so, observe the rules that I set down.
Come again to my little village to see me,
And there from among seven girls
Pick one for yourself as wife
And make a family with her."

Peasant on Obrók[99]

"Thus I took leave of the bárin,
And with sorrow left the village.
But resolved to contemplate our lot:
Bondage is a heavy burden to us all!

"With horror and despair, I wonder:
By what strange turn of fate
Did Rus' win this similarity
To the ancient people of Israel?
How did we come to be seized
By the evil of Egyptian bondage?
It would seem that we are Christians,
No devotees of idols—so where did all
These tyrants come from? They keep the light
Of Christ from the world, asking that
The people pray to them, and venerate,
Through them, the golden calf.[100]

99. Subtitle added.
100. P.'s note: "The golden calf is a symbol for money."

And hearts in torment are bent so low
That all goes just the way they want it.

"But what are we doing, we slaves?
We fulfill the orders of the masters,
And in ignorance brought by our
Cruel fate, we fill the world with vice.
Do you [know] why God the Father merely
Turns his face away from us,
And why the people suffer in confusion
Unobserved by that all-seeing eye?

"Oh, will our tribe be waiting long
For the arrival of our warrior king?
Already we drag along a burden of torment,
Tarrying till all patience is expended.
We must all pray to God, that to the tsar
He might give of his wisdom; that he might
Command the tsar's attendance to
The deliverance of his people."

Stepan

"I responded to his words in full accord—
'Yes! Long ago, 'twas time for us
To turn to this, to pray to the holy Trinity,
That it might bring wisdom to our tsar,
And free us from this yoke.
This land would enjoy renewal then—
Fine grain in the fields, thick grasses in
The meadows—and earth would show itself
In all fertility. New freedom would improve
Our homes, our buildings and our stock,
And our children would learn to live
By strength of their own labor.
And all the world would be filled with light
And pleasant air: little birds would sing
And gambol in the forest groves,
Amid the sound of breezes rustling through

The leaves; the herd in the valley would rise
To rejoice at the sound of the herdsman's pipe.
And all nature would say with us:
"Flourish, Russian land!
Freedom is yours, bondage is no more!"

"'The old times would be forgotten,
[Payment would be made for land,]
And harmful clouds would not be seen.
Can we believe this darkness will not end?
Will the sun's rays be quelled forevermore?

"'And so, dear groom, it's time for us
To end our conversation. Your words
Have made me happy, and I've forgotten kids
And manor house alike! You, my dear one,
Sorrow not that our bárin is so proud
And strict, and do not fear his villainies—
God will give payment to him who endures.'

"I looked, and there the peasant stood in tears,
Musing deep on certain thoughts.
He took leave of me then, as though from a friend,
And rode away from our field.

"I walked up to the desiátskii, and told again
To him our conversation. He had his own response
To make to our words, often casting glances
In the direction of the village."

The Words
of the Desiátskii

"Already twice we've heard rumors of freedom,
Heard that the tsar had wanted to make us happy.
But will our rusty chains in fact be opened,
The yoke of slavery fall from our necks,
And our wounds heal? It would be as though
Almighty God had hoisted us from swamps

Into the firmament, and after this, we'd
Even more desire to serve the tsar.
Our debt to him would be our obligation
To obey him in all things, to pay taxes
On our land, to fight against the enemies
Of Russia, not sparing ourselves in battle.
But don't say a word of this out loud,
My friend, for boiars ride us like before.

"Stepan, step forth and shout![101] The grave is
The only nest we'll find in the good life.

"Once I set myself to work, and took
To chasing out my horse, skinny as a twig.
Suddenly I heard a voice in the forest—
A peasant on obrók had broken into song,
And my ragged cattle pen was near
That bit of forest where mournfully he sang.
The peasant expressed his sorrow, and I
Had no time to listen to him, but all the same
Rode with ears wide open. Here's the song,
"If you'd like to hear it: with my soul,
I understood it."

Song of the Peasant on Obrók

"Tell me, soul, why do you suffer?
What sort of pangs have seized you?
Do you foretell for me some new fate,
Or torment with the old one?

"And you, heart, say your piece:
Why do you moan so in my breast?
You're not announcing woe too, are you?
Wait a bit before wasting away with disease!

---

101. P.'s note: "To shout [here] means 'to plow.'"

"And you, tears, why do you water?
Hair, what made you lose your curl?
The days of spring have darkened:
The fields, meadows, and the trees.

"I see only thick clouds that turn
The light into terrible darkness.
Everywhere, fateful troubles are there,
Running along beside me.

"And so I must settle down, and make
The choice of that bride, the one
I'm ordered to marry, the unwanted wife
With whom I'm ordered to live!

"Not knowing family happiness within
Our lives, the path to love is blocked to us;
Human autocracies turn us
Toward a life of vice.

"Was it for this, that we were born,
That we should wear the chains placed on them by power?
And that the powers themselves should sin because of us,
And live within the darkness of their evil deeds?

"And so, if this must go on, and we're
To suffer from one another forever,
Then why are we born upon this earth
Merely furiously to pursue new torment?

"O God, God almighty!
Show us the lie, exposed before the truth,
We who live with you ask
That you preserve the world from ruin.

"We glorify you within the Trinity:
Raise our praise once more to the tsar,
Preserve the orphans and the poor,
And maintain your laws."
[*End of song.*]

P. (Petr O.)

Stepan

"Then he rode further into the wood,
And his voice vanished on the air. . . .
After that I worked for a long time,
And good people along with me,
But the day ended, thank God,
And we were sent to our homes."

Solomónida

"So Stepan spoke his piece; I understood,
And grieved over the slaves' fate.
But afterward I said to him:
'I've delayed you here, and you're
Already wearied from plowing, moaning all
The time from your troubles—you even
Ended up in the manor house—in that whirlpool,
Friend, you'll drown. We've angered God, that's sure:
For there's no end to transgression there.'"

Stepan[102]

"Oh, marvelous creation of God—
Lord of all earthly things—the human being!
What are we to do? We're called 'property,'
And those same humans . . . oh, it's a strange time!
Wretched is the law that rules in Russia—
The human, created in blessed immortality,
Is bought and is sold like cattle or plants
Of earth! Because of this we languish;
For this we must bear all pain—
Live in poverty, as ignoramuses,
Together with the boiar's beasts. . . ."

102. Subtitle added.

Solomónida[103]

"My muzhík then let tears flow
And began to straighten out his reins;
From me, the old woman, he took his leave,
And went to his home to sleep.
I too returned to my house
And soon laid down to rest."

The Groom[104]

So this is the fate of all serfs—
A single fate for all the condemned!
They're punished for their faults—
But what do we, the innocent, have to do
With such faults? Or are we criminals before God?
Must we wear the chain of bondage?
Here, in spite of all restriction,
We can ask something of God—
Did the Creator really grow furious
At our grandfathers when they lived,
Ordering them into ruin at last,
And us as well, congenitally and forever?
Oh God! Clean the arch of heaven,
And heed the prayers of slaves!
Make more broad our narrow path
On earth, take off our bondsman's chains,
And then with free hands
Shall we restore earthly labor;
God and tsar will be with us,
And the hearts of Russians will blossom.

103. Subtitle added.
104. That is, P., the main narrator of the poem (the putative author).

Nikolai Shipov

The Story of My Life and Wanderings

The Tale of the Former Serf Peasant Nikolai Shipov, 1802–62

The following narrative, one of the longest published autobiographies by a Russian serf, appeared (like so many other memoirs) in the pages of *Russian Antiquity* (*Russkaia Starina*, in 1881). The translation that follows provides an abridged version of that text, with annotations clarifying Nikolai Nikolaevich Shipov's[1] complex and detail-laden tale.

We know nothing about the author, apart from what he tells us in "The Story of My Life and Wanderings." Besides containing what is surely one of the most astonishing tales of captivity and escape on record, Shipov's "Story" includes some priceless digressions, particularly his descriptions of Russian frontier and colonial life in the early nineteenth century, and what is probably the most detailed first-person *peasant* account available of a Russian peasant wedding. The peripatetic Shipov writes of his experiences in virtually every corner of European Russia, from his own village south of Nizhnii Novgorod to the cities of Moscow and Saint Petersburg to Bessarabia, culminating in the Caucasus during the colonial wars of 1829–59. In terms of sheer wealth of detail and breadth of geographical coverage, Shipov's autobiography is unrivaled among Russian serf narratives.

---

1. Pronounced "SHEE-puff."

G. V. Soroka, "View of the Dam on the Estate Spasskoe," 1840s. (courtesy of the Russian Museum, Saint Petersburg)

In publishing the story of my life in the pages of *Russian Antiquity*,[2] I hope to meet with sincere sympathy from all those who have chanced to encounter trouble and injustice during their lives. During the course of my life, filled as it was with much wandering and misfortune, I endured many hardships, but always bore them with nobility and sobriety, never losing my presence of mind even in the saddest and most difficult situations. I

---

2. In Russian, *Russkaia Starina,* the journal of historical and memoir material in which Shipov's autobiography appeared: *Russkaia Starina* 31 (1881), 133–148, 221–240, 437–478, 665–679. (The last section [pp. 665–679] recounts events in Shipov's life following his manumission and is not included in this translation.) It was reprinted in 1933 together with another nineteenth-century memoir as V. N. Karpov, *"Vospominaniia"; Nik. Shipov, "Istoriia Moei Zhizni,"* ed. P. L. Zhatkin, intro. by N. V. Iakovlev (Moscow: Academia, 1933), 362–523.

convey here the facts pertaining to my life from childhood onward, in the form in which those facts have been preserved in my memory. In submitting the story of my adventures to the judgment of my readers, I place all my trust in their gracious indulgence—

Nikolai Shipov

1802–1813

I was born in 1802 in Vyezdnaia,[3] near the city of Arzamas, in the province of Nizhnii Novgorod. My father was a landlord's peasant, but well to do. He was involved in the cattle trade and went every year to the Simbirsk and Orenburg provinces to buy sheep. He was a literate and erudite man, honored and respected by all.

When I was six they sent me to a local priest to learn to read and write. As far as I can recall, my grandmother brought me to the church just as they were concluding the service in honor of the prophet Nahum. That's how it was usually done in the old days.[4] I quickly learned to read, and in a year or two had already "gone through" (as they say) the entire Psalter. With writing, however, I had less success: no matter how I tried, I still wrote in an old-fashioned hand, much like that of my parents. Thus passed four or so years.

[. . .][5]

[Following the disruption associated with the War of 1812], my father recommenced trading cattle. He went to the steppes of the Simbirsk and Orenburg provinces to buy cattle, now taking me with him. (This trip [in 1813] was my first to the steppes of the northeast provinces.) Later he often brought me along to Orenburg Krai,[6] gradually teaching me the secrets of his trade. Here, it might not be out of place to speak about some of what I heard, saw, and experienced during that time.

---

3. Today known as Vyezdnoe, it is now a suburb of the city of Arzamas; see map on page 2.

4. In Russian Orthodox tradition, Nahum is the patron of learning ("pokrovitel' ucheniia").

5. Here and elsewhere, I indicate my abridgements of the text with ellipses in square brackets. Occasionally, I also incorporate summaries and clarifications in my own words, also placed within square brackets.

6. An administrative division in Russia and the former USSR, with central administrative offices located in some main city (here, Orenburg).

1814–1819

We made our trips to the Ural steppes at various times of the year, but usually left home in March or in the early days of April—both in order to buy cattle well in advance of other traders and because it would be easier to drive them home during the summer.

A little way from the city of Simbirsk, on the far side of the Volga, begins the steppe; it stretches to the city of Ural'sk and beyond, and from thence all the way to the Caspian Sea, expansive and vast. Across the steppe flow small streams abundant with every kind of fish; wild fowl are to be found there in great numbers, and Father and I never missed an opportunity to go hunting. To the north along the Ural foothills lived a multitude of wild goats; hunting them, however, was difficult and dangerous.

Small settlements of Ural Cossacks were scattered through the steppe at considerable distance from one another. Along the so-called "line" along the Ural River, Cossack outposts like small fortresses made of earth had been built for protection against raids by hostile Kyrgyz.[7] (These Kyrgyz brought no small amount of trouble; they stole away cattle and sometimes people, whom they usually sold in Khiva.)[8]

For the most part, the Cossacks were raisers of cattle and fisherman; they planted melons, watermelons, and various vegetables, but in insignificant amounts. They were crude men, though quite hospitable. They strongly disliked the Orthodox Russians and wouldn't eat from the same plates as they did (they always gave us special plates from which to eat); they would, however, drink wine and vodka from the same glasses. The Cossack women were kind, gracious, and devout. Across that vast expanse, from Ural'sk to the town of Iur'ev, everyone great or small spoke Kyrgyz—this was because they lived in close proximity to the Kyrgyz and often carried out business with them.

[. . .]

[Among the many other problems we faced while driving cattle across the steppe], we had to deal with bandits, who ruled those areas unimpeded by authority. On this side of the Volga, for example, near the village of

7. The Kyrgyz are a west-central Asian people who now live primarily in Kyrzyzstan; it is doubtful that the people Shipov refers to here are "Kyrgyz" in the contemporary sense.

8. Khiva (in present-day Uzbekistan) was the capital of the Khivan Khanate from 1592 until 1920.

Sobakino (Simbirsk[9] province), the retired soldier Bezrukii robbed and plundered together with his audacious comrades.

In 1816, my father sent our salesman Baranin (who was a loyal and responsible man) home together with two herds and seven helpers. They stopped with their herds one night near a forest about four versts[10] from Sobakino. In the morning, Bezrukii rode out of the forest with his lads and demanded money from Baranin. The workers began to quail, and Baranin fell to his knees, telling the bandit that he had no more than ten rubles on him. After receiving twenty or so blows with the whip, Baranin gave him all the money he had and his best horse.

The robbers went off into the forest, but the faithful steward, after ordering the laborers to drive on the cattle, rode immediately to Sobakino and told the village authorities what had happened. And what response did he get? "Ah, my dear fellow," they told him, "those bandits have robbed not only you, but many others as well. And they've taken a lot more money than you just lost. We can't do anything for you; it's possible that they're already wandering along the Penza highway.[11] Be off, and God be with you." And so Baranin left.

On the other side of the Volga in the Obshchii Syrt,[12] where the roads run in the direction of Orenburg and Ural'sk, the Cossack Ivan Grigoriev Mel'nikov and his men preyed on passersby. Mel'nikov was an object of fear for all who traveled, and various tales about him and his feats circulated among the people, tales that mixed fact and fable. It was said, for example, that he possessed a charm protecting him from guns, making it impossible to kill or even wound him with a bullet. It took years for the local police to catch him; on those occasions when they did succeed in imprisoning him, he would escape, no matter how vigilant the guard or sturdy the lock. Mel'nikov would kill only in rare and exceptional circumstances. He loved obedience and submission, and whipped anyone who disobeyed his orders and refused his demands, taking from them even more plunder than he otherwise would have.

---

9. Now known as Ul'ianovsk: city west of the Urals, south of Kazan'.

10. An old Russian unit of measurement; one verst (in Russian, *versta*) is equivalent to about 1.06 kilometers.

11. That is, already several hundred kilometers away, in the district of the city of Penza (see map).

12. Name for a system of plateaus in the southwest Ural area (between the cities of Samara and Orenburg).

On one occasion, a group of peasants from Vyezdnaia—more than twenty men on ten carts—left for Orenburg to buy rams. When they reached the Obshchii Syrt, they agreed among themselves not to submit to bandits in the event of a raid. After a time, the peasants noticed a group of armed men riding fast toward them—none other than Mel'nikov the robber chieftain and his gang.

"Stop!" cried Mel'nikov to the lead peasant, riding up to the string of carts; but the peasant refused to obey and rode on. Mel'nikov then ordered one of his comrades to beat the unsubmitting peasant on his back with the whip. At this, the peasants grew terrified and forgot their vow not to give in to bandits. Mel'nikov ordered that a piece of felt be brought for him; it was laid out on the ground, and he sat down.

Silently, the peasants stood before him, surrounded by Mel'nikov's men. Their leader addressed the terrified peasants with the following words: "I know that you're traveling to Orenburg to buy cattle; and I know that every one of you is carrying cash. I could simply clean you out, but as you displayed your obedience to me, I'll take only five rubles assignat[13] per cart. On the return trip, I'll ask nothing of you, except some mutton for soup." One of the peasants immediately pulled out his wallet and gave Mel'nikov the money.

"What's your name?" asked Mel'nikov.

"Ivan Grigoriev Minev," replied the peasant.

"My old chap," said Mel'nikov, "you're my namesake, we share the same name! Take off your crucifix, give it to me, and take mine—we shall be 'brothers by the cross.'"

They traded crucifixes, and Mel'nikov returned the money to Minev, saying: "Take your money back, brother—we're of one family now. But you, my lads—fork it out!"

After collecting the money, the gang leader requested wine and something to eat, and ordered everyone to drink. He then left, paying two rubles for the peasants' hospitality. They were pleased that they'd gotten off so easily.

Later, Minev recounted how he met with Mel'nikov again on the return trip from Orenburg. Mel'nikov never took a kopeck from him. They

---

13. A form of paper money, in use from 1769 to about 1840 (*Oxford Russian Dictionary* [Oxford and New York: Oxford University Press, 1993]).

dined and caroused together, and Mel'nikov once even invited him to his camp, where he gave Minev a horse and 25 rubles in bronze.

I should add that Mel'nikov was eventually caught by a local police chief about fifty versts from Samara, whence they transported him, his arms and legs in wooden stocks. They hung the stocks on his neck as well, and on the road to Samara, he suffocated. On that sensational note, the legend of Ivan Mel'nikov passed out of memory . . .

[. . .]

Though mostly involved in the cattle trade, my father also dealt in tallow, furs, and skins. We sold these items mostly in Moscow and at the Makar'evskaia market in Rostov. My first trip as a trader took place in April 1816, a trip I undertook together with one of our old and experienced salesmen. Before I left, my father and grandmother (my mother having already died by this time) asked that I write out a psalm called "Live through the help of the Almighty." They told me to learn it by heart and read it every day, and instilled in me the idea that I would avoid attacks from bandits and other evil people by reading that psalm.

We traveled to the cities of Murom and Suzdal', where we visited nearly every church and kissed holy relics. In Rostov, after having sold a good many items, we went to pray to that great Russian miracle worker, Dmitrii of Rostov,[14] and asked the prelate if we might hear the service. We then ascended the bell tower and heard the tuned bells[15] before leaving Rostov for the glorious first capital, Moscow.[16]

Although I was young and ignorant, I had been hearing a great deal about our "mother built of white stone"[17] over the course of the previous three years. My trip there, undertaken when I was twelve years old, remains firmly stamped in my memory. On arriving there I bought, on the advice of the salesman, a newfangled peaked cap and beautiful silk sash. We went off to see the sights of the city, and everything there surprised and

14. Metropolitan Dmitrii of Rostov (born Daniil Grigor'ev, 1651; d. 1709), Russian Orthodox saint.

15. Between 1682 and 1688 the Moscow bell makers Philip Andreev and Flor Terentiev cast three bells weighing eight (metric) tons, sixteen tons, and thirty-two tons in the city of Rostov (see map). Rung together, these bells produce a major chord; they are also mounted horizontally on a special bell tower with large open arches—the peal of these bells can be heard some twenty miles away.

16. "First capital" in contrast to Saint Petersburg, the "second capital."

17. "Matushka-belokamennaia," a traditional epithet of Moscow.

astonished me: long, winding streets filled with people riding and walking; huge, high houses, some of which were either singed or unfinished—a sad token of the recent French presence in Moscow;[18] a multitude of churches; and the golden-topped Kremlin with its cathedrals, palaces, and halls; and the "Ivan the Great" bell tower, the highest of them all, in front of which lay an enormous bell.[19]

We spent about three weeks in Moscow, and so I had the opportunity to get fairly well acquainted with the city. I was very pleased with myself as I wandered about the city, thinking, "so now, I've visited Moscow—when I get home, I'll tell everyone about what I've seen." And so it was—there was no end to my stories.

In May of the same year, my father married for a second time. He took as his bride a neighbor girl, fourteen years of age, with whom I'd played children's games up to that time. After the wedding, my father ordered me not to refer to his young wife as "mother." So I didn't.

1820–1828

Four years later, when I turned eighteen, my father decided it was time to find me a wife as well. Any merchant from Arzamas would gladly have offered his daughter to me, with a large dowry and gifts of money to boot; but the landowner allowed us to marry only other serfs. In Vyezdnaia there were three potential brides, all daughters of well-to-do peasants. According to established custom, my father called our close relatives in for a family council. They called me and asked, "Which girl would you like to ask for her hand in marriage?" I replied that, as I didn't know any of them, I had nothing to say in the matter. They decided to arrange a marriage with the daughter of a rather wealthy peasant named Lanin.[20]

On the morning of November 2, my uncle, a merchant named Feoktistov, was sent to Lanin's house to begin negotiations. After hearing out

18. That is, during the War of 1812.

19. Shipov is referring here to the famous third "Tsar-Bell" or Great Dormition Bell, which fell down and cracked (because of a fire in the Kremlin) in 1701.

20. What follows is a detailed description of the premarriage transactions and various ceremonies making up a traditional Russian peasant betrothal and wedding. For an excellent scholarly account of peasant marriage rituals, see Christine D. Worobec, *Peasant Russia: Family and Community in the Post-Emancipation Period* (Dekalb: Northern Illinois University Press, 1995), 151–174.

"Betrothal," etching by N. Shakhovskoi.

Feoktistov's proposal, Lanin said that he was unable right then to give a positive answer; it was necessary, first, to go to church and attend the service, then assemble all the relations for a family council. He told Feoktistov to come back the following evening. My uncle returned with this news to our own council, and they decided to wait.

At the Lanin family council, as it was later recounted to me, some of the relatives were opposed to my marrying the daughter. They criticized my past conduct and noted that I had a young stepmother, with whom it would prove difficult for my wife to live in a single household. But the better part of Lanin's relatives thought that the daughter should be given to me in marriage, for we Shipovs were a wealthy family, one of the foremost in Vyezdnaia.

On November 4, our relatives again gathered at our house and once again sent uncle Feoktistov to see Lanin. He was respectfully received and seated in a place of honor; a priest read a prayer out loud. After this, they gave my uncle five kerchiefs and a towel adorned with rich lace, as a kind of deposit; my uncle received another fine kerchief for himself and was entertained by the Lanins as an honored guest.

My father and relatives awaited his return. When my uncle arrived with the kerchiefs and in fine spirits, I was summoned again; they congratulated me and showed me the kerchiefs, one of which was meant for me—that is to say, I was to wear it wrapped around my cap. I was then ordered to bow before my father and uncle, which I did. Then began the festivities, which lasted long into the night.

The next day (November 5) we awaited the arrival of the "shirt woman."[21] This was a woman from the family of the bride's father, who would come to fetch one of my shirts—based on its size and form, new shirts would be sewn for me by members of my fiancée's family. The "shirt woman" was usually one of the bride's close relatives and was regarded as a guest of honor; she had to be met by the groom's closest relatives and shown the best possible hospitality.

She arrived at three in the afternoon and turned out to be the wife of my future father-in-law's brother, that is, the aunt of my betrothed. My relatives immediately went out to greet her, led her into the *górnitsa*,[22] and zealously began to entertain her with food and drink. She stayed with us until

---

21. In Russian, *rubáshechnitsa*.
22. That is, the tidiest part of a peasant hut, functioning like a sitting room.

six in the evening, during which time it was determined when the *smotré-nie*,[23] *zapói*,[24] *devíchnik*,[25] and the wedding itself would take place. The *smotrénie*, it was decided, would happen later today. After these discussions, this new matchmaker took my shirt and left for the house of Lanin. Along the way, she was obliged to sing songs nonstop; the bride would greet her in the front yard, inviting her to come into the main room.

Following the "shirt woman's" departure, we gathered together to go to the bride's house for the *smotrénie*. With me rode uncle Feoktistov (who now became my "best man") and his wife. We took with us about twenty pounds worth of gifts, with each pound in a separate package; apart from this, my father gave me two half-imperial coins wrapped in paper, five silver rubles wrapped in little bundles, and five rubles in one ruble pieces, wrapped in paper. This money was provided so that when my betrothed approached me and began giving me gifts, I would offer the money to her on a tray and kiss her three times.

We arrived in the Lanin's yard, met by my father-in-law-to-be, his wife, son, and close relatives. They first bestowed kisses upon my uncle and aunt and then upon me. We then passed into the *górnitsa* where a priest was waiting. They sat me down at the head of the table; next to me on the right sat the priest and my uncle, with my aunt on the left; around the rest of the table the Lanin relatives distributed themselves. A sweet pie, covered in various decorations, lay on the table. For several minutes we sat there in silence, until my aunt said—"It's time for us to look upon the pie-maker,[26] the one who prepared this pie for the table"—in other words, my bride. Allegedly I grew timid when I heard these words.

One of Lanin's female relatives immediately led my betrothed out of a neighboring room. She was dressed in a silk *sarafán*,[27] stitched with gold, and a shirt as white as snow. On her neck were forty threads with pearls of various sizes; in her ears, earrings of pearl; on her head, a band of pearls; and a whole bundle of scarlet ribbons tied into her pigtail.

---

23. Also called the *smotriny* (from the verb *smotret'*, to look at): Russian folk rite of inspection of a prospective bride (*Oxford Russian Dictionary*).

24. Also called the *pripoi* or *zaruchiny*: a betrothal party held among family and friends where everyone drank in honor of the bride-to-be. See Worobec, *Peasant Russia*, 159–162.

25. Party for girls given by a bride on the eve of her wedding (*Oxford Russian Dictionary*).

26. In Russian, *pirózhnitsa*.

27. A sleeveless Russian peasant women's dress, buttoning in front.

Everyone stood when the two women entered. The women said a prayer to God, received a blessing from the priest, and exchanged kisses with my aunt and uncle. Then my bride took up a tray, on which lay a gift for me (a vest); she walked up to me and bowed. I took the gift and in exchange laid two half-imperials on the tray, and also bowed; then we kissed three times and bowed again to one another.

The priest then asked us: "Do you wish to join in marriage?" We replied that we very much wished to. The priest blessed us and read out a prayer. I was then seated, with my betrothed next to me, and everyone began to take refreshments, except for us; we just sat there, although tea was served to us as well. In a special room, my fiancée's young girlfriends sang wedding songs and kidded the best man about being miserly in his gifts for them. After taking tea, my fiancée gave me some kerchiefs, and I gave her money—with every exchange of gifts we kissed three times. This went on for several hours. A supper was offered after midnight, after which all the guests went home. I remained there with my fiancée and the girls; we played games, sang cheerful songs, and I remained there till break of day.

The *zapói* was to take place on November 7 [at the Lanins]. My father invited all of our close relatives, several honored guests, and the priest and his wife—altogether, about fifteen people. The food and drink had to be brought by the groom's family, and Father didn't skimp on a thing. [. . .] [Upon arriving later at the Lanins], we exchanged kisses with our hosts and their guests and were invited into the *górnitsa,* where we sat down according to the usual arrangement. The table was laid for forty people; on it were four gammons and a pie—big, white, sweet, and round—covered with various figurines and decorations.

Suddenly it fell silent in the room. We sat for about five minutes without saying a word, after which time my stepmother turned to Lanin and his wife and said, "you, who are proposing this match—where is the pie maker, who baked such a wonderful pie for us?" Lanin replied that he would summon her, if the guests so pleased. At this my betrothed came out of another room, all dressed up and richly ornamented, accompanied by her aunt (who had previously performed the function of "shirt woman"). They made a prayer to God, bowed down low to all the guests, approached the priests in attendance for their blessing, then kissed, first, my father and stepmother, then everyone else in the prescribed order.

After the kissing was over, my betrothed was given a tray, upon which lay a beautiful neckerchief. She approached me with the tray and bowed from the waist; I took the kerchief, answering with the same bow. Then I laid a half-imperial piece on the tray and, holding her chin with one hand, kissed her three times, side to side, after which we again bowed to one another. My betrothed then began bestowing various gifts upon all of my relations, in gratitude for which they answered with pieces of money. Finally, she sat down beside me.

The time for *proshchénie*[28] had arrived. The father of the bride took the first glass around to the guests, after which our relatives took care of entertaining them. All the while, my betrothed and I kissed many times at the request of the guests: one would say "we still haven't seen how our young ones kiss each other"; another, "the wine's really bitter, it needs sweetening"; and a third party would think up something else. More than an hour passed like this before tea was served. The girls took to singing happy songs, and a riotous feast began; our meal began at midnight and lasted about four hours. Halfway through the meal, my betrothed and I were pulled away from the table to sing, revel, and play games. The festivities ended at six in the morning, when all the guests went home. I stayed until dawn, however; my betrothed and her girlfriends accompanied me with songs to the gate.

The preparations began for the wedding itself, which was to take place on November 10. The day before, my fiancée's girlfriends came over to get some home-brewed beer, which they would use to add steam to the bath (by pouring it on the bathhouse stove) when they would steam-bathe her for the last time, singing songs of farewell.[29]

Then the "box men" and "bed women" arrived:[30] four men and two women, together with a male relative of my future father-in-law. With three pairs of horses, they brought the belongings and bed linens of my betrothed, setting the trunks down in a specially prepared stall in the

---

28. Here in the sense of "giving permission": the part of the ritual devoted to a show of public approval of the match.

29. Shipov is referring here to the *devíchnik,* or "girls' evening," a gathering for the bride-to-be and her female friends and relatives. During the *devíchnik,* songs and lamentations would be sung, the bride's braid (a sign of maidenhood) unplaited, and the bride herself ritually bathed. (For an excellent account of the *devíchnik* rituals, see Worobec, *Peasant Russia,* 159–162.) Here Shipov is referring to the ritual steam bath; apparently beer would be poured over the stove or heating element in the bathhouse (the "kamenka" or "stone") to increase the amount of steam.

30. In Russian, *korobeinik* and *postel'nitsa* (or *postel'naia-svakha*), respectively: titles used for those performing the ritual functions described here by Shipov.

entryway, and bringing the bed linens into the bedroom (where the "bed women" began unpacking it). Afterward we entertained all these men and women well with food and drink.

That same day, my father sent couriers to all his relatives, friends, and acquaintances with an invitation to our wedding table, which was being made ready for eighty people. My father was revered as a true Russian *khlebosól*,[31] and so he made sure that everything would be provided in abundance. On the evening before the wedding, around midnight, I went to the cemetery to take leave of my deceased relatives and to ask a blessing of my late mother. I did this and let my tears flow upon her grave.

On the 10th, as evening approached, all of our relatives and acquaintances, along with the priest, the deacon, and the sacristans, assembled at our house. Two of our unmarried male relatives were meanwhile sent to the house of my fiancée with shoes, stockings, soap, perfume, combs, and other things; they were invited in, given kerchiefs, and treated to food and drink.

At home, my father put my boots on me; he placed three rubles in the right one, so that my young wife might take them for herself when removing my boots later. When I was fully dressed, Father took the icon of the Mother of God, set in a framework of silver, and blessed me, weeping. I shed tears as well—it's not in vain that people say that "a wedding is a person's final happiness." Then my godfather and godmother blessed me with their icons and sat me down in the corner where all the icons stood. Beginning with my father, everyone then took their leave of me, after which the priest, having uttered a prayer to God, led me to the church, where a multitude of people was waiting. Several people, so-called "escorts," followed behind.

Meanwhile, the matchmaker and my best man[32] rode over to my fiancée's house, carrying bread and salt. On arrival, they found bread and salt on the table as well. The matchmaker took the salt, sprinkling a bit for herself, and handed over the bread and salt she'd brought with her. My fiancée, covered in a shawl, was seated at the table, and after she received the parental blessing with icons, everyone took their leave of her, giving her gifts of money whenever possible. The priest then led her out the room and went to the church with the matchmaker, the best man, and the

31. A hospitable person (from "bread and salt," *khleb i sol'*, traditionally given guests upon arrival).

32. Shipov's aunt and uncle.

candle-bearer; this last person bore the icon of the bride and some wax candles. Following them rode men and women, so-called "members of the procession," on a number of horse-drawn carriages.

At the conclusion of the sacrament of marriage, we newlyweds carried the icon of the Mother of God from the church to my father's house, as is customary. It was completely dark outside, and the snow was falling hard; taking this as a sign, the people gathered there predicted that the new couple would be happy. (Alas! This prophecy was not entirely fulfilled.)

My father greeted us at home with an icon and with bread and salt; we exchanged kisses with my father, after first kissing the icon. [After the conclusion of the service in honor of God's Mother], the matchmaker led us to the bedroom, sat down next to us, and gave us some communion bread. Then, as we had fasted this day, we were given something to eat after tea. Then the matchmaker did up my bride's hair the way it is worn by married women.[33]

We went out again to the guests, and the wedding feast began soon afterward. There were ten different courses, and all in the purest Russian taste, without any soups or sauces. Near the end of the feast a sweet pie was brought out that we newlyweds were to distribute among the guests. A pearl *kokóshnik*[34] was put on my young bride's head, and we passed around the pie, together with the matchmaker. All the guests congratulated us on having joined in lawful marriage.

The feast ended long after midnight. The matchmaker and best man then led us back to the bedroom, made up the bed, and commanded my bride to remove my boots; having put us to bed, they went away.

The next morning I got up early, only to find the door locked from the outside. There was nothing to be done—I had to wait. Eventually the matchmaker unlocked the door and led us (along with the best man) to the bathhouse, once again locking the door from outside. They led us back to the bedroom, where tea had already been prepared and was waiting for us. After a while, a woman (a so-called "pancake woman")[35] came [on orders] from my father-in-law, bringing hot pancakes and various pastries, and we ate. Then a relative of my bride arrived with gifts to be given by my bride to my father and stepmother, who, after receiving the gifts, showed their gratitude with money.

33. That is, in two plaits. See Worobec, *Peasant Russia,* 167.
34. A Russian peasant woman's headdress.
35. In Russian, *blinnitsa:* another ritual role (from *bliny,* pancakes).

That evening, my father invited over our relatives and friends for the evening, but we newlyweds, along with the matchmaker and best man, went to my father-in-law's; afterward we visited one another in turns. And with this, our wedding ceremony came to an end.

I have already mentioned that we were serf peasants and paid *obrók*[36] to our *bárin*.[37] This landowner, Saltykov by name, did not live in Vyezdnaia. He spent the winters in Saint Petersburg, the summers in Sergeevskii, his estate near Moscow; he came to visit us only rarely. In Vyezdnaia lived an estate manager[38] and a bailiff[39] who dealt out punishment to the peasants and kept busy extracting the bárin's obrók from them.[40]

As a wealthy and respected person, my father was designated as bailiff more than once. Others regarded this as an enviable duty, but neither my father nor I had any liking for it. This was, first, because our trading business required father's frequent absence from home, while the job of bailiff demanded that he stay continually in Vyezdnaia. Furthermore, the task of exacting obrók meant that one necessarily got into unpleasant conflicts with peasants, thereby making enemies. At the same time, my father was always in danger of incurring the wrath of the landowner and suffering some punishment or other. As the bárin was a rather unbalanced person, the meting out of punishment was no rare occurrence on his estate.

Once, for example, in 1820—I forget exactly what the situation was—a peasant from another estate was sent by the landowner to my father. He was given orders to chain the peasant up and to feed him nothing but one pound of black bread once a day until further notice. Father was further informed that he would be called to strict account if the prisoner escaped or was better fed than the order prescribed. The *muzhík*[41] was chained to a wall in our old house and someone was appointed to guard him; out of humane feeling, my father ordered that he be given enough to eat. Six months passed.

36. Pronounced "ahb-ROHK": quit-rent, an obligatory payment to the landowner in money or in kind.

37. Pronounced "BAH-ren": a noble landowner.

38. In Russian, *upravliaiushchii.*

39. In Russian, *burmistr.*

40. For an outstanding study of the dynamics of interaction among landowners, managers, bailiffs, and peasants, see Steven L. Hoch, *Serfdom and Social Control in Russia: Petrovskoe, a Village in Tambov* (Chicago: University of Chicago Press, 1986), esp. chapters 3–5.

41. Pronounced "moo-ZHEEK": a male peasant.

Then Father left home for a short time on business, and during this absence the prisoner fled. The landowner was informed of this, and he ordered that 7,000 rubles immediately be seized from my father as a penalty. After a time, the escaped peasant was recaptured, but the money remained, of course, with the landlord.

The bárin might also send strict orders for Father to immediately appear before him with the collected obrók—say, 30,000 or 40,000 rubles worth. All the money would not yet have been gathered from the peasants, but failing to fulfill the landlord's orders put one in danger. My father handled such cases in the following way. If he had enough of his own money at hand, he would offer up whatever was missing; if not, he would borrow from Arzamas merchants and pay the interest out of his own pocket. This way Father would get out of this jam, though not without loss to himself.

Once, however—indeed, in the year I got married, 1820—Father was unable to produce the full obrók. To justify himself, he noted that all the peasant traders and craftsmen had suffered big losses that year, making the payment of obrók more difficult. But the landlord would hear none of it; he threatened to imprison Father in a punitive workhouse or send him off to settle in Siberia. However, the whole affair ended when the landlord decided to remove Father as bailiff. We were overjoyed at this decision, not least because year by year the amount of obrók (always dependent on the whim of the bárin) only increased.

The bárin often had strange reasons for increasing the obrók. On one occasion, he came to Vyezdnaia together with his wife; as was customary, rich peasants, dressed in holiday garb, appeared before him, bowing and presenting him with various gifts. Women and girls were there as well, all dressed up and decorated with pearls. The *barynia*[42] regarded all of this with great curiosity and told her husband: "Our peasants have such elegant dresses and jewelry; it must be because they're so very rich—for them it's nothing to pay us obrók."

Hardly pausing to think, the landlord raised the amount of obrók right then and there.

It reached the point where each "inventoried soul"[43] had to pay more than 110 rubles assignat per year, together with contributions toward the

---

42. Pronounced "BAH-ryn-yah": the bárin's wife.
43. In Russian, *revizskaia dusha:* a male serf who had been entered into the last census.

mir's[44] expenses. The landlord determined how much obrók would be required from his entire estate; Vyezdnaia was to pay 105,000 rubles assignat per year. There were just under 1,840 "inventoried souls" among us, but by no means were all of them equally able to pay. It happened, for example, that a wealthy peasant would have to pay for only one or two souls, while a poor one would have to cover for five or six. Then there were the old and the crippled, and those who had been sent into the army as recruits, and those who had fled—none of these people could even make an appearance in Vyezdnaia, but obrók had to be paid for them.

Again, the bárin would hear nothing of all this, and insisted that the appointed obrók be paid in full. This meant that a certain [additional] amount would be apportioned from the well-to-do dues payers; thus it turned out that my father and I paid the landlord more than 5,000 rubles a year in obrók. Another peasant paid nearly 10,000.

In such conditions, it would apparently make sense for well-off peasants to buy their freedom from the landlord. Several tried to do so, indeed, but without the slightest success. One very rich peasant who had seven sons offered the landlord 160,000 rubles to manumit him and his family; the landlord didn't agree to the offer. When, a year after my wedding, a daughter was born to me, my father had the idea of redeeming her for 10,000 rubles. The landlord refused.

What could be the reason for the refusals? It was said that they had something to do with one of our lord's peasants, a certain Prokhorov who had lived on the estate near Moscow. In the village there, Prokhorov owned a small house; he carried on some petty, quite unenviable trade in textiles in Moscow, went around in a sheepskin coat, and generally gave the impression of being a person of modest means. In 1815 Prokhorov proposed to the bárin that he free him for a small sum, under the condition that some merchants from Moscow pay the deposit. The bárin agreed to this.

Afterward Prokhorov bought a large stone house in Moscow that was richly decorated; he also built a vast factory in the city. On one occasion, Prokhorov happened to meet his former master and invited him over. The bárin was more than a little surprised when he saw Prokhorov's magnificent

---

44. Pronounced like "mere": the peasant community, the lowest level of village governance. For information on this crucial institution, see David Moon, *The Russian Peasantry 1600–1930: The World the Peasants Made* (New York: Addison Wesley Longman, 1999), 199–236; Hoch, *Serfdom and Social Control,* passim; and the introduction to this volume.

house and factory. Filled with regret for letting such a man free, he vowed never to manumit another of his peasants. And he never did.[45]

Toward the end of 1823 my father was named bailiff once again. [. . .] At the time I was in the Orenburg Krai and knew nothing of what was going on. When I returned and learned the news, we conferred to see by what means we might rid ourselves of this hateful job of bailiff.

During this time, our lord's chamberlain and personal favorite occasionally stayed in Vyezdnaia. This man would sometimes find ways to arrange peasant affairs in ways satisfactory both to us and to the bárin. With this in mind, my father asked the chamberlain to petition the bárin to relieve him of the duties of bailiff and gave him 1,000 rubles to do it. The chamberlain wrote to the bárin and received the following response: "If Shipov even thinks about getting out of the bailiff's job, I'll do something to him that he never dreamed I'd do: I'll ship his whole family out to settle in Siberia and send his son into the army."

We received this answer with lamenting and in a burst of bitterness I told Father that it would be better if I went off to the army: time spent in service to the tsar would never go to waste.

"No," replied Father sadly. "I'd never be able to bear separation from you. We shall live together—whatever sadness and suffering we have to put up with, we'll endure and carry out the Lord's will."

[. . .]

Later, after some pondering, Father said: "Yes, I guess I will step in and manage peasant affairs—you, in the meantime, carry on the trade and manage things as best you know how. You're able to run things yourself now."

With nagging heart, I heard out my father's resolution and said nothing, knowing that if he had so decided, that's the way it would be.

1824–1831

Starting in 1824 I began to travel frequently away from home to carry on our trading business. As before, the trade was in Ural cattle and furs. [. . .]

45. There was a very famous family of textile producers (descended from serfs) named Prokhorov, whose founding member, Vasilii Ivanovich Prokhorov, died in 1815. The dynasty lasted into the twentieth century, but I have found no evidence linking it to the serf mentioned here by Shipov. See *Prokhorovy,* ed. P. N. Terent'ev (Moscow: TERRA/Ekonomicheskaia Gazeta, 1996).

I. V. Boldyrev, "Holiday Market in Tsymlianskaia Stanitsa," 1875–76.

[Upon returning from Orenburg once in 1828], I learned from my father that a house serf named Tarkhov had been named as father's assistant in administering the affairs of Vyezdnaia. This was exceedingly unpleasant news, for this Tarkhov always did everything he could to harm my father and our family as much as possible—both out of malice toward my father and because he had his eye on the bailiff's job, or so it seemed.

Right around that time Tarkhov began to spread rumors to the effect that all of our cattle and wares were going to be confiscated in order to recover unauthorized expenditures made by my father while the administration of the *vótchina*[46] was in his hands. The rumor was altogether false, but it reached the ears of the merchants with whom we did business, and they found it plausible. At the Makar'evskaia trade fair, where I went soon after my arrival back home, the merchants refused, in light of this absurd rumor, to entrust me with any credit. It took me a lot of trouble and effort to maintain our credit [with them]; although I did manage to do this, we still suffered a loss of around 18,000 rubles assignat in 1828.

46. That is, the master's estate.

The following year Tarkhov continued his insidious plotting against my father. He convinced several peasants to file various complaints against my father to Raguzin, the estate manager. Living in Vyezdnaia at that time was a man named Raev; he was my father's nephew and godson, and Father loved him scarcely less than he loved me. At the incitement and instigation of Tarkhov, Raev submitted a petition to Raguzin, claiming that my father hadn't given him all the money that remained and was due to him after the death of his mother. My father fell ill upon hearing this news, so unpleasant was it for him.

Our business was going badly; again we incurred significant losses, and our obrók was not reduced. For the right to conduct trade we paid, as before, 800 rubles assignat per year, but I could see that we would soon be completely ruined if things continued the same way. We had to think of some way to improve the situation—but how? We attempted to make a formal plea to Raguzin, asking him to petition the landlord to free me for 50,000 rubles assignat, under the condition that my father would remain a serf. (My stepmother was already dead by this time.) The estate manager categorically refused, however, even to inform the landlord of our request. After this, I began to consider running away from home, never to return to see my father again; I wanted to try my luck in some alien land. This was during the last part of 1830.

I prepared myself for the road, speaking to neither my wife nor my father about my intentions. I took 13,000 rubles with me and told my father that I was heading to Ural'sk to buy tallow and fish. When I took leave of my father, I grew intensely sick at heart; my eyes welled up with tears, no matter how hard I tried to hold them back. Saying goodbye, Father repeated to me, over and over again, "come back soon." My wife accompanied me to Arzamas, and before parting we exchanged wedding rings. I was sad.

I rode to Ural'sk, and from there to Uzen' in order to get some business affairs in order. I arrived in Samara on January 10, 1831, and there I met with one of our salesmen.[47] He told me that my father was very ill and was being treated by a doctor. I was stunned by this news; all kinds of thoughts started spinning round in my head.

"If I don't return home," I thought, "and if they hear nothing from me, Father will immediately send someone to look for me in Ural'sk; they won't

47. In Russian (here), *prikazchik*.

find me there, of course, and will inform him that I'm missing. He won't withstand such a blow, and with his condition, he'll die—and then I can regard myself as his murderer."

I felt sorry for my kind father, not to mention the wife and six-year-old daughter I'd left behind. I left Samara with the aforementioned salesman. Along the road I struggled with my thoughts for a long time and burst into bitter tears. Again I asked the salesman, "What is my father's condition?" He repeated, yet again, that my father was very weak.

At the third station there was a fork in the road: one branch led to Syzran', the other to Simbirsk. Here I ordered the coachman to stop. My heart beat violently, and I could not decide: should I turn right, back to my parent's home, or left—to who knows where?

Finally, I said to myself: "Let Your will be done, o Lord! I will not abandon my father while he's dangerously ill. With God's help, he'll recover, and then I'll finish what I'd planned to do." I ordered the coachman to go right along the Simbirsk road.

At home, I found father lying in bed; he was suffering from dropsy, but took joy in my arrival with all his heart. For the first few days the sickness was in remission, and he began to recover. But then Raguzin arrived unexpectedly with new peasant complaints, incited by Tarkhov, against my father. This had a strong effect on him; he was gripped by a fever, and within nine days my never-to-be-forgotten father passed away.

I will not describe the grief that seized my heart. I had only one thought: that my dear father, my adviser and guide through life, was no more. "Now, live as best you can," I thought. "Act as you best know how." Already at that time I had a presentiment that my dead father's enemies, headed by Tarkhov, would not leave me in peace and would try to harm me as well—and my hunch did not deceive me.

In repaying my last debt to the deceased, I arranged a rich and magnificent funeral. I invited the archimandrite of the Spassky monastery in Arzamas; Antonii, the superior of the Vysokogorskaia hermitage; and sixteen priests and their associated clergy. A multitude of people assembled. Choristers sang during the liturgy and the requiem; the priests uttered homilies and eulogies. After the burial, more than one hundred friends and relatives of the deceased attended the meal. A granite monument engraved with a cross in pure gold was placed on the grave under a canopy. I forgave the debts of several poor creditors, gave away more than one hundred rubles to the destitute and poverty stricken, and paid for the manumission of two poor girls.

Afterward I went to see Raguzin and informed him that my father left behind absolutely no deficits in the accounts during his time as bailiff of the estate. Soon after this, Tarkhov was named my father's successor as bailiff.

A few days before my father's death, I had already, out of a sense of caution, passed 15,000 rubles on to the Arzamas merchant Podsosov in exchange for a promissory note, and sent our most valuable personal property in fourteen trunks to our relatives, uncle Feoktisktov and Potekhin. I decided not to trade in cattle or tallow anymore, so I sold thirteen cauldrons from my tallow boilery to Podsosov and ordered one of our salesmen to transport them to Podsosov's factory in Arzamas. This was on the first of March.

[. . .]

A while later the salesman arrived and said that when he and the other workers were carrying the boilers away, several peasants, under Tarkhov's orders, stopped them and bid them return to my house. I was not a little astonished by this news. The village elder, Pavel'ev, my friend and godfather of my child, came to me with an order for me to appear right then and there before Tarkhov in the village office. The office was in fact located in my house, and took up one of the corner rooms. I went home but did not go into the office, although they sent for me more than once.

Toward evening of that day, the following commands were issued: all our salesmen and workers were sent off of our premises; the door of one of the porches was shut with a lock, and a guard was posted on the other—thus, I was unable to leave. Sentries walked around the house during the night as well. The next day Tarkhov asked for my passport, and I gave it to him. My friends and relatives were not allowed to see me. In this way, two weeks passed.

I wrote to the landlord and to Raguzin about my unjust imprisonment, but no answer or order from them followed. The fortieth day after my father's death arrived, and I wanted to pray on his grave—this, too, was denied me. I spent the days and nights in sadness and despondency.

On the morning of March 29, exactly one month later, I looked out the window and noticed that the guard had disappeared. I couldn't figure out what was going on, but everything soon became clear. Village elder Pavel'ev came in and gave me my passport and a letter in my name from Raguzin. "The administration of Vyezdnaia noticed something suspicious, for which they decided to arrest you. I have ordered Tarkhov to release you from custody and to keep as much distance from you as you please. Carry on your trade as before."

I immediately went outside to check the yard, the storerooms, the granaries—everywhere, the locks had been broken and a great deal had been stolen. I wrote a declaration of this fact and sent it to the *Zémskii Sud*,[48] and went myself to Saint Petersburg for a personal clarification of the matter with Raguzin and the landlord.

On arriving in Saint Petersburg, I stayed in the master's own house, where Raguzin was living as well. Raguzin greeted me kindly and rendered his condolences regarding my father and all that had happened to me; he promised to get back my lost property from those who had taken it and to recover my credit. I didn't put much faith in Raguzin's promises, but I could do nothing but wait and hope. Besides, I had decided at this time to try once again to buy myself out of serfdom.

Once over tea, I began to speak to Raguzin about this, telling him that if the master didn't free me now, life would become unbearable for me in Vyezdnaia. With a displeased look, Raguzin told me that I had to wait a bit before petitioning the landlord about this, that I could still continue to live in Vyezdnaia perfectly well, and that I might just be named the bailiff in my father's place. Determinedly I told Raguzin that I would never accept the duty of bailiff: through it, I said, my father died, without receiving the slightest favor from the master for all of his services. With that our conversation ended. I didn't dare go to the landlord for a personal discussion of my case, for this would have gone completely against the wishes of Raguzin.

I remained in Saint Petersburg for five days and visited the Kazan' cathedral, the Aleksandr Nevsky monastery, and the Petropavlovsk cathedral, where I bowed down before all the late emperors and empresses at rest in God. I had already prepared to go home when I heard that there was going to be an inspection of the troops on May 15 in Tsaritsyn Meadow, where the lord emperor,[49] the heir to the throne,[50] and Count

48. The Lower Land Court of the district.
49. Tsar Nicholas I (1796–1855).
50. The future Alexander II (1818–81), who declared the end of serfdom in 1861.

Paskevich-Erivanskii[51] (only just returned from Tiflis)[52] would be present. I waited until the 15th and in the morning went to the Pavlovsk barracks.

There was a multitude of troops on the parade ground, and the number gathered to watch exceeded even that number. The emperor and Paskevich arrived around noon on horseback and began the inspection; the heir, dressed in a Hussar's parade uniform, commanded a platoon. After the inspection was over, all the people rushed onto the parade ground.

[. . .]

I succeeded in arriving there before the crowd and got a good look at the emperor, at Paskevich, and at the heir. The Sovereign had a strict, imperious gaze, and it seemed to me that, having seen his gaze once, one could never forget it. I gazed long and intently at the heir, and never tired of looking at him. It's like I can see him now: exceedingly lovable—white, round-faced, and ruddy as a ripe red apple; his smile was kind and indescribably pleasing; his face seemed to express something important, something regal. I had a premonition then that this tsar would be great—the protector of all the oppressed. The next day, I returned home.

At this time my trading business was going badly, but there was no way I could simply abandon it. On returning home from Saint Petersburg, therefore, I sent all the remaining furs to the Korennaia [Pustyn'] trade fair (in the province of Kursk) with a salesman. I went there myself a few days later—allegedly, in order to sell the furs. In fact, I went there in order to find Stepan Lanin, my brother-in-law. Five years earlier, this Lanin had run away to Bessarabia; he then went to Wallachia,[53] where he worked as

---

51. Ivan Feodorovich Paskevich (1782–1856): a Russian army officer and administrator. He was created count of Erivan, Armenia, after conquering (1827) Persian Armenia in the war with Persia (1826–28) and became field marshal after his successful campaign in the Russo-Turkish War of 1828–29. After the Polish insurrection of 1830, Paskevich captured Warsaw from the rebels (1831) and was made prince of Warsaw and viceroy of Poland by Tsar Nicholas I. Brutal and authoritarian, he followed Nicholas's policy for the Russification of Poland ("Ivan Feodorovich Paskevich," in *The Columbia Encyclopedia*, 6th ed. [New York: Columbia University Press, 2001–2007]).

52. Now called Tbilisi: the capital of Georgia.

53. A region corresponding to the southern part of contemporary Romania, located south of the Southern Carpathian mountains and north of the Danube River. The region was under Russian control on and off between 1829 and 1851.

a sutler[54] during the Russian army's campaigns. I had to find Lanin because, with his assistance and instructions, I hoped to realize my ambition
of going into hiding, considering that he was experienced in these matters.
I didn't know where he was exactly, but I knew the address of a merchant
in Odessa through whom Lanin received letters from relatives and friends.

So when trade at the Korennaia market started going very badly (due
to a cholera outbreak), I went with our wares and with a salesman to the
Il'inskaia trade fair in Romny (in the province of Poltava). Here we sold
about 8,000 rubles worth; the remaining wares I sent to the Uspenskaia
fair in Kharkov with the salesman, and I went myself to Odessa, where
with the help of the previously mentioned merchant I found my brother-
in-law Lanin.

He had arrived there not long himself with some wine from Constantinople, which he sold in a cellar at the Rybnoi bazaar in Odessa. I
explained my situation to Lanin and asked him to help me escape from
Vyezdnaia, which he joyfully agreed to do. I gave him 2,000 rubles assignat
to pay for expenses; he promised to register my wife and I [as residents of]
Kishinev (or whatever town turned out to be most convenient), and to secure passports for me to travel to the Kreshchenskaia fair in Kharkov in the
following year, 1832. Of course, all of this was to remain secret.

From Odessa I went to Kharkov, and from thence returned home, arriving around the beginning of September. I explained my long absence to
friends and family by saying that I fell ill with cholera on the road from
Romny and took a long time to recover.

On the day after I arrived, I was approached for the obrók I owed for
the last third of the year; they asked for 1,500 rubles assignat. I sent Raguzin a tearful letter asking him to reduce the obrók even a little bit, considering that I had incurred great losses and ruin that year. From Raguzin I received an answer to the effect that I was to pay the required obrók without
voicing any contradictions; he'd deal with my case and reduce the obrók,
he said, on his next trip to Vyezdnaia. There was nothing to do, so I gave
them the obrók.

After this, what could I expect from Raguzin's promises, which he gave
me in Saint Petersburg about recovering my lost property from the ones
responsible for my arrest and ruin and in regard to reestablishing my

---

54. "One who follows an army or lives in a garrison town and sells provisions to the
soldiers" (*Oxford English Dictionary,* 2nd edition (Oxford: Oxford University Press, 1989).

credit? Nothing, of course—nor was this the end of it. On the side, I began to hear rumors that all of my property would soon be confiscated, and I myself sent, if not into the army, then probably to a more distant vótchina. Perhaps these rumors were exaggerated and untrue, but who knows? Anything can happen to an enserfed slave—such were my thoughts at the time.

In December I began to prepare for my flight from Vyezdnaia and made the final arrangements. I resolved to travel with my wife, and to leave our seven-year-old daughter in the care of her grandmother Lanin for the time being. When 1832 arrived, I had to welcome the New Year without joy . . .

1832–1835

On the night of January 1, 1832, my wife and I left by post chaise for Kharkov. There we met with my brother-in-law Lanin, who brought us passports for one year under the names of Grigorii and Elizaveta Kislov, residents of Kishinev. The three of us then left for Mogilev on the Dnestr River,[55] where I arranged with Lanin that he would travel immediately to Kishinev, where he would obtain foreign passports for us and send them to the small town of Brichani[56] in Bessarabia, where we would have to wait. Lanin left, no sooner said than done.

The next day I hired a Yid[57] to take us to Brichani. The sleigh trail had already disappeared, but it was impossible to travel on wheels; it was, in short, that time of year when roads are bad, and only with difficulty did we make it to Brichani. It turned out that there wasn't a single Russian in the town—they were all Jews, but there was nothing to be done; we rented an apartment from a Jew. The room was most unappealing, with a heavy and peculiar smell; my wife had never seen such a nasty chamber and it disgusted her. We lived there for over a week, and the boredom was unbearable. Shrovetide arrived, and somehow my wife contrived to bake *bliny*[58]—and that gave great pleasure to both of us.[59]

---

55. Now known as Mohyliv-Podil's'kij, on the Ukrainian side of the border between Ukraine and Moldova, southwest of Kiev; see map.

56. Now called Briceni, located in Moldova just south of the border with Ukraine, southwest of Mohyliv-Podil'sk'ij.

57. In the original, *zhid:* a well-known anti-Semitic term of abuse.

58. A kind of pancake, eaten during Shrovetide.

59. Given the character of Shipov's comments here, it is worth noting that the Jewish community in Brichani, present from 1817, was among the largest in the region by the

On the Sunday of Shrovetide week we received the foreign passport from Lanin, and the next day we left for the Moldavian border; on crossing the border, we spent the night in the premises of a Moldavian. We rented two carriages from him, loaded our possessions onto them, and went down the road into this (for us) unknown country, to its main city of Iassy.[60] We went up mountains and down valleys, and stopped in taverns where there was nothing but wine and vodka to be had. I neither knew the Moldavian language nor could I understand their way of counting money; at that time, I had about 14,000 rubles with me. However, I managed to dodge any bad situations and little by little got used to things there.

Finally, we arrived in Batashany, the first city of Moldavia; we stayed here in the coaching inn of a tavern owned by a Yid. We carried our things from the carts into the big room and put them in one corner. In that room were a lot of half-drunken Yids and Moldavians, and they sold vodka and wine there. I left my wife there with our things and went off to the bazaar. In some of the stalls, pure Russian muzhíks with beards were busily trading away; I was glad to see this, and began speaking with them.

It turned out that they were confirmed Old Believers[61] and long since citizens of Moldavia: their fathers and grandfathers had come there from Russia during the time of Peter the Great. According to them, there were many Russians in Moldavia, living in their own settlements, involved in raising grain and gardens, and especially in trade. They lived there in freedom; they didn't have to pay many taxes, and weren't conscripted into the army. The Old Believers asked me in their turn about Russia, and I told them that free people lived well in Russia, but that serf peasants had it very bad: poverty, *bárshchina,*[62] and obrók had worn them all out. The Old Believers were very sorry to hear this.

[. . .]

[*Shipov and his wife spend less than one full day in Batashany, returning to Iassy on March 1, 1832.*]

---

middle of the nineteenth century, with 7,184 Jewish residents in 1897 (96.5 percent of the total population), and about ten thousand in 1940. Most of them were murdered in the Holocaust; only one thousand Jews returned to Brichani at the end of the war.

60. West of Kishinev; see map.

61. Sometimes called *raskolniki:* those Russian Orthodox believers who retain the liturgical forms in use prior to the reforms instigated by Patriarch Nikon of Moscow (1652–58).

62. Pronounced "BAR-shcheenah": "corvée," dues paid in labor.

Just before Easter, I received a letter from a relative in Arzamas, inform-
ing me that my persecutor, Tarkhov the bailiff, had finally realized that I
had run away and had made a report to that effect. My house and everything in it had been confiscated; my in-laws had been harshly interrogated
about me and threatened in various ways; a guard had been posted outside
their house to prevent me from taking my daughter away. This news saddened our hearts.

Easter arrived. On Holy Sunday we went to the matins in the Russian
church and to the metropolitan see for the mass, where the gospel was read
in twelve different languages. But for us, this High Holiday was a dreary
and sad one. The Moldavians for the most part were in the taverns, where
they danced and drank wine; gypsies were playing various musical instru-
ments, and the music they produced sounded strange. Near the taverns
festive swings were set up,[63] next to which Yids were selling various kinds
of fruit. None of this cheered us up, however.

To complete our unhappiness, from Arzamas I received word that the
administration of Vyezdnaia had sent three peasants to look for us. Then
and there we left for the banks of the Danube and the city of Galats, which
had a wharf for seafaring ships arriving from Greece and Turkey. We met
with Lanin there, who had decided to go to Constantinople to buy various
wares. I wanted to go with him, but my wife was afraid of traveling by sea,
and there was no place to leave her, so I wasn't able to go.

[. . .]

After this my wife and I returned to Iassy, where I left her with a certain
Skopéts [64] whom I knew named Dubrovin. I purchased six pounds of attar
of roses[65] (at 100 rubles per pound), hoping to sell it at a profit in Russia,
and traveled across the Austrian border to the city of Chernowitz.[66] I
hoped to convey the oil in secret to avoid paying any duties, but this didn't
work out; the customs officials found my oil, confiscated it, and escorted

---

63. Swings were often erected for amusement around Easter time.

64. That is, a member of the religious sect known as the "Skoptsy" or "self-castrators,"
one of the most notorious and persecuted of dissenting groups in Russia. For an outstanding study of the Skoptsy, see Laura Engelstein, *Castration and the Heavenly Kingdom: A Russian Folktale* (Ithaca, NY: Cornell University Press, 1999).

65. "A very fragrant, volatile, essential oil obtained from the petals of the rose" (*Oxford
English Dictionary*).

66. Now Chernivtsy, Ukraine. Chernowitz was the capital of Bukowina, or Buchen-
land, province of the Austrian Empire from 1849 to 1918.

me to Chernowitz. I had divined by this time that things might turn out very bad indeed, so I revealed the truth about my scheme to the customs commissioner through my translator (a man named Lamikovskii). The officials weighed the oil, gave me a receipt in exchange for it, and let me go in peace.

Lamikovskii assured me that the oil would eventually be returned (though not anytime soon), and so I gave him a warrant to petition for it, and went off through Kamenets-Podol'sk to Romny. I wasn't able to receive the money [from] my brother-in-law there, but learned for certain that I was being pursued; Tarkhov had offered 1,000 rubles for my capture. I grew cautious: I changed my outfit, shaved my beard, cut my hair in the German fashion, and went out only in the evenings. It was still dangerous for me there, however, so after making some arrangements I hurried off back to Iassy.

Sometime later I received a letter from Lanin in Constantinople, in which he informed me that he had spent 7,000 rubles on various grocery products and had sent them to a merchant in Odessa. At almost the same time I heard from Potekhin (a relative in Arzamas) that he had purchased one hundred poods[67] of Russia leather and sent it on to another merchant whom I knew in Odessa.

Potekhin also informed me that Tarkhov had sent a Vyezdnaia peasant named Pavel'ev to find me. Pavel'ev had been empowered with a warrant stating that I had left and taken with me a great deal of money and property; it was left unsaid in the warrant whether this money and property belonged to the landlord or to me.

On receiving this news, I began to think about going to Odessa, for my presence there would soon be essential. But I had to postpone that trip for a time. There was one acquaintance there, a peasant named Kozhevnikov who had run away from Vyezdnaia before I did and was also in hiding. We saw one another from time to time, and carried on a secret correspondence about my affairs and my business—I paid Kozhevnikov well for all his services and his trouble.

He was in Odessa at this time, and I received a letter from him saying that Pavel'ev had arrived there, intending immediately to find me or perhaps Kozhevnikov himself. Forthwith I told Kozhevnikov to come to the small border town of Skuliany, where I would give him instructions in

---

67. A Russian measure of weight: 1 pood equals 16.38 kilograms.

person. There we arranged for Kozhevnikov to follow Pavel'ev in turn, as well as watch over my wares sent from Arzamas and keep abreast of Lanin's activities; he was to inform me about all of this regularly and without delay. I gave Kozhevnikov 25 chervontsy[68] and he left for Odessa.

Soon I began to receive reports from him, one after another, but none of them were good. I learned that the salesman who was bringing my Russian leather from Arzamas had secretly sold it and hidden the money somewhere. The city authority of Odessa received word from the Russian consulate in Constantinople that my brother-in-law Lanin had died in Constantinople from the plague raging there at the time. Because no documents had been found indicating what was to be done with Lanin's property, it was decided that it would be sold and the money handed over to the Office of Social Charity.

This news saddened me greatly, for my main hopes had rested on Lanin. I didn't know what to do. I thought about going straight to Constantinople myself, but many considerations stood in my way: the length of the trip, the cost, and the plague. So it was impossible for me to travel to Tsargrad.[69] Soon (but after much trouble) I secured a warrant in the name of a certain Odessa merchant I knew. I sent the warrant to him together with Lanin's receipt for the 6,000 rubles and asked him to petition for the money lost in Constantinople. With that, I left the whole affair in the hands of God.

I was heavy at heart . . .

On February 19, 1833, a son was born, whom we named Nikolai. I took great joy in this, but my happiness was darkened by sad thoughts.

Not long before this, my relative from Arzamas sent a letter saying that my daughter, by order of the Vyezdnaia administration, had been taken from her grandmother and sent to the vótchina where estate manager Raguzin was living. I had no idea what the point of this directive was, but I could clearly imagine how unhappy my daughter's life would be there, and could do nothing to improve her lot. And what could my newborn son await in the future? I had, it is true, hoped to establish a better life—surely, I thought, I wouldn't be persecuted and pursued by my foes forever? But when would the precious moment arrive? . . .

68. A chervonets (plural: chervontsy) is a gold coin worth three, five, or ten rubles.
69. "King city": alternative Russian name for Constantinople.

During Shrovetide I received news from Kozhevnikov in Odessa saying that my pursuer Pavel'ev was no longer there and had probably gone to Kishinev. Thinking of ways to avoid welcoming that unpleasant guest to where I was staying in Iassy, I spoke about my situation with my host, Dubrovin; I gave him 2,000 rubles and asked him to protect me, if the need arose, from Pavel'ev's inquiries. He agreed.

A few days later, Dubrovin anxiously ran into my room and told me that he'd seen Pavel'ev together with a civil servant from the consulate and some other man; they were headed in this direction, no doubt, and so we had to hide. We immediately got my wife and child ready, put them in a carriage and ordered that they be taken to the home of a certain Skopets whom we knew. Then I arranged for Dubrovin to tell Pavel'ev that I had left for Constantinople, and left my property with him for 4,000 rubles. I locked the door, gave the key to Dubrovin, and hid in the hayloft.

A little later, Pavel'ev and several other people walked in the yard, and Dubrovin went out to meet him. (I watched the whole thing through a small crack in the wall of the loft.)

"Where's Kislov,[70] and where's he living?" Pavel'ev asked Dubrovin.

"He left for Tsargrad," answered Dubrovin, "and his quarters are here. I've got the key to his room. He left his property with me for a deposit of 4,000 rubles."

"I saw Kislov myself, today," said Pavel'ev. "He must be here."

"If you saw him," replied Dubrovin, "why didn't you seize him and take him to the consulate?"

"Where's Kislov's wife?" asked Pavel'ev.

"How should I know? Ask her husband," replied Dubrovin.

At this someone told Pavel'ev that my wife had been taken to the home of a certain Skopets; they went off to find her—of course, without success.

After Pavel'ev left, I crawled down from the loft, but didn't remain in my apartment, going instead to the home of Aleksandrov, still another Skopets I knew. Soon many Skoptsy knew our story and took an interest in us, trying in every way possible to conceal my wife, my child, and me from Pavel'ev. So we hid in the homes of various Skoptsy for a while.

It turned out, however, to be an uncomfortable arrangement, however, for the simple reason that the Skoptsy have no children in their homes, and we had a child. We then decided to leave Iassy; with the help and support

70. Shipov's note: "At this time I was living under the name of Kislov."

of the Skoptsy we knew, we got ready to travel. They managed to get me a passport from the Prussian consulate under the name of Peter Johann, his wife Aleksandra, and his son Nikolai—that is to say, I had become, by this time, a citizen of Prussia.

They bought us a little caravan and a pair of horses, supplied us with provisions and gave us a letter of recommendation addressed to Father Konstantin, the Father Superior of Pungaratsy monastery;[71] a Moldavian was hired to be our guide. We took leave of the hospitable Skoptsy on March 2 and went on our way.

[. . .]

[On arriving at the monastery], Father Konstantin welcomed me with kindness. In Moldavian I explained to him that I had a wife and small child; that we had come here to fast, and therefore needed some place to stay. Father Konstantin ordered a special "cell," or room, to be prepared for us, and we moved into it.

A week later, my wife and I began our fasting; we gave our confession and took Holy Communion. Strange as it seems, the communion bread was made of black flour—this must have been because it was difficult or impossible to get any white flour there. Easter arrived, and on the first day, following the mass, a monk was sent for us at ten in the morning asking us to join them for lunch, and we did. The lunch included foods forbidden during the fast, including some meat, and it was well and tastefully prepared.

[. . .]

Father Konstantin had to travel to Iassy during St. Thomas's week.[72] I used this opportunity to send a message with him to the Skopets Dubrovin and his friends; I asked them to inform me about Pavel'ev's doings and to obtain another passport for me to travel back to Russia through Austrian territory. A few days later, Father Konstantin returned with 330 chervontsy (a bit more than 4,000 rubles) for me, together with a passport permitting "Nikolai Nikolaev" to cross the Austrian border into Russia. The money had been sent through Dubrovin to me by one of my friends from Moscow; they had in turn been received in Moscow from Podsosov, the merchant, with whom I'd left 15,000 rubles prior to my flight from home.

Dubrovin wrote further that Pavel'ev was not in Iassy; apparently, someone had told him that I was in Bucharest, so he'd gone there. This

71. I have been unable to discover where this monastery was located.
72. The second week after Easter.

news couldn't have come at a better time. We began to travel immediately, and on the first of May said goodbye to the Pungaratsy monastery and to its kind Father Superior, Konstantin.

[. . .]

[*Shipov, his wife, and child successfully cross the border, and after passing again through Moldavia (Chernowitz, Mogilev) and Ukraine (Odessa, Kherson), arrive in Simferopol', where one of his wife's grandfathers, a peasant named Markov who had escaped thirty years previously, was living. After living for a while in Kherson and returning briefly to Bessarabia (where he almost runs into Pavel'ev), Shipov decides to go to the Caucasus. He buys one thousand bottles of red wine and travels through Stavropol' to Piatigorsk where, by the end of 1834, he is living and working as a merchant.*]

1835–1836

A year passed. Neither the Vyezdnaia administration nor my pursuer Pavel'ev bothered me during all that time, and I traded peacefully. I traveled to Mozdok and Kizliar[73] to buy the local wine (which went by the name of *chikhir'*) as well the so-called "Kizliar vodka"; I also bought fresh *shamai,*[74] which I salted and smoked in the Armenian manner; I also prepared *shashlyks.*[75] Most of the other items I sold were ordered and brought in from Moscow. My business went rather well, and so I declared my intention officially to register as a merchant of Piatigorsk and presented the required amount of capital. For some reason, however, my petition got tied up in the administrative offices of the Stavropol' oblast'.

Thanks to my business, I got to know many people, among them a *sotnik*[76] from the Don regiment named Vasilii Sukhorukov. Sukhorukov was a clever, deft, enterprising man and was widely respected. In the Caucasus he rented post offices, took on contract work for the government, and was generally involved in a variety of commercial enterprises. This Sukhorukov offered me a job as a commission agent, with a salary of 1,000 rubles assignat

73. Cities in the north Caucasus; see map.
74. A kind of fish.
75. That is, kebabs. Nowadays shashlyks are a common and popular summertime food all over the former Soviet Union. Shipov's note: "This is lamb fried on a spit; [they also eat] shashlyks with 'tiuriatina,' which is the meat of a wild mountain ram."
76. A lieutenant of Cossack troops.

per year, and another 2,000 for the right to sell from out of my store. This offer could not have been more to my liking, and I agreed.

At this time tenders were posted for government-owned oil wells, located in the mountains near the fortress of Groznyi.[77] Sukhorukov wanted to lease these wells, and gave me the task of going, first, to the auctions in Stavropol', and later to the wells themselves; there I was to begin working in the oil business. This was at the beginning of 1836. I hired a salesman to take care of my store and, leaving him to carry on the business with my wife, went off to carry out Sukhorukov's orders.

Sukhorukov ended up with the wells during the auction, and I left for Groznyi. There I took over the wells from the colonel in charge, arranged with our workers for the transfer of the oil from the wells into barrels, and ordered the oil to be transported to a storage area in a *stanitsa*[78] called Naur. I soon followed them to Naur in order to take the oil to trade fairs in Mozdok, Ekaterinograd, and Egor'evsk. At those three markets I sold a lot of oil, and profitably too.

After this I returned to Piatigorsk with the account books and presented them to Sukhorukov. He was pleased with my success and asked me to find a specialist in distilling crude oil. Such a specialist soon turned up, and he began working as a distiller near the storage area in Naur.

[. . .]

[Following this, Shipov makes a brief trip through various southern Russian cities to check on the oil market for Sukhorukov, visiting another monastery along the way. Upon returning, Sukhorukov sends him off again into the Piatigorsk area to buy cereal flours.]

Within three days [after arriving back in Piatigorsk] I got ready to leave again for Kislovodsk. Right then I received a visit from one of my good friends, a former police clerk from Piatigorsk named Kastychenko. It turned out that he was headed to Kislovodsk himself, and so I asked him to buy about two hundred quarters of rye flour for me (for I had no desire to travel all that way for such a trifling amount). I reckoned that one could buy the flour in Egor'evsk and in the settlements along the Kuma River,

77. An important fortress town founded by Cossacks in 1818, and today the capital of the Chechen Republic in Russia. On the beginnings of the petroleum industry in Russia, see Pavel Natanovich Apostol, *La Lutte pour le Pétrole et la Russie* (Paris: Payot, 1922).

78. A large Cossack village.

and Kastychenko agreed to do it; I gave him a 200-ruble advance and my
Black Sea–bred saddle horse. We parted, and I went to Kuma.

After buying a good amount of flour in the [local] settlements, I arrived
in Egor'evsk, where I heard that the Circassians[79] had attacked Kislovodsk
during the night several days earlier (this was in the middle of October).
They cut down Cossacks standing at their posts, and plundered and
burned the stanitsa; a number of people were taken into captivity. This
rumor shocked me and worried me to no end: what had happened to Kastychenko? After all, it would have been so easy for me to be in his place!

I immediately went back to Piatigorsk, and thence to Kislovodsk, where
I learned that the rumor about the Circassian raid was true; they had taken
Kastychenko and my horse into captivity. In fact, in those places and in
those years, residents friendly to the Russians were often subject to raids by
various mountain plunderers.

Sukhorukov then received a letter from a postal inspector named Klement
in Tiflis, inquiring as to whether Sukhorukov would like to participate in a
tender for the lease on all the postal stations in Georgia. Sukhorukov called
me over and asked me to go to the auction, but not in order actually to win
the lease; rather, he wondered if I might find a way to get some money out
of the current postal station proprietors.

This assignment was a difficult one, and the road I would have to take
was both unknown to me and (most important) dangerous. I didn't have
any time to think about it, however: Sukhorukov pressed for my departure, so I took some money from him, said goodbye to my wife and son,
and on October 17 set off down the route taken by the postal relays.[80]

At sundown I arrived in Ekaterinograd. The postmaster there, because
I was carrying a letter of attestation from Sukhorukov, immediately provided me with a saddle horse and summoned ten Cossacks and a Cossack
NCO[81] as escorts for me; for protection from nighttime raids, he also sent
ten soldiers and another NCO. Together with this convoy, I set out.

We crossed the bridge over the Malka River. It was a clear, moonlit
night; the stars glittered like diamonds, and here and there giant, silvery

79. In Russian, *cherkes:* a term that Shipov uses to refer more-or-less indiscriminately
to the peoples of the north Caucasus.
80. That is, at this time, the mail was carried by relays of horsemen.
81. A noncommissioned officer (in Russian, *serzhant*).

mountains rose up, among which the Kazbek and magnificent Elbrus stood out sharply. On our left side roared the seething Terek River.

We went quietly, not saying a word, listening to every rustle, to every tiny sound. Involuntarily I lapsed into thought, and my thoughts were sad.

"What is going on in my dear native land," I thought, "where the abundant Volga flows, where the Ural steppe stretches wide and free? And where am I dragging myself off to now? To the mountains of the Caucasus, where I'm in danger from bandits, anticipating death any minute . . . O freedom, freedom! Where are those happy people who have never known persecution, never known constraint—under what star were they born? They live as they want to, by their own free will, and fear nothing—but I? Whether asleep or awake, it always seems that I'm being followed. They put me in a dungeon, take away my money, separate me from my wife and son and daughter, rule inside my home, and give orders as they please; they send me away from my dear native place, and forbid me from shedding tears on the dust of my parents . . .

"Oh, Father, never to be forgotten! Arise, and look upon your son, whom you loved so much. What is happening to him? Look now, there: the plunderers attack—and mountaineers cut me up with their sharp sabers. My bloodied body will not lie next to your precious dust, and no one from my family will come to water my distant, lonely grave with their tears. Perhaps only some traveler passing by, someone like me, will see my hillock of a grave and say, 'here, no doubt, lies some unfortunate, killed by bandits.'" This was hard and sad to contemplate, and tears fell from my eyes against my will.

The NCO broke off my thoughts as he began to tell of how bandits killed a company scribe and coachman traveling from Ardon to Ekaterinograd about four days ago in this very place. I said to him: "And perhaps we will meet the same fate?"

"Yes," he replied, "we will, if a big gang of mountaineers attacks us." I got scared, no joking about it. A while later we arrived safe and sound, however, in the fortress of Ardon.[82]

[*Shipov wends his way through the Caucasus, finally arriving in Tiflis, the Georgian capital.*]

---

82. Founded in 1824, today a town in North Ossetia.

[On arriving in Tiflis], I lost no time in going to see Klement, the postal inspector, and gave him the letter from Sukhorukov. He welcomed me gladly and was evidently pleased that Sukhorukov had sent me to lease the Georgian postal stations. In the course of our chat, Klement asked me in a serious tone whether Sukhorukov indeed owned a lot of horses, and whether, if Sukhorukov did obtain the lease, he (Klement) might become their caretaker.[83] Recalling Sukhorukov's order, I answered in the affirmative, and on hearing this, Klement replied that he would do everything in his power to help me.

Meanwhile, the various proprietors of the stations had gathered in Tiflis. They had seen Klement and learned from him that I had come as Sukhorukov's deputy to take out a lease on all the Georgian posts. They wanted to talk to me about this, and fixed a meeting time at the home of one of the proprietors. Klement, who informed me about the proprietors and their proposed meeting, suggested that if they offered me a decent sum of money, then I might just forget about the lease and go back to Sukhorukov without any more bother. I took good note of this suggestion and went to see the proprietors on the evening of the appointed day.

They asked me to enter the grand hall of the house, where Armenians, Georgians, and Tatars were gathered—around thirty people in all. I bowed to them and they invited me to sit on the sofa. There were princes seated among them; others were wearing silver and gold medallions. In a word, they were all important, imposing personages.

Several of them knew Sukhorukov personally, and asked about his health and business affairs before moving on to discuss the upcoming tenders. I told them decisively that I had come to lease the post offices, for Sukhorukov had plenty of horses and didn't need any help running this business. They offered tea followed by rum, but I told them that I didn't drink strong liquor. At this they were most surprised and said that it was hardly possible that a Russian wouldn't drink!

After this, they began to tell me (through a variety of hints) that I shouldn't involve myself in the lease, and that they would offer their gratitude for my nonparticipation in monetary form. I said that if they didn't want me to get involved, they would have to give me 10,000 silver rubles.

83. Because the mail was carried by horse at this time, it would have been crucial for the lessee of the postal outlets to have a large number of good horses on hand.

They said nothing positive in response to this, and began to serve me various European wines, hors d'oeuvres, and finally champagne. Finally noticing that I was stubbornly rejecting their overtures, they got completely drunk themselves and then went their separate ways.

The next day I went to see Klement and told him about this meeting. He praised me and said: "Now I will do everything I can for Sukhorukov and use all my powers to help him. If he doesn't send you any money soon, I can give you up to 10,000 rubles of my own; with it you can buy barley, hay, and barley straw here. But tell me something, in all honesty: will Sukhorukov actually maintain the outlets? By the first of January (of the following year, 1837), we have to have 360 *troikas* and 360 Russian coachmen in place at the stations. If Sukhorukov doesn't get them there, what will I tell Baron Rozen?[84] For I'll expose myself to serious trouble, and might even end up being tried."

Seeing these kind-hearted feelings and Klement's disposition toward Sukhorukov, I struggled with my thoughts. I knew that Sukhorukov had sent me on the basis of deception, but I wasn't sure that I would be able to get anything from any of the postal station proprietors. And time was running out—the auction was tomorrow.

I told Klement: "Vasilii Mikhailovich! I see your good intentions. But if I tell you the whole truth and Sukhorukov learns of it, I'll be in trouble."

"Don't worry," replied Klement briskly. "I'll protect you from Sukhorukov's attacks."

Then I told Klement that Sukhorukov had neither money nor horses, and that he had no intention whatsoever of leasing the postal stations. Klement was pleased to learn this, and asked me to appear at the auction only for appearance's sake. He promised, too, to get something for me from the proprietors.

The auction took place the next day, but Baron Rozen didn't ratify the result and gave all the stations to his favorite, a Georgian merchant named Zubalov. The deal included a big reduction in the postage prices paid by the state.

I continued to live in Tiflis until the middle of November. By that time I had very little money, and Sukhorukov wasn't sending any more. Klement gave me some cash for the road, and soon afterward I left Tiflis. I was

---

84. Shipov's note: "At this time, Baron Rozen was the commander in chief in Georgia."

traveling for a long time, for I had to spend fourteen days in a quarantine station near Ekaterinograd.

On arriving in Piatigorsk I went to see Sukhorukov and gave him a fair account of my trip. This time, Sukhorukov said nothing bad to me; but his evil designs against me soon revealed themselves.

1837–1841

In January I overheard a rumor to the effect that Sukhorukov was writing to his friends in Tiflis to find out whether I had taken any money from the postal station proprietors during the auction. Nothing had so far confirmed these rumors, but in the middle of April, Sukhorukov called me into his quarters and told me that I'd received 4,000 rubles assignat from the proprietors. In support of this assertion, he handed me a letter he had received from a retired colonel named Gorodinskii.

I affirmed, of course, that Gorodinskii had written a lie about me. On hearing my denial, Sukhorukov suggested that I write a letter to my wife, saying that I had left to Egor'evsk on business for him. Sukhorukov instructed me to tell her to send me the money back to me with the bearer of the letter—who was, as it turned out, a mutual acquaintance, a sergeant named Globatskii. Suspecting nothing, I did as Sukhorukov asked, and Globatskii went with the letter to see my wife. A while later he returned, and in another room discussed something or other with Sukhorukov.

After this Sukhorukov came out and said: "Well, Nikolai Nikolaevich, it's certainly true that Gorodinskii lied about you, for it turned out that your wife had no money at all in her possession." Of course, I knew this without his telling me.

So Sukhorukov and I parted friends. When I returned home, I learned that my wife was not a little surprised by what had happened; she said that as she had no money, she had gone to the home of an acquaintance to borrow some, asking Globatskii to wait for her. It turned out that the acquaintance wasn't home, so she returned with empty hands, and Globatskii left.

I looked into a box I had sitting on the table, where I usually kept various papers and documents. Many of these papers, especially the ones concerning Sukhorukov, were gone; even a diamond ring stored there was missing. I understood then the dirty trick Sukhorukov and Globatskii pulled on me. I went the next day to submit a complaint to a commandant named Simborskii, hoping to protect myself from any more of Sukhorukov's searches and oppression. Later, however, I regretted that I had made the complaint, for Sukhorukov became furious with me when he found out about it, and resolved to harm me no matter what.

A brave soldier named Baron Gan, who was in all respects an honorable person, was at this time the commander of the Kislovodsk line; he was also acquainted with Sukhorukov for a short time. The latter asked Gan to send Simborskii a document allegedly indicating both that two bandits carrying ten pounds of gunpowder had been captured, and that they had revealed that the powder had been purchased in my store. There was a sufficient quantity of powder kept in my store, and therefore they had to conduct an appropriate search of my store and lodgings, and thereafter prosecute me.

On one unhappy day the commandant, the chief of police, a solicitor, and a group of witnesses appeared to conduct a search. They found no gunpowder, however; they asked the owner of my apartment and the neighbors about my peddling any gunpowder, but they said that they'd never seen or heard anything of the sort. And with that the matter ended.

Then Sukhorukov made use of another opportunity. My relatives and friends addressed their letters to me "care of " Sukhorukov, indicating that the letters were to be passed on to me. Sukhorukov now began to read through all my letters before giving them to me. On one occasion he received a letter from Kozhevnikov, who wrote that our mutual pursuer, the peasant Pavel'ev, was in Odessa. Kozhevnikov wrote that he would almost certainly not be able to conceal himself from Pavel'ev, and would thereby end up in the stockade.[85] Thus he asked me to send him some money in exchange for his not revealing my location to Pavel'ev. Sukhorukov showed this letter to the police chief, and I was arrested and jailed in the police station.

Three weeks went by, and I asked a clerk in the station if I might not at least occasionally call upon my family. I learned from him that Sukhorukov had filed a complaint against me with the police, claiming that I owed him 500 rubles assignat and asking that my property be confiscated. This was done, and my store was closed up; those who owed me debts from the store refused to pay me. Finally, Sukhorukov succeeded in having my wife, my son, and me deported under guard from Piatigorsk to Stavropol'. Here I was transferred from the police station to the stockade, and my wife sent to the prison for women. This occurred on August 1, 1837.

85. That is, in the sense of "prison."

I was placed in a barrack, on whose doors hung a sign bearing the legend: "For Vagrancy." And here began an unspeakably bitter period of my life—so bitter, indeed, that even now I began involuntarily to weep when I recall it . . . But I will continue my story.

A month passed, and my wife was released from prison on bail. From time to time she and our son visited me, but this didn't make it any easier for me. She went to work for a merchant, and at the same time was going to give birth again within days. I could do nothing to alleviate her bitter lot, but was able to take our four-year-old son to live in the stockade with me.

In October a rumor reached our barracks that the Emperor Nikolai Pavlovich[86] would soon be stopping by Stavropol'[87] on his return trip from Georgia, and that he would visit the stockade. All of the prisoners were set in motion by this news, despite the fact that we were forbidden from bothering the sovereign with any written or oral requests. Many, however, stored away various written petitions, hoping to hand them over to the sovereign in person. I also decided to tell the never-to-be-forgotten monarch about the abuses I had suffered on the Caucasian line, certain that he would show me some sort of mercy.

On the day of the tsar's arrival, the whole administration of the stockade was on its feet from early in the morning. The whole place was cleaned up, the trash swept away, and the floors sprinkled with sand. Each of the prisoners received a new knee-length sheepskin coat, and they cooked up *kasha*[88] and beef for us—it was, in short, a real holiday.

The sovereign arrived at noon, and I stood next to the very door of our barracks. As soon as the door opened and I saw the sovereign, I fell to my knees and said, "Your Imperial Highness!" But that very second, the door was locked shut again—the tsar didn't come into our barracks. And so I had to carry on as I did before.

Religious dissenters were jailed in the barrack next to ours, about thirty-five in all. I got to know some of them, and they told me the following story about themselves:

86. Tsar Nicholas I.

87. City in southwestern Russia, founded in 1777 as a military encampment during the Russo-Turkish War.

88. A dish of cooked grain or groats.

They were all state peasants from the Mikhailovka settlement, fifteen versts from Stavropol', and were hard-working, well-to-do people. A few years earlier, they got it into their heads to ascertain which faith in Rus'[89] was the real, true faith. With this goal in mind they sent two old men off to Moscow and to various other cities and places. When the old men returned home, they declared that there had never been and never would be a better faith than the old "*Pomórskaia*" faith[90] — so people said in Moscow, and on the Unzhe River,[91] and everywhere else . . .

These residents of Mikhailovka then selected a preceptor for themselves, a man named Gavrila; they began living according to the Old Belief and no one bothered them. But at the beginning of the previous year (1836), a wanderer[92] named Lipatov arrived in Mikhailovka and asked a peasant if he might live in his house for a time, to which request the peasant agreed. Soon the Old Believers heard about the recently arrived wanderer and began to visit him and listen to his speeches "from the book of Holy Writ."

Lipatov said that in the Word of God it was written: "If you want to achieve perfection, go, sell your possessions, distribute them among the poor, and follow Me."[93] His adepts were to leave behind their homes and possessions and run into the mountains, beyond where the hostile Circassians lived, into unpopulated, desert areas, and there settle down.[94] One could take only what was necessary for the trip. If they came with him, Lipatov would baptize them all, but their names would remain the same;

89. Traditional name for "the Russian lands" (as opposed to the more modern "Rossiia," or Russia).

90. That is, the Old Belief (see note 61), here designated by an allusion to the name of its main theological work, the "Pomorskie otvety" ("Replies of the Shore Dwellers") of Andrei Denisov (1672–1730). One early group of priestless Old Believers (led by Denisov and his brother Semyon) was called "shore dwellers" because their famous settlement, the "Vyg wilderness," was located on the shores of Lake Onega in northern Russia; see Robert O. Crummey, *The Old Believers & The World of Antichrist: The Vyg Community and the Russian State 1694–1855* (Madison: University of Wisconsin Press, 1970).

91. A river in the province of Vladimir, east of Moscow.

92. Here, a religious pilgrim.

93. Shipov's note: "From Matthew 19:21, Luke 28:22."

94. Lipatov's directives here strongly recall the practices of the self-exiling Old Believer sect known as the "runners," so called because of their doctrine of abandoning all worldly property and living in total isolation. Shipov, however, does not use the Russian name for these sectarians (*beguny*) to describe them.

he would be their main preceptor and leader in all things. They would call themselves brothers, and their wives would be called sisters. If they happened to get caught along the road, and if attempts were made to return them to their homes, they would refuse to go and would denounce [their captors] as Antichrist. Lipatov's teaching seduced the residents of Mikhailovka, and they decided to follow him.

Little by little they sold their cattle, grain, and other belongings, and during the night of Easter Sunday, 1837, they departed from their settlement on a number of carriages. After traveling about forty versts, they stopped by a stream to water the horses. Here Lipatov baptized them all, and they began to call one another brother and sister.

They arrived in the Kuban',[95] where they encountered Cossack military posts. It turned out that the Cossacks living there were Old Believers as well, and the people of Mikhailovka soon made a deal with the Cossacks to allow them to pass beyond the Kuban'; the Cossacks even found a Circassian guide to go with them. At night the wanderers went [southwest] across the Kuban' and their guide led them further into the mountains. Led by him, they spent the days in the forest, the nights on the road. After a while, however, the guide disappeared, and they found themselves alone in a completely unknown locality.

One day as the sun was dawning, they saw a Circassian village not far away. They went into a large forest and settled down to spend the day there. From the village (which turned out to contain Circassians friendly to the Russians) a Circassian came into the forest to look for his traps, which he'd set there to catch wild goats and deer. He noticed the Mikhailovka encampment and informed the boss of the village, a Circassian officer in the Russian army, of their presence. The officer and some armed Circassians immediately went to see the wanderers and began to ask them who they were, where they were going, and so on; in response, however, they received only rude remarks and swearwords. The officer ordered them to be driven into the stanitsa, where the regimental staff was located.

The colonel went out to see the Old Believers and asked, "Who is your leader?" "I am," replied Lipatov, who then began making various coarse remarks. Right then and there the colonel ordered him to be given two hundred blows with a Cossack lash. While receiving these cruel strokes, Lipatov

95. An area in the northwest Caucasus, centering on the city of Krasnodar on the Kuban' River and bordering in the southwest on the Black Sea.

neither groaned nor moaned, saying only "My brothers! Pray for me, a sinful man." His companions went down on their knees and prayed toward the east.

After the punishment was finished, Lipatov got up, turned to the east, crossed himself, and said, "Glory to You, O Lord, that you took away all my uncleanness." The colonel didn't like this comment, and ordered that Lipatov be whipped another seventy times, after which the wanderer could no longer get up; his companions had to lift him. After Lipatov's punishment, Gavrila was also given eighty blows.

The next day they were all driven back to Stavropol', and there various interrogations took place; priests came to see them, trying to persuade them, to admonish them, but with little result. About ten of them, however, returned to their homes, with the rest being imprisoned in this stockade, where I dragged out a miserable existence together with them.

Their preceptor Lipatov was kept separate from them in the guardhouse, in heavy irons; he was seen only in the bathhouse of the stockade, where he met and spoke with his companions. I saw him—he was of average height, broad shouldered, and, it seemed to me, far from stupid. Subsequently several of the Old Believers passed away, others returned to their homes; about fifteen were sent to Siberia, and the others sent to serve in the army.

At the end of 1837 my enemies began to gather information from all the places where I had received foreign passports. For this reason, no doubt, my pursuer Pavel'ev learned (whether in Bessarabia, Odessa, or someplace else) that I was being held in a stockade in Stavropol' and came there. My meeting with him was brief but extremely taxing and unpleasant for me. Pavel'ev told me that if I returned home to Vyezdnaia, the landlord would forgive me. I replied that since the whole affair had already reached the courts, let the courts settle our dispute. I would rather live in Siberia, I told him, and I won't return to the landlord. With that our conversation ended.

More than a year passed. During that time the administration of the province of Stavropol' collected information about me from various places I had worked, and my case went before the Uyezd[96] Court for consideration, and from there (or so I heard) on to the Chamber of the Criminal

---

96. A Russian regional administrative unit.

Court. Thanks to petitions on my behalf by one General Rebrov, the whole affair was finally to be decided in my favor. So I waited and I hoped.

But my foes weren't dozing either. In either February or March 1839—I don't recall exactly—the stockade administration received a memorandum from the court of the Arzamas Uyezd. They were demanding that I be sent to my native area of Arzamas for a legal confrontation with the peasant Kozhevnikov, who was being held in the stockade at Arzamas. (This no doubt came about through the intrigues and insistence of Tarkhov and Raguzin.) My wife, my child, and I were sent under guard from Stavropol' to Arzamas on April 19. I was imprisoned in the Arzamas stockade, where they shaved off half my hair and beard and shackled me in irons. By Tarkhov's orders, my wife and son were sent to live in the village of Larionovo, one hundred versts from Arzamas, where estate manager Raguzin lived and where my daughter was located.

Soon my relatives, friends, and other peasants in Vyezdnaia learned of my sad arrival and condition; although they were all forbidden to visit me, this prohibition was not always observed. For this reason, life in this stockade wasn't particularly harsh—I even got together a fair amount of money from my former creditors, thanks to which I was released from the stockade on bail in October 1839.

I moved into the home of my uncle Feoktistov, and my wife and son came as well.[97] In December another daughter was born, and in memory of my release from prison on bail on October 10, gave her the name of Evlampiia.[98] My son began to learn to read and write, and we began to live not too badly, especially in comparison with what we had just undergone.

But only six months passed, and I began to hear more rumors that Tarkhov (on Raguzin's orders) was petitioning and demanding that I be sent again into the stockade. And indeed, on July 30, 1840, I was called to the Uyezd Court, where the judge read me a decree from the Criminal Court of Nizhnii Novgorod sentencing me to imprisonment once again in the Arzamas stockade. There was nothing to be done—I had to submit to necessity.

Meanwhile, my case was being considered in the Uyezd Court, which decided that my punishment should be exile to Siberia. The Criminal

97. Shipov's note: "Raguzin forbade me from bringing my daughter as well."
98. Name of a Russian saint and martyr; the name means "good light," and her feast day is October 10.

Court affirmed this decision, but the Senate, in accord with petition made by Panov, the governor of Nizhnii Novgorod, resolved that I should be reinstalled with my landlord, Saltykov.

I was released from the stockade on November 5, 1841.

1842–1844

In January our estate manager Raguzin came to Vyezdnaia, and I asked him for a six-month passport in case I were to travel away from home. I tried to gather together some money, just under 1,000 rubles, from my former creditors; I then received the passport from Tarkhov and left for Moscow on May 15. There I found the wife of a deceased friend, in whose care I had once left some money and some of my possessions. It turned out that this woman had already remarried; she told me that she knew nothing about any money or possessions that I might have left with them, and that there was no mention made of these things in the will. I shed a few tears and left.

In Moscow I found a few friends who helped me with whatever money they could afford to spare, and with those funds I traveled through Korennaia market to Kherson,[99] where my cousin served as a military clerk to the town major. [. . .] I hadn't seen him for more than eleven years, and with what joy we met again now! Although he was a soldier, he breathed freely; he was loved by his superiors for his faithful and conscientious service and was assigned tasks with which few of his fellows were entrusted. Whereas I, on the other hand, remained burdened down by my persecutors, dragging out a miserable existence, like a blade of grass all withered from lack of rain. And why? Simply because I wanted freedom above all else; because I sought not honor, glory, or wealth, but simply my and my posterity's independence from that cruel-hearted landlord. But I was still to suffer much sadness and loss before I reached that long-awaited hour . . .

I was with my cousin in Kherson for about two weeks, then left for Odessa, then through Tiraspol' to Kishinev. I learned by chance that a certain Godunov [who had assisted Pavel'ev in looking for me], had his own house there, the building of which was paid for by his crooked dealings. I

99. See map.

had nothing to fear from him now, in contrast to the time when he was looking for me with Pavel'ev in Iassy. So I went to see him. He knew me only through the portrait that Pavel'ev had carried around with him.

"Once, you and Pavel'ev dearly wished to look upon a certain Shipov," I said. "Now if you wish, you can see him for free, and without even looking for him. I am Shipov."

Godunov seemed glad to see me and asked me to stay in his house. I agreed, and in conversation we recalled all those moments in my life where Godunov's participation had been so unwelcome to me. Beyond this, I learned from him that my late brother-in-law Lanin had left some of his money and possessions in the hands of a Kishinev merchant. It had all been given over to the police, but I had no success in recovering it; they said that everything had been stolen. [. . .] On December 12 I returned home.

In and around April 1843, potential suitors from good, wealthy families began courting my daughter, under the condition that my house would be given over as dowry, a condition to which I assented. But the landlord refused to give his permission. Seeing that well-to-do peasants would not accept my daughter in marriage, I decided to give her to one Puzakov, a peasant and bootmaker of modest means in Vyezdnaia. The wedding was of the poorest, and soon the young couple went to the market in Nizhnii Novgorod to set up shop as bootmakers.

At this time, I was in the most disastrous state. No one would accept me into their service, for they were so frightened of me, I might have been a bear. Besides, I was obliged to pay 400 rubles of obrók and had no way of getting this money together. In this extreme situation I again decided to turn to my uncle Feoktistov, who still had some of my belongings in his possession. When he refused to give them to me, I petitioned the local magistrate, who decided that all my property now belonged to Feoktistov because he had already held it for ten years. I then complained to the civilian court, which concluded that only the landlord himself, or his manager, could plea for the return of the property. I then asked Tarkhov to help me in my case, but he flatly refused. So that was the end of that.

But in the course of pursuing my case, I became acquainted with a civil servant, and this man gave me some law books to read. On one occasion, he brought me the ninth volume of the Code of Laws. There I found a statute declaring that serfs who had been captured by mountain plunderers would be freed along with all their family upon escaping from captivity.

Those freed serfs would then have the opportunity, within nine months of escape, of selecting whatever type of life and work that best pleased them.[100] I decided then to attempt this severest of remedies, if only that I might be rid of the bárin's power over me. Concealing my intentions from everyone, I somehow obtained in December a six-month passport from Raguzin; I collected 25 rubles for the road from some generous friends and left home on January 3, 1844.

I will not, indeed cannot, describe the feelings that filled and agitated my poor heart at that time. I only remember that my lips were whispering a single phrase: "Almighty God! Make me wise, and hear the howling of my soul—if not for my sake, then for that of my son and heir. Merciful Creator! Give me the strength and patience to endure all misfortunes . . . let, however, Thy will be done!"

[*Shipov travels through Tambov, Voronezh, Kharkov, then west through Bessarabia and ending up eventually in Odessa.*]

At about this time, General Lüders[101] set out with the Fifth Infantry Corps from the province of Kherson for a campaign in the Caucasus. I decided to follow, with the intention of either getting hired by the sutlers as a worker or being taken on by the sutlers as one of their own. On arriving in Odessa, I sold my horse, bought a ticket to Kerch' and, at the end of April, left for the Caucasus on the steamship *Successor*.

During the trip the weather was clear and warm, the sea quiet and peaceful. I was delighted to see a multitude of porpoises playing on the surface of the water. [. . .] From the distance we could see Alupka, the estate of Count Vorontsov.[102] As our ship drew up to the city, a cannon by the harbor fired in salute, and we replied in kind.

---

100. In this crucial passage, Shipov is actually referring to several laws: the principal one, statute 1089 in the 1842 Code of Laws, mandating the manumission of serfs (and their families) following their escape from mountain bondage; statute 5704 of the *Polnoe Sobranoe Zakonov Rossisskoi Imperii* (1832), mandating the nine-month limit for choosing a "way of life" (e.g., as merchant, free peasant, etc.) following the manumission; and statute 18515 of the *Polnoe Sobranie* (1844), restricting manumission to the serf's immediate family members.

101. Aleksandr Nikolaevich Lüders (in Russian, Liders): on his activities during the war in Chechnya and Daghestan, see Moshe Gammer, *Muslim Resistance to the Tsar: Shamil and the Conquest of Chechnia and Daghestan* (London: Frank Cass, 1994), 150–158. The setting for this next, last part of Shipov's narrative is the 1830–59 war for control against the Caucasus; see later text.

102. Alupka is a town on the south tip of the Crimea (just southwest of Yalta), the site

The view of Alupka from the sea was an enchanting one: beautiful buildings of fanciful design; wonderful gardens surrounding them, covered in fresh spring verdure; streets that wound like snakes, with flowers in bloom everywhere, like the finest Persian carpet. The wind brought us their aromatic fragrance and the songs of nightingales.

[After arriving in Kerch'], I traveled by boat to the town of Taman'.[103] As a town, Taman' is worse than any village, but from it you have a wonderful view of Kerch', Erikal, and Evpatoriia.[104] From Taman' I hired a carriage to Ekaterinodar,[105] and from there to Stavropol'.

[. . .]

In the meantime, I noticed that my passport would cease to be valid within a month, and I began to wonder how I might acquire a new one. I decided to write the following note to estate manager Raguzin in Saint Petersburg:

"Traveling through Ekaterinodar, I saw four peasants in flight from Vyezdnaia, all of whom are fit for military service. I want to catch these peasants and hand them over to the local police, who will then dispatch them back to Vyezdnaia. However, I am unable to do anything without your official warrant. I am therefore asking if you might forward me such a warrant, together with a [new] passport."

I hoped that Raguzin and the bárin would fall for this fabrication, and I wasn't wrong: two months later I received both the warrant and the passport. All I needed was the latter, of course.

From Stavropol' I went to Piatigorsk on foot, for I neither had enough money to rent a cart nor any traveling companions [with whom I might share the expenses]. [. . .] Just beyond Aleksandrov Station, the magnificent

---

of the famous Vorontsov palace (completed 1827), built by Count (later Prince) Mikhail Semyonovich Vorontsov (1782–1856), governor general from 1823 to 1854 of what was then called "New Russia" (originally Bessarabia and Southern Ukraine, later expanded to include the Caucasus). Educated in England, Vorontsov participated in the campaign against Napoleon (1806–15) and was one of a series of generals to serve (1845–54) as commander in chief of the Russian forces fighting against Imam Shamil in Chechnya and Daghestan; see later text.

103. A town immortalized by Mikhail Lermontov in his tale of the same name in *A Hero of Our Time* (1840). The story begins by calling Taman' "the nastiest little hole of all the seaports of Russia."

104. These are all places around the Strait of Kerch', between the Black Sea and the Sea of Azov.

105. Now called Krasnodar.

mountains of the Caucasus unfolded again before me; I saw familiar sites and familiar roads.

In one place I sat down on a stone to rest. Shedding a few tears, I thought, "Lord! Once again, you've brought me here to see these giant forms. Within view of them, I endured the saddest events of my life . . . But where one suffers unhappiness, there, too, must one await joy." I took a piece of bread out of my sack, had a bite, and walked on.

[. . .]

After passing through Piatigorsk], I eventually arrived in the stanitsa[106] of Naur. I went into a *dukhan*[107] and sat down on a bench to rest. I asked a fellow working there who owned the place; the owner, it turned out, was a merchant from Rostov, a Jew named Osip Borisovich Favishevich. This last name struck me as familiar, and I suddenly recalled that, back in 1836, when I was working for Sukhorukov, there was a Jew working there as a shop assistant—we called him "Os'ka," but his last name was Favishevich. I began asking the fellow in more detail about his boss and ascertained that our Os'ka had indeed become Osip Borisovich.[108]

The inn laborer said that his employer would arrive in Naur tomorrow. I thought to myself, "In the old days I rendered Osip Borisovich all possible aid and kindness at a time when he was still poor. Even though he's a Jew, he's certain not to have forgotten what I did for him." So I decided to stay on and see Favishevich.

The next day around noon, the inn laborer told me that his master had arrived together with Leon Borisovich, his brother (we used to refer to him as "Leiba"). I immediately walked out to meet the Favishevichs. There in the courtyard of their lodgings was a carriage, harnessed to a troika of excellent bay horses. "So much for Os'ka!" I thought.

Entering their lodgings, I greeted both brothers and said: "Do you recognize me, Osip Borisovich and Leon Borisovich?"

"No," they replied. "We don't know you at all."

106. See note 78.
107. One of the names used in the Caucasus for an inn.
108. Shipov's note: "In the Caucasus (and indeed in some other places as well), poor people and especially Jews are often called by diminutives [of their first names]—and if and when any of these poor people happen to grow rich and influential, their names are expanded to include the full name and patronymic."

"But surely you do recall, Osip Borisovich—I'm Nikolai Shipov, the one who recommended you for work in the oil trade in 1836, while I was with Sukhorukov as a trader."

On hearing this, both brothers rushed toward me and began to kiss me, saying, "Oh, our dear friend! However did you end up here?"

"There was a rumor," continued Osip Borisovich, "that that rascal Sukhorukov had injured you in some way, and caused you a lot of problems. I was sorry to hear this, in my very heart I was; but I could do nothing to help, because I didn't know where you were. We even heard that supposedly you'd been sent to Siberia after committing some serious crime or other. Please sit down, dear Nikolai Nikolaevich."

I sat down and told the brothers about all the troubles that had befallen me because of Sukhorukov's doings. Having heard my story, Osip Borisovich said: "I sincerely sympathize with you in your misfortune and want to help you—because I remember the boon you once performed for me."

Favishevich proposed that I become his partner in trade. He said that he and the Belev merchant Kuznetsov had made a three-year contract with the Kabardinsk[109] chasseur regiment to provide it with supplies. The general staff of this regiment was stationed in Fort Vnezapnaia,[110] beyond the Terek on the Aktash River, near an *aul*[111] called Andreevskii.[112] The battalions were located in various strongholds not far from Vnezapnaia. Osip Borisovich was already occupied with other business, so he resolved to provide me with a warrant [for trade]. I would be allowed to sell goods at my own discretion, whether at the headquarters themselves or traveling with the regiment on its campaigns, which were to commence that very month

109. Regiment originating in the Kabardá area of the Caucasus, between the Terek and Kuban' rivers (see map). The regiment suffered severe losses later on in 1845 in battles near Dargo (Darghiyya), Chechnya.

110. Vnezapnaia means "sudden" or "surprise," and was one of the forts—along with Groznyi ("menacing") and Burnyi ("stormy")—built under Russian General Ermolov in the early years of the Caucasian conflict (1819–21). See Gammer, *Muslim Resistance to the Tsar;* and John F. Baddeley, *The Russian Conquest of the Caucasus* (New York: Russell and Russell, 1969; original work published 1908). The fort was in ruins by the early twentieth century (see Baddeley, *The Rugged Flanks of Caucasus* [London: Oxford University Press, 1940], 1:59).

111. Pronounced "ah-OOL": a mountain village in the Caucasus.

112. Now called Endirei, located southwest of Khasavyurt on the Aktash River in Daghestan (see map).

(June). Of course, I could only accept Favishevich's offer with rejoicing. The next day I went with him to Fort Vnezapnaia and immediately began to carry out my duties.

[. . .]

And thus, in the middle of July 1844, I began buying and selling goods in Vnezapnaia on Favishevich's behalf.[113] This wasn't an easy job; you had to watch out for the interests of the master and at the same time get along with the various regimental authorities, starting with the company sergeant major.

One of our traders worked together with Kuznetsov in a fort called Taskichi, where one battalion of our regiment was stationed. For some reason, this trader didn't hit it off with the battalion's physician. This physician reported to the colonel that the trader had purchased bad beef for the battalion, from which many soldiers had fallen ill. The colonel flew into a rage, called in Kuznetsov and dealt with him so roughly that he ran back to me in Vnezapnaia in tears and half out of his mind, begging me to set things straight. I went to Taskichi, met with the physician, presented him with a "gift," and duly entertained him with food and drink. After that, he never made another unfavorable report.

And I may as well own up to it—this sort of situation could crop up often. Either the beef would be bad, or the hay would be rotten, or the vodka watered down too much—well, what does it matter anyway? The regimental quartermaster would often learn that we didn't have some item or other in our store, despite the fact that we were obliged to have it according to the contract. He would run to the store and demand that we get whatever it was we didn't have by the next day without fail; he would start to roar and shout so that even Favishevich wouldn't dare appear before him. What was to be done? Usually I would go and visit the enraged quartermaster in the evening, when I wouldn't be noticed, and arrange

---

113. Shipov's note: "Sometimes I would end up traveling from Vnezapnaia to Bogomatov Bridge, a Circassian village whose residents were friendly to the Russians, about fifty versts from the fort. [. . .] Here I bought hay and various wildfowl, of which there were many to be had around the small lakes and creeks. Huge reeds almost like forests grew there, and in them lived wild hogs that were mercilessly slaughtered by the Tatars. Swine are an abomination of their law, and when a Tatar kills a pig, he never grabs it himself; instead, he slips a rope around its muzzle, ties it to his horse's tail and drags it along. The meat from these pigs was sold at a very cheap rate."

matters so that his hostility would change to favor. Afterward he would say: "You should have done this long ago—as it stood, we'd had nothing but trouble and dissatisfaction with you!"

The next day the quartermaster would send his batman[114] to fetch his free provisions. The parade and regimental adjutants also received substantial gifts—and Favishevich himself ordered that the company commander be given anything he wanted, gratis and duty free.

Mobile detachments would leave and return to Fort Vnezapnaia on brief sorties. I would either send the shop manager to accompany them with bullock carts laden with provisions or would go myself. At one point near the end of August, a detachment of three thousand foot soldiers and artillery left Vnezapnaia under the command of Colonel Kozlovskii, and I fitted out two carts with various supplies for them.

The detachment went upward along the Aktash River; having gone about six versts, they encountered armed bandits and a crossfire ensued. The next day, the Circassian mountaineers took the river, barring our path to the water; sitting behind large rocks in the ravine, they shot at us. All of Kozlovskii's effort to drive the Circassians from the ravine proved futile, while at the same time they caused us a lot of grief, as our bivouac was sitting out in the open. It was even difficult for us to get water from the Aktash.

The whole affair ended on the fourth night when Kozlovskii made a disorderly retreat back to Vnezapnaia.[115] In all of this turmoil, the axle of one of the carts broke, and all of that cart's provisions ended up in the hands of the mountaineers. But what does a cart matter, when all you're thinking about is how to escape whole and unharmed! Oh, the life and labor of a sutler . . .

1845

I traveled rather often from Vnezapnaia to Andreevskii, whether to check up on the sales in the two dukhans owned by Favishevich or to buy cattle

---

114. "A military servant of a cavalry officer; an officer's servant" (*Oxford English Dictionary*).

115. For an account of a battle right around this time (September 1844) in the Vnezapnaia area involving Russian forces under Colonel Kozlovskii, see Baddeley, *The Russian Conquest of the Caucasus*, 368.

and various supplies. On Friday (market day) I'd be in the aul without fail. For the most part I traveled alone and sometimes ended up walking about rather late. Several Tatar acquaintances warned me that I was putting myself at risk by going around at night. I paid little attention, however, to their words of caution. The only thing I feared was death, and although I was scared of being captured by the mountaineers, in the depths of my soul—I wished for it. Then Friday, February 8 arrived . . .

February 8

On that day I was at the market in the aul as usual; I bought whatever we needed and just before evening set off home for Vnezapnaia, where I gave all the money and accounts to Favishevich. Thanking me, he said: "We've got absolutely no butter in our stores; the last of it was taken by the regimental commander today. And tomorrow morning, the colonel and the officers will be asking for more."

"I did buy some butter today from a Tatar," I said, "but only conditionally: I didn't give him an advance."

Favishevich then asked me to go back to the aul and give an advance to the Tatar, stipulating that he bring the butter early the next morning. Having spent the whole day on my feet running around the aul, I wasn't keen on going back, but I knew the regimental commander very well, and Favishevich's request seemed fully justified. So I left for the aul.

The sun had descended behind the mountains, down from which a terribly thick fog was beginning to spread. Near the guardroom I ran into an NCO I happened to know, who asked me, "Where are you headed? It's getting on."

"To the aul," I replied.

"Now look, Nikolai Nikolaevich," said the NCO. "It's dangerous walking around at this time—the Chechens could snap you up anywhere. Those damned savages are cunning; they know you've usually got money on you. They'll catch you, send you off into the mountains, and from there—to the next world."

"Oh, what nonsense," I replied. "I've gone out late before, and everything went smoothly. Perhaps nothing will happen this time, either." And with that, we parted.

It was already very dark when I reached the aul, and I had a hard time finding the *saklya*[116] of the Tatar with whom I'd bargained for the butter

---

116. Pronounced "SACK-lia": a Caucasian mountain hut.

that morning. I gave him the deposit and asked him to deliver the butter early the next day. [. . .] When I left for home, it was so dark, you may as well have plucked out my eyes. As I was leaving the gates of the aul, the watchman hailed me with a "Who goes there?" — "A sutler," I replied.

From the gate I descended down a hill; on my left was a cliff, on the right, a steep bank down to the Aktash; I walked close to the cliff's very edge. Exactly halfway between the aul and a smaller community on its out-skirts, I was seized by some people who began dragging me downhill to the river. I ended up rolling down the bank with them in the snow and would have cried out to the guard, but the bandits bared their daggers and drew them up to my chest. [For a moment], I lost consciousness.

The bandits then put some sort of hood on my head and tied it so that I couldn't see a thing. Then they bound my head with a belt and led me onward. We went past some sort of water-driven mill where I overheard a conversation in Kumyk.[117] We crossed a river, probably the Aktash, on foot, and proceeded further, but I didn't know where.

Somewhere in the distance I heard the barking of a dog. At this sound, my companions began speaking in Chechen, a language I barely under-stood. As we continued through the snow for about another four versts, the barking became more and more audible. We waded through another river, though I supposed that it was the Aktash yet again. We seemed to climb upward for a while, then stopped when the bandits began calling someone. A response was heard from somewhere up high, and something was thrown down from above; I was bound with a rope around my midsec-tion, my hands were untied and I was told in Kumyk, "usta arkan" ("hold on to the rope"), which I did. After being pulled up about three sazhens,[118] I was grabbed by two men who then led me along for another fifteen min-utes or more. Finally they stopped, tied my hands behind back, pushed me into some sort of storeroom, slammed the door shut, and put a chain on it.

My new lodgings didn't turn out to be very warm, and a frigid wind passed through the walls, whistling as it went. I was wearing a *beshmet*[119] and a wadded overcoat; my wet legs grew cold and my bound hands became numb. I stood up but was nervous about walking or even moving.

---

117. A Caucasian language of the Altaic group, of which the best-known representa-tives are Azeri and Turkmen. Kumyk is now mainly spoken in the Daghestan Republic of the Russian Federation.

118. One sazhen equals 2.13 meters.

119. A kind of quilted coat.

[. . .]

Then someone led me to another place and removed the hood. I saw before me the interior of a large saklya, illuminated by some heated tallow set upon a stool. In front of me stood a Kumyk—tall, well built, broad shouldered—whom I had never seen before. He asked me: "Tanisman meneke?" ("Do you know me?")

"Bel'meima" ("No, I don't"), I replied. Indicating a stool, the Kumyk told me "ultar" ("sit down"), and I did as he said.

The Kumyk drew a knife from his pocket and began sharpening it against a whetstone. On seeing this, my hair stood on end and my heart beat so hard that I'm sure the Kumyk could hear it. In my thoughts I said farewell to all my family and the world, under the assumption that the last minutes of my life had arrived.

The Kumyk finished sharpening the blade, came over to me, pulled my head toward him and said "korkma" ("don't be frightened"). He began shaving my head, and my heart grew quieter when I realized that this was his sole intention. He shaved off my hair and beard, placed a hat upon my head, tied that selfsame hood back on, led me back to the previous storeroom and silently shut the door. I spent the night in extreme disquiet; it was so cold that I could barely close my eyes. Roosters were crowing in the aul.

February 9

Suddenly I heard people making a racket, bullock carts squealing, dogs barking; the sun must have risen. I alternated between stretching my benumbed limbs and, by either sitting or leaning against the wall in a standing posture, dozing off.

Someone opened the door and said "aman, Mekelei" ("hello, Nikolai"). I was very glad to hear someone addressing me by my name and impatiently waited to hear what he would say to me. But the door slammed shut, and I heard nothing more.

It was already evening, no doubt, when I was led back to that same saklya where the Kumyk had shaved my head. They removed the hood, and I saw him there again before me.

"Akhcha barma senike?" ("Do you have any money with you?"), he asked.

"Iok akhcha" ("No"), I replied.

He then proceeded to search me, but found no money. Then he withdrew my notebook and pencil from the pocket of my beshmet and said: "Zzhias Osip kagas" ("Write a note to Osip").

"Ne zzhiazdym?" ("What shall I write?"), I asked. He replied, "Men cheberdym sagan, ber akhcha chus tiumen kumysh" ("I'll let you go if you hand over 100 silver rubles.")

I pulled a leaf from the notebook and wrote to Favishevich, "I'm a captive but don't know where—they're asking 300 rubles for my redemption. For God's sake, please help unhappy N. Shipov."

The Kumyk took the note and shut the door again. I spent that night in much the same way as I'd spent the one before, with the exception that I was dying to have something to eat.

February 10

No one came to see me during the day. Late in the evening, after everything had died down in the aul, a Tatar came and led me out of my dungeon. After a while we stopped, and suddenly four men appeared next to me. They untied my hands, which had been rubbed raw by the belt, and tied a rope around my midsection. After telling me to "hold on tight!" in Russian, they pushed me over a cliff and began to lower me down. "It was here that I was pulled up the first night, no doubt," I thought. Two other men received me at the bottom and spoke quietly about something or other with those up above. Tying my hands again with the belt, they led me across the river and through the snow, walking with quick steps.

[. . .]

Eventually, we seemed to arrive at a forest, and there my bonds and blindfold were removed. Before me stood two middle-aged Tatars, both of whom were carrying sabers, pistols, daggers, and a rifle. They looked me in the eyes, and I looked back at them.

"Do you know this place?" they asked me in Kumyk—I told them I didn't. Looking around, I saw a small wood on both sides of our path; the farther we went along this road, the narrower it became. The night was starless and overcast. Laughing at me, the Tatars said, "Sogom sagan kerek, akhcha bar" ("You need to buy cattle—so you're bound to have some money!"). I only told them that I had no money with me at the moment.

The wind blew in my face, and I began to feel better; we went for a few versts more through the forest. Suddenly the Tatars emitted a whistle, to which another, distant whistle replied. A young Tatar came up to us and greeted my escorts with "salamalikam."[120] They shook hands and began

---

120. An Arabic greeting meaning "peace be upon you."

speaking in Chechen, while the newcomer greeted me as well with an "aman-ma" ("hello"), to which I replied in kind.

We set off along a narrow little path, and the forest became thicker, the path more sinuous and winding as we descended. At one point I noticed what seemed to be a Tatar graveyard a little way ahead, where various stone monuments were standing. When we came up to it, the Tatars stopped and said loudly, "salamalikam."

I asked, "Ne bu monda?" ("What's this?") One of them replied to me, in a strange mix of Kumyk and Russian: "Kardash umrit, kon saldat ubit, monda bardym aul" ("Our brothers died, many soldiers were killed—here an aul once stood").

Then I understood—the Tatars were paying homage to their dead relatives.

[...]

Finally we approached some gates made of wattle; on either side of them were shallow ditches and an earthen wall on which prickly blackthorn was laid. The gates were opened, and we were hailed by an armed Chechen who led us to a guardroom that was also made of wattle. A fire burned brightly nearby; around it, four Circassians were sleeping as we approached. They got up and greeted us, then sat down again and began speaking in Chechen. Then they all lay down to sleep, and I too curled up to the fire. But I had no longing for sleep, although my companions soon dozed off; various ideas were roiling in my head.

"If God wills it," I thought, "I'll somehow manage to escape from captivity—I will be a free man, and my descendants will be grateful to me forever. And what will my pursuers think, when they learn that I am free, together with all my family? They will be most unhappy that they let me slip out of their hands, and for nary a kopeck too! They'll never forgive themselves or me. Or perhaps I'll never live to see my native land or dear family again . . ."

The watchman woke my companions, and we went on.

[...]

We came to a river, and my escorts told me that it was called the Yaman-su. We crossed it and followed it upstream; on the sides of the [surrounding] hills, scattered saklyas could be seen within the scrubby forest, and from which fierce, angry dogs emerged and ran after us.

[Eventually we saw] a small aul situated at the bottom of a mountain. Smoke emerged from the scattered saklyas, mixing with the fog and spreading through the forest and low-lying plain. A small creek flowed down the mountain into the Yaman-su.

[We descended] and entered a saklya equipped with two chimneys. We were met there by a very pretty young Circassian woman carrying an infant in her arms. She looked charmingly at my companions, of whom one (as it turned out) was her husband. Occasionally she cast her fast-moving, fiery black eyes upon me as well.

[...]

[Later, after falling asleep by the fire], I was awakened by the master of the house, who told me "tur" ("get up"). I saw before me a saklya full of Circassian men and Circassian children of various ages; both men and boys were armed with daggers, and some with pistols. Their black eyes were all gazing upon me with curiosity and hostility, while I, as the captive, looked at them mournfully. Among themselves they spoke Kumyk, Chechen, and Tavlin.[121] The woman of the house withdrew some small, round, flat cakes made of wheat flour (called *chureki*) from the ashes of the fire and, wiping them off with a dirty rag, passed them out to my companions. She gave one to me as well, which I ate with enormous appetite; I held it up above my cupped hand as though it were a piece of communion bread. After all, I hadn't eaten for three whole days.

After putting some wood on the fire, the woman hung over it a small pot with water, into which she threw some flakes of barley and a bit of lard. When this dish was ready, she poured a ladleful of it into each of several bowls and handed them round to all of the men, including me. She gave me another churek as well. I ate my food with great relish, then handed the bowl back to her and sat in silence. People came in and out of the saklya; the door was squeaking incessantly, like an ungreased wheel.

About three hours later they led me to another saklya, in which rifles, sabers, and saddles hung on the walls. There was an anvil in the corner, in regard to which I asked my escort: "Kem darkhan monda bar?" ("Who's the blacksmith around here?")

"Kardash magan" ("My brother"), he replied. I now realized that I had been led to this place by two brothers, one of whom was single, the other married.

Soon people began arriving in this saklya as well. Among the arrivals, one Kumyk sat with me and began conversing in decent Russian. It turned

---

121. I have been unable to discover anything about the Tavlin language Shipov is referring to here.

out that this fellow (whose name was Mustafa) was a resident of Andreev-skii, where he had a house, a wife, and two children.

This Mustafa had once purchased a pair of horses in Taskichi from an unknown Tatar. The horses turned out to have been stolen; Mustafa was arrested and told that he would be tried in the military court if he didn't track down the missing Tatar. As it was, of course, impossible to find him, Mustafa escaped and fled to the present aul, where he had already been living for more than a month, although he made secret trips to Andreevskii to visit his family.

I was very happy to have run into this Mustafa fellow and spoke to him in detail about my captivity. On hearing my story, Mustafa observed that I wouldn't likely succeed in escaping soon; it was probable, he said, that I'd be brought to Shamil[122] in the "Red" aul (also known as Dargo), located about forty versts away.

Right then a Circassian entered the saklya—an elderly man, but tall, well formed, and handsome, and dressed in a yellow Circassian coat[123] adorned with silver galloon. Across his chest he wore cartridges of superb quality, on his left side a dagger with a costly hilt, on his back a pistol. He sat down next to me, threw his eagle-like gaze in my direction and said: "Aman, saldat" ("Hello, soldier").

I replied with an "aman," and asked Mustafa who the man was.

"A Chechen," replied Mustafa, "the chief of this and the surrounding auls. He's called the 'chiliarch,'[124] in the event of an order from Shamil, he's

---

122. The Imam Shamil (born ca. 1797, Gimry, Daghestan [now in Russia]; died March 1871, Medina, Arabia): leader of Muslim Daghestan and Chechen mountaineers, whose fierce resistance delayed Russia's conquest of the Caucasus for twenty-five years. Shamil was the third Imam (political-religious leader) of the Muridis, a Sufi brotherhood that had become involved in a holy war against the Russians after the latter formally acquired control of Daghestan from Iran in 1813. Establishing an independent state in Daghestan (1834), Shamil reorganized and enlarged his Chechen and Daghestan forces and led them in extensive raids against the Russian positions in the Caucasus region. Only after large, well-equipped forces under generals N. I. Evdokimov and A. I. Baryatinsky had been deployed (starting in 1857) were Shamil and his supporters compelled to surrender (on September 6, 1859). Shamil was taken to Saint Petersburg and then was exiled to Kaluga, south of Moscow. With permission from the Russian tsar, he made a pilgrimage to Mecca in 1870. See Gammer, *Muslim Resistance to the Tsar.*

123. In Russian, *cherkeska:* a "long, narrow, collarless coat worn by Caucasian high-landers" (*Oxford Russian Dictionary*).

124. That is, the commander of a thousand men (in Russian, *tysiachnyi* or *tysiashnik*).

Portrait of Shamil.

the one who gets the armed men up and out of the auls and tells them where to go."

Mustafa spoke with the chiliarch in Chechen for about ten minutes. When they'd finished, the chiliarch asked me (though Mustafa) how many troops the Russian tsar had. I answered that he had two million, a reply that greatly surprised my interlocutors; the chiliarch had supposed that

Russia had no more troops than the ones who were fighting with them in the mountains.

[. . .]

Toward evening the chiliarch together with most of the Circassians left the saklya; only four young Circassians, one old man, and Mustafa remained. The latter said: "You're getting bored here; I'll bring some cards and we'll play a bit."

He left, and while he was gone one of the Circassians brought over some leg irons and fettered me with them. Soon Mustafa returned with a nearly brand-new deck of cards, and we sat down by the fireplace, where a fire was burning brightly. Two Circassians joined us, and we began to play a game of "fools."[125] The Circassians played badly, but I played "the fool" deliberately; they were pleased [with my ineptitude] and laughed at me, saying "saldat ten'tiak" ("this soldier's a fool").

[. . .]

February 12

[After my companions awoke and left the saklya], I too stepped outside to breathe the fresh morning air. The sky was overcast, and a thick fog spread down from the mountains through the aul; silvery dew hung in the tall trees, and in the distance the Yaman-su roared over the stones. I returned to the saklya and sat by the fire.

After a while the master of the house came with some kind of apparel; with miming gestures he explained that I was to change my outfit, and to that end he opened my fetters. I put on a shirt as filthy as the ones worn by chimneysweeps, a sheepskin coat full of holes, wretched *cheviaki*[126] on my feet, and a tattered hat upon my head. In this attire I probably looked like one of those scarecrows that stand in village gardens. The master of the house closed my fetters again, took my clothes, and left.

A little later his wife brought me some thin gruel and lard and a bit more of the familiar churek. I had just finished my meal when Mustafa arrived; he told me that he'd been with the chiliarch, who said that it was likely I'd be taken soon to Shamil. Apparently the chiliarch was delaying

125. Also called "simpleton" (*prostoi durak*), the objective of this game is to get rid of all your cards; the "fool" is the last person left with cards after everyone else has run out.

126. A kind of leather shoe.

my transfer only at the request of the master of the house, who had also promised the chiliarch a gift in return for the delay. I wondered, then, if Osip Favishevich was petitioning anyone in regard to my redemption.

There was no one in the saklya but Mustafa and I, and so I asked him if it was really impossible for me to escape from this place. He replied that he would be sincerely happy to help me with such an endeavor, but that he could do nothing on his own and was afraid to speak to anyone about the matter. He was planning, however, to go to Andreevskii the following night to visit his family, and thought that he might find out something there regarding my liberation.

My regular companions then walked in, along with several other Circassians. We started playing cards again, and I played "the fool" just as I had done the day before—to the evident satisfaction of the Circassians. The evening I spent alone with Mustafa; the four young Circassians didn't show up, and Mustafa said that they had gone off to do some pillaging. "But where do they go?" I asked, my curiosity piqued.

"They don't know themselves where they're headed," replied Mustafa. "Usually they just ride and wander like hungry wolves along various roads and near auls friendly to the Russians. If they meet anybody, they rob him; if they find some cattle, they herd it away. They're fearless, and they live [by pillage] alone. One other thing: whomever they take captive, they either kill or sell him."

At this Mustafa looked sadly at me—but I was sadder than he was.
[. . .]

February 13

[In the morning] I stepped out of the saklya and started walking up the mountain with heavy steps; the master of the house went past me without saying a word. Like a lark I sat down on a thawed patch of earth near an enormous chanar tree[127] and began examining the area. The sun had fully emerged from behind the mountains and began warming the earth with its beams; water purled down the mountains, the Yaman-su made its distant noise, and dew showered down from the trees. In the woods, the Circassians cut down one-hundred-year-old chanars, which fell with a crash to earth; afterward they transported them on oxen to the aul.

---

127. Apparently a deciduous tree, common in arid climates, of the genus Geoffroea decorticans.

The larks were singing and the eagle owls crying out in a strange sort of voice. Circassian women drove cattle to the watering hole, and some of them carried jugs of water from [a nearby] channel on their shoulders. Kids came over to me, carrying daggers and small pistols; they sat down next to me and looked at me in a most unfriendly manner. They spoke among themselves in Chechen, and I didn't understand them.

Then they left, and I was alone. I sat there looking at the ground and suddenly noticed something shiny, like a little star. It struck me that this must be some kind of metal in mineral form! I thought: "May God enable our Tsar quickly to subjugate Shamil and his plundering peoples, and to conquer this rebellious land, where no small amount of wealth and abundance might be found. If God wills it, an end will come to this never-ending fighting and bloodshed, and our tsar will take possession of this wonderful land . . ."

During these meditations I noticed in the distance two men in white turbans heading down the mountain to the aul, leading two saddled horses. On seeing them, the master of the house approached them with quick steps and spoke with them about something for a long time—they kept looking in my direction while they were conversing. After the two men left, the master came over to me and, sighing, asked: "Senike katan bar?" ("Do you have a wife?")

I replied, "Bar katan ulu nike kyz" ("I have a wife, son, and two daughters"). The master of the house sighed again and went off to his saklya. Meanwhile, I was completely lost in guessing and riddles: why would he have asked me about my family? I wondered if there was any connection here with my note to Osip Favishevich, in which I asked for a redemption sum of 300 rubles. I knew from experience that the bad arrives easily, while the good takes a long time to show up; and Favishevich, I thought, would pay scarcely any attention to my note. But if he had guessed what my situation was and written to my wife in Vyezdnaia, everything would be different—my wife might gather together the requested sum from relatives and friends in Arzamas. But that might take a long time . . .

I began to weep inconsolably.

[. . .]

February 14

Mustafa came early in the morning and told me that he'd just arrived from Andreevskii, where he'd seen his wife. As far as I was concerned, she passed on the following information to him: On the morning of the day after I was captured (February 9), Favishevich apparently told Kozlovskii, the regimental commander, that I did not return the previous night from Andreevskii, where he, Favishevich, had sent me on business. Kozlovskii surmised that either I'd been killed by the Andreevskii Tatars or sold to [other] plunderers in the mountains, and so ordered his soldiers to search for me in all the suspicious saklyas in the aul. Naturally, these searches were carried out in vain.

The following day (continued Mustafa's wife), the little note I'd written was found on the road leading to the aul. At the request of Favishevich, the colonel was now petitioning for either my redemption or my exchange for one of the bandits being held in the guardroom. But no one knew when any of this might come to pass. All the same, of course, I was very glad to hear this news.

After this, my host (the master of the house) brought me my usual dinner, and I ate while he spoke with Mustafa. Then he left, and Mustafa conveyed to me the substance of what he'd said. Yesterday (my host said), two Circassian merchants going past our aul learned that he had a captive in hand (me, that is) and offered to buy me for one hundred rams. My host, however, didn't consent to this, saying that he'd rather wait it out and see whether some scout from Andreevskii wouldn't come and offer money for me. This would be more convenient for him, because he could always keep the money with him, whereas maintaining cattle was a risky business; they weren't even safe from raids carried out by the Russians.

We spent the rest of the day playing cards. Upon leaving, Mustafa said that it seemed likely that he would soon be absolved of any wrongdoing; then, he said, he'd be able to steal me away from here. These words, too, gladdened me, and I fell asleep dreaming pleasant dreams.

In my slumber I saw my deceased father coming toward me in that very saklya, and saying, "Nikolai, why are you sitting here? I've been looking for you for a long time; come along now, hurry up." And taking me by the hand, he led me out of the saklya. We stepped onto a clean and level road; on both sides, broad meadows with tall, succulent grass exposed their verdure, flowers bloomed . . . I was so happy—and then I woke up.

[. . .]

February 15

[That morning, while I was sitting outside], an elderly man came up to me; in one hand he held an unfinished wooden spoon, and in the other a small axe that he was using to put the finishing touches on the spoon. He greeted me, sat down and began speaking in broken Kumyk—indeed, I had a hard time understanding him. He explained that he was a Tavlin living in this aul (he indicated his saklya with a gesture of the hand) and had all kinds of excellent weapons, sheep, horses, cattle, and (in addition) a daughter.

Following this explanation, he entirely unexpectedly suggested that I take his daughter in marriage and remain in the aul forever. I explained to him, as best I could, that I already had a wife and children, and that our law forbade marrying again with another wife still alive. The Tavlin shook his head, sighed, and fell to thinking; he then began working on the spoon, and I praised his work. He walked away without saying another word.

[. . .]

[A little later] I spoke with Mustafa, who translated for me a conversation [he had just had with my host]. The host had said that everything was expensive now for them in the mountains because of the long-standing conflict with the Russians. If it weren't for this fighting, he said, everything would be the other way round; even the bread wouldn't cost anything, for the soil here was of the richest. Life had become difficult because they had to be afraid of both Shamil and of the Russians, the latter of whom could attack unannounced at any moment and utterly exterminate them. Therefore (my host continued), if he succeeded in selling me or securing a redemption payment from the Russians, he would quit this place and adopt Russian citizenship.

Afterward we began to play "fools" again, and while we were playing a tall, fully armed Circassian came into the saklya; he was received graciously by both my host and Mustafa, and respectfully they asked him to sit down. This Circassian glared at me fiercely, like a beast; it seemed that he wanted to devour me with his darting eyes. His gaze was hardly a surprise to me, however, for only rarely did any of the savages look at me with pity or a smile. This was understandable. All mountain peoples had lived freely and independently from time immemorial; only with Russians did they have to struggle so continuously and for so long. During that time a lot of Russian blood had been spilt. But from among the mountaineers, you might find only one from every ten who hadn't had a grandfather, a father, a son, or some other relative killed by Russians. So how could a savage stare at me, other than with hate?

[. . .]

February 16

[That evening] there was a frost outside, and it got cold inside the saklya, so I added wood to the fire and silently warmed myself; [the four Circassians, returned from their thieving, slept, as did the old man.] But the old man had forgotten both to lock the door and to block it with the anvil. I decided to run for it.

Quietly I left the saklya and headed toward the stable, which also turned out to be unlocked. I returned to the saklya and began to think about carrying away and hiding all of the weapons hanging on the wall. "If the Circassians wake up after I've left, no problem," I thought, "for they'll have no weapons. With that in mind, I'll take two rifles, a pistol, and a dagger with me; I'll saddle up a horse, lead her away forty sazhens from the aul, break my bonds with the dagger, get on the horse, and ride away. If I run into any bandits, he'll have three shots to contend with."

I was just about to get a saddle and some weapons when one of the Circassians turned over, lifted up his head and, looking at me, asked: "Ne turassan" ("What are you sitting for?")

"Bek suvuk" ("It's very cold"), I replied, shaking as though I had a fever.

The Circassian got up, went out of the saklya, and returned a few minutes later. Although he'd laid down to sleep, he rolled over all the same . . .

"No," I thought, "the hour of my flight has not yet arrived," and I began to remove the rag I had wrapped around my fetters. I laid down right next to the fire, but was so agitated and filled with thoughts of my loved ones that I didn't fall asleep until dawn.

February 17

The day began with the usual activity in the aul. Mustafa came early to see me; pulling a pipe and some tobacco from his pocket, he said: "Although Shamil has forbidden the smoking of tobacco in the mountains," he said, "the rule applies only to his subjects. You're a captive, not a subject; one day you're here, but the next day you might be with the Russians."

"Your words are like music to my ears," I said.

[. . .]

We played cards again that evening. It's true that card playing is a waste of time, but I was grateful for it in my situation. Without that distraction, I would have been gripped in fatal depression and bitter thoughts.

Toward midnight we stopped playing and, wrapped in my tattered coat, laid my head upon my fist and fell asleep, and in my sleep I dreamt that I had been brought to Shamil. In my dream he appeared to be no longer young, but still lean, with a tinted beard and wearing a motley-colored turban, a white silk beshmet, a belt adorned with silver, and a dagger studded with precious stones. He sat on a marvelous Persian carpet, his legs folded beneath him. I bowed to him, and he did likewise, saying "aman, moskov" ("greetings, Russian"); I replied "aman," and suddenly awoke.

"Yes," I thought, "my dream might be realized even today. And what will happen to me? I've heard that Shamil is rough with any of our officers who fall captive to him. And I can forget about any shows of mercy or leniency in my case. But all the same: did I do any harm to him, the master of the mountain peoples? Why should he want to torment me? . . . Well, whatever will be, will be."

February 18

In the morning, my host came to see me as usual and, after the usual greeting, said: "Monda turassan sigas kun" ("It's already your eighth day here").

With that, he left. "It's true," I thought. "My host is calculating my worth."

Mustafa then appeared and said that I would be brought by the chiliarch to Shamil tomorrow—and if not tomorrow, then the next day. I said nothing, and only recalled my recent dream.

The wife of my host brought me some more than the usual helping of churek and gruel; it was as though she knew that my road to meet the leader of the mountain peoples would not be an easy one. After eating, Mustafa passed me a pipe and said: "Smoke, smoke to your heart's content. Smoking is prohibited around Shamil."

We left the saklya and sat down on a hillock. "Your face has really changed," said Mustafa. I agreed that this might very well be true and began speaking to him about my sadness, as suggested by the proverb: "if you're suffering, speak to someone about it." Then Mustafa left.

[. . .]

February 19

When I awoke it was already bright inside in the saklya. My companions got up, put on their fighting armor, saddled their horses, and left to practice their robber's trade. Soon Mustafa arrived, followed by my host, who told me through Mustafa that the chiliarch was bothering him about getting me off to Shamil; with that he left in distress. One can only surmise that his chagrin was due to the fact that no scout had arrived from Favishevich with a redemption payment. Besides, he might receive nothing for dispatching me to Shamil—in short, all his work and everything he spent in keeping me there came to nothing for him. Mustafa offered me a pipe and said he'd come by early the next morning, when I was to be carried off to Shamil; he promised to see me off and discuss my situation. Then he left.

Having finished my churek and gruel, I left the saklya and, after walking up the mountain a bit, sat down on a rock. Familiar scenes! I began looking in the direction toward which they'd be taking me: there I saw the blue of high mountains, topped with white snow and swirls of thick fog; the clouds floated with the noonday winds toward the north. The sun peeped out from behind, but my lamenting heart found no joy in that . . .

A Circassian came up to me; he was a rather short man and bore a single dagger. He approached and said in perfect Russian, "hello, brother." This surprised me, and I became curious to know who he was.

"I'm a Tatar," he said, "a soldier in the Kabardinsk regiment. I ran away from the regiment about three years ago, and now I live here in the aul. There's my saklya (and with his right hand he indicated its position near the edge of the aul). I saw how you were brought here by the two brothers, the Kumyks—from Andreevskii, they say. I own a splendid dog, by the way—the best one in this aul."

"I saw your dog, brother, when they brought me here," I said. "It's a fierce one. If you brought it to Russia to work with herders, they'd have no qualms about offering 100 rubles for it—no greedy wolves would get to the cattle with that dog around. What province and uezd are you from?"

"From the Orenburg province," he said. "I lived in Kargala sloboda."

"My dear fellow," I replied, "I know Orenburg very well, and Kargala sloboda included! Merchant and Tatar friends of mine live there, I bought sheep from them. In 1828 a salesman working for me had a shop at the market there—he used to trade rams for textiles with the Kyrgyz."

"And what was the salesman's name?" the Tatar asked.

"Ivan Semis,"[128] I replied.

"I worked for him for four months that same year!" said the Tatar. "I used to bring the Kyrgyz to his store, precisely in order to trade sheep for other items. And I got a good salary from him, too. But I don't remember seeing you in the shop—I began working for him in August of that year."

"I wasn't in Orenburg at that time," I said. "I'd already left. But look here, my dear friend—what a strange coincidence, meeting one of my own workers here, in the mountains, among the plunderers! However did you end up here?"

128. Shipov's note: "His last name is Kyrgyz; 'semis' means 'oily.'"

"I joined the army in my brothers' stead," he said, "because they have children. I was assigned to the Kabardinsk regiment, and they herded us off down here to the Caucasus. But I was used to a life of freedom and didn't want to serve, so I left, came here, and live just fine. I'm called to serve Shamil only when there's a big disturbance. And truth to tell, I shirk that duty too—what am I, fool enough to shoot at my own people? That's disgusting and sinful. I live here by myself in that saklya I acquired; I make a few kopecks, and want to get married. Maybe I'll die here."

He asked me to tell him the story of my life, which of course I did, with pleasure. I ended my sad tale with the following words: "So as you can see, right now I'm the captive of mountain bandits. I still have a dear, sweet family, and I pity them to the bottom of my heart. And now," I said, "now that you've eaten my bread and heard my story, heard who I was—my dear workman, help me in my misfortune: help me escape from here. Once I'm there, I can give you 200 rubles in return."

With that I seized his hand and began bitterly to weep.

"I heard, honored master," said the Tatar, "that they're taking you to-morrow to Shamil. From there, it's difficult to escape. I would help you, only . . . (Here he fell to thinking.) Look: the Circassians often ride out from this damned aul to rob and plunder, or else they go and visit their friends and relatives in Andreevskii. If you run into any of them, you'll meet with certain death. And the road is nowhere near. Let's suppose that it's possible to get to Vnezapnaia—all the same . . ."

Here the Tatar took to thinking again, and then resumed: "I feel sorry for you, master," he said, "and I want to do you a good turn. But I don't need your money: it would be hard for me to claim it anyway, dangerous . . . When you escape from captivity, it would be good, at least, to say that a Tatar freed you, just because he had a soft heart."

My interlocutor fell silent again. Then, having looked around, he said: "Yes, so it is—I want only to help you. Here's what I'll do: I'll open the fetters on your legs and take over two shifts from the watchman; then I'll show you where the road is, and return in time to my own saklya. Run to Vnezapnaia as best you know how. If you get caught along the way by plunderers and are brought back here or to any other hostile aul alive, don't ever let them know who unlocked your bonds and showed you the way out of here. No dilly-dallying on the way."

"You," I said in a burst of joy, "you are my second father—my protec-tor, the one who delivered me and all my family from persecution forever."

"Go now to your saklya," said the Tatar, "they might notice us. I'll come by just before evening, while your hosts are in the mosque, and

I'll bring something for you to break those fetters with. Let me look at them."

He looked at the irons on my legs, muttered "good," and said: "Later, when you leave the saklya, go over there along this path (he pointed to it) and wait for me—I'll whistle."

I felt as though I were drunk—could it be true? It didn't seem possible! . . . With my hand I wiped off the tears rolling down my face and went to the saklya; there I lit a fire and began looking down on my fetters. Would the promised key ever arrive? I was on tenterhooks waiting for my Tatar benefactor.

Suddenly he rushed into the saklya and said: "Let me open the fetters now—your hosts will be arriving soon from the mosque."

He pulled four pieces of iron out of his pocket, of which one deftly opened the lock on my fetters; I took that piece of iron with me.

"Go quietly," said the Tatar. "Try not to let the dogs hear you." And hurriedly, he left.

My hostess came in, bringing me the usual churek and gruel. I thought to myself, "Perhaps I'm enjoying this meal for the last time." After finishing, I looked over my cheviaki, and they were full of holes. I had no socks, no foot bindings. I tore apart my unattractive shirt, and with shaking hands hurriedly wrapped my feet with the pieces and put the cheviaki back on.

My guard, the old man, came in and sat down by the fire to warm himself as I was doing. Then he looked over my fetters, blocked the door with the anvil, and lay down to sleep.

"Lord!" I thought, "this may be the little old man's last evening of patrolling. [. . .] When I leave, he'll no doubt receive a cruel beating." I felt sorry for him, but (I won't conceal it) even more sorry for myself.

I lay down next to the old man and pretended to be sleeping. After a while, as though sleeping, I kicked the old man, but he lay there like a dead man. I got up, crossed myself, opened my fetters with the piece of iron given me by the Tatar, took a small stick with me and quietly, carefully left the saklya. The dogs didn't smell me.

I got out of the aul and went up the mountain by the path the Tatar had shown me. Near a large chanar tree I stopped, and sat there listening for about ten minutes. Suddenly I heard someone coming toward me along the path until, stopping for a second, he quietly whistled. This was my benefactor, the Tatar, armed in the Circassian fashion.

We walked along together quickly. I didn't feel my legs beneath me—I floated like a feather in the breeze. We waded across the Yaman-su and climbed up the hill into the forest. Here my good companion said that a guard was stationed up ahead; it would be necessary to travel three extra versts, lest I avoid the guard only to fall into the hands of the plunderers returning to their auls.

"For God's sake, lead me as you know best," I said. "I'm ready to travel not three extra versts, but twenty."

We went further into the forest, now without a path and in snow that collapsed under our feet. My cheviaki, filled with holes, were filled with snow as well, but my hot feet didn't feel it. We went from the big forest into a smaller one, along a narrow, almost invisible path. Then my companion ordered me to sit to one side, under a bush, and went along the path to find out whether the sentries were sleeping.

In fifteen minutes or so, my benefactor came rushing back and said that all the guards were sleeping. We went quietly, with caution. I could see those gates through which my former hosts had led me into captivity. I gazed at the guardhouse, in which a small fire was burning, and my heart began to beat.

Carefully we passed through the gates, and from there the road went downhill to the Erak-su River. We didn't go far, however, for my good escort stopped and said: "Master, I can't escort you any further. There's your road. Don't go to your right—you'll end up in the hostile aul of Aukhi. If you go to the left and cross the Erak-su, you'll end up in the aul of Aktash, friendly to the Russians, although it'll be the same distance to Aktash as to Fort Vnezapnaia. If you don't leave the main road, you'll escape directly to Vnezapnaia. Be careful, keep your ears open. If you hear anything coming, jump over to one side and hide. If you get caught by bandits, don't resist: get on your knees and ask for mercy, they like that. And don't lose any time—it's precious for you now. Goodbye"—and he squeezed my hand tightly and said: "If you succeed in getting to Vnezapnaia, remember that I did this for you out of soft-heartedness. Goodbye."

I bowed down to the ground and kissed him.

After he left, I went downhill like an arrow. I ran to the Erak-su, crossed it, and went on, again downhill. On both sides were bushes and small stone cliffs. Suddenly it seemed that people were running after me. I stopped for a minute, listened—and ran further. The road began to get narrow. I saw the Tatar graveyard and hurried past. My feet began to get all gummed up in those cheviaki filled with snow. Sweat fell from me like hail, and I had a terrible thirst that I quenched with snow grabbed in handfuls along the way.

I ran this way for about twenty versts until I had to sit down in the snow from exhaustion. Steam was rising from me as it does from a horse after a long ride in cold winter. I suddenly heard someone going along the path, and my wet hair stood on end. The thought flashed through my mind: "I won't be able to avoid death this time." I began peering ahead, where I could clearly hear some kind of rustling, and suddenly saw a huge wild hog. What was I to do?

When the hog drew another two sazhens nearer, I cried out with all my might. The hog dashed off the path to one side and, after doing a few jumps, got stuck in the snow and crawled away. I quietly went along the path, never taking my eyes off that wild animal. After another ten sazhens or so, I took off running, as they say, as fast as my legs would carry me.

I don't remember how long I was running. I even forgot about the Circassians. I stopped and turned around—"is the hog running after me? No," I realized, and ran on at a gallop. My wet coat started to get heavy, and I would soon have to throw it away. Snow was continually flying into my mouth, like water from a bathhouse stove.

By the time I'd put ten versts between myself and the hog, my trousers and cheviaki were soaked. [. . .] The sun started to set, but the road ahead seemed to grow wider and wider, and it became easier for me to run. The forest got thinner, too. Then I noticed a sleigh road, one that led my direction—to Vnezapnaia, no doubt. Here I caught my breath a bit and said: "Lord! Deliver Your sinful slave. Don't allow beasts or enemies to tear at my unclean body on alien ground. And bring me to stand at Your holy tomb in Jerusalem, that I may pour out all my heartfelt tears, for all Your rich and generous mercies."

And morning dawned again. It occurred to me, then, that the plunderers might catch sight of me from somewhere far away and that it would be impossible for me to conceal myself from them. I ran with all my remaining strength, weeping from the wind hitting me in the face, but unmindful of it . . .

Suddenly in the distance, on my right, I saw the tower of Fort Vnezapnaia and on the other side—Andreevskii aul. Soon I had passed through the forest entirely and ran onto the main road, where I could see the sentry standing on the fortress wall. I ran up to the outermost gates and collapsed in a dead faint . . .

Favishevich was terrified when he saw me in such a deplorable state and was very happy that I had returned. He took me back into the same service as before. Although my head had been disfigured,[129] my mind was still sound, thank God.

After a month, I began to submit petitions concerning my captivity. I went to the regimental commander Kozlovskii, told him about the whole business and asked him to attest to the fact that I had indeed been held captive by plunderers. The commander gave me a strict dressing-down for having gone late at night to Andreevskii. However, he did order a detailed account of the events to be taken from me in the regimental office and that an appropriate formal attestation be given to me; it was to be delivered to General Hasfort[130] as well, the commander of the left flank.

Soon after this, Favishevich sent me along the front line to Stavropol' to find out the prices of cattle. This assignment could not have come at a better time. On March 21 I rode off, making use of the opportunity to travel first to Terek and then alone along the main road to Piatigorsk, my old home. There I spent the first three days of Easter with some old, old friends, then left for Stavropol'.

When I arrived there on the Monday of St. Thomas's week, I gave my petition, along with the attestation of my captivity, to the investigating magistrate—with these documents I applied for "my liberation from the landlord's proprietorship." Then I returned to Fort Vnezapnaia.

As I recall, it was rumored during the first days of May that the general commander, Count Mikhail Semyonovich Vorontsov,[131] would be visiting Vnezapnaia soon. He was inspecting all the fortresses in the mountain region;[132] apparently he was traveling to Tiflis through Temir-Khan-Shura and the auls of Kasiyurt and Kustiaki, and then on to Andreevskii.

On the appointed day we all left the fortress gates to meet our exalted guest. There were shots from the fortress guns when the Count arrived along with his multitudinous escort and retinue. Adorned with gray hairs, he rode on a white Circassian horse and wore an affable smile that never left his face. Riding up to us, he asked: "Is there anyone here who has been offended or oppressed?"

---

129. That is, by having his hair and beard shaved off.

130. Hasfort was the commander of the Fifth Infantry Division; see Gammer, *Muslim Resistance to the Tsar,* 164.

131. See note 102.

132. See Gammer, *Muslim Resistance to the Tsar,* 158; and Baddeley, *The Russian Conquest of the Caucasus,* 387.

Portrait of Count Vorontsov.

At this, Colonel Kozlovskii presented me before the Count. His Highness spoke very affectionately with me and asked about my time in captivity. At the end he said, with a smile: "Well done! You escaped from them quickly—I suppose you didn't much like it there."

And with that he rode away from me. There was a mounting of the fortress guard, with which the Count was very pleased and for which he thanked Kozlovskii. The next day he left Vnezapnaia and went along the main line of fortifications through Batashyurt to the Kastychenskii fortress.

After the Count's departure, troops from all the forts gathered together at Fort Taskichi. We dragged ourselves there as well, along with our bullock carts loaded with various provisions; almost thirty thousand troops had assembled.

Soon Count Vorontsov arrived and set out from Taskichi to Vnezapnaia.[133] At one point the troops stopped for a rest—it was unbearably hot, and everyone was intensely thirsty. I was asked for some porter for the Count, and with a dozen bottles I appeared before him. He asked me which division I was working for, and Kozlovskii answered that I was working for his men.

"That's the prisoner of the mountains," said the Count with a smile. "How much does a bottle of porter cost?"

"Two rubles," I replied. The Count was surprised that it was so expensive, so I enumerated all the expenses that a trader has to pay for a single bottle of porter. The Count shook his head and said: "Here you go—that's for ten bottles" (20 rubles). I bowed and went back to the carts.

On May 29, the troops under Vorontsov set out from Vnezapnaia to the Metlinskaia Ford across the Sulak River. Favishevich went himself with these troops; I received my discharge, and on June 12 I left for Stavropol'.

There in the regional government office my case was getting dragged out with various inquiries, transcriptions, and, yes, delays. Meanwhile I had received a letter from my wife; rumors had apparently been flying at

---

133. Shipov's note: "Before this, the Count sent a battalion of the Kabardinsk division, along with several hundred Don Cossacks, into the Chechen mountains under the command of the brave Colonel Dombrovskii, with the goal of joining forces with the main detachment. [. . .] Dombrovskii, however, was killed in a skirmish with the plunderers—and our workman and his helpers barely escaped."

home about my captivity, and the new bailiff (Tarkhov had died by this time) had written to the regimental office at Vnezapnaia, requesting that I be deported under guard back to Vyezdnaia. The office, however, replied that I was not there and that no one knew a thing about my ever being there. Meanwhile, I was peacefully trading away in the store of some merchant friends of mine and waiting for the outcome of my case.

October 16 arrived. That morning, a civil servant I knew came to me, congratulated me on being freed from the landlord's yoke, and asked me to go to the Regional Government Office to receive certification of my manumission. I heard his words, but couldn't utter a word to him, my bearer of good news. I have experienced joy in my life, but none like that I experienced at that moment. "Just God," I thought, "how strongly I feel Your infinite mercy . . . from this moment on begins a new life for me . . ."

As though on wings, I flew to the Regional Government Office. The desk chief brought out my certificate of manumission, I signed my name in the record book for "outgoing paper," and bowed deeply—I had nothing else with which to thank him.

Afterward the desk chief told me that within days the Administration of the Nizhnii Novgorod *guberniia* would be informed of my case, and that they would announce the results to the landlord and to my wife and children. I bowed low again and left.

I went over to see some friends and began to read the certificate aloud, but tears of joy confounded my vision, and I couldn't make out a thing. Yes, such rare and happy moments are remembered for a lifetime. Even now, as I stand on the edge of the grave, I recall them with indescribable pleasure.

By then I had only three rubles and an unimpressive silver watch (which I later raffled off in a lottery for 15 rubles) to my name and I began to think—how should I set out now, where should I register myself? I soon received a letter from my cousin in Kherson, inviting me to come to him. (I'd already informed him that I was petitioning for my freedom in Stavropol'.) This I did. I registered myself among the *meshchâne* of Kherson[134] and told my wife to come with the children.

As she later told me, they tried to detain her and keep her down in Vyezdnaia, but the local officials were powerless against the law and against

134. That is, as a member of that urban lower-middle class comprising small traders, craftsmen, junior officials, and so forth (*Oxford Russian Dictionary*).

justice. This was especially true because my main persecutors, the landlord and estate manager Raguzin, had right around this time turned their sinful souls over to God. My wife and children came to me in Kherson and we began to live a new life.[135]

135. Shipov's narrative ends with a brief account of the years 1846–52 (not included here).

M. E. Vasilieva

Notes of a Serf Woman

The following autobiographical sketch appeared in 1911 in *Russkaia Starina (Russian Antiquity)*, a Saint Petersburg journal that published an abundance of invaluable historical, biographical, and testimonial material from 1870 through 1918.[1] At least two other, considerably longer, memoirs written by ex-serfs—by Aleksandr Nikitenko[2] and Nikolai Shipov (the latter included in the present volume)— were published in *Russkaia Starina* (in 1881 and 1888, respectively), but M. E. Vasilieva's "Notes" are distinguished by more than their brevity; they are one of the only serf narratives composed by a woman.[3]

Vasilieva's account, which was supposed to continue in later issues of *Russkaia Starina* but apparently did not,[4] contains many elements that are familiar to readers of U.S. slave narratives: descriptions of the serf-owning family (in this case, of course, Russian nobles, who are absentees at the outset of the piece), anecdotes about cruelty and exploitation, an

---

1. "Notes of a Serf Woman" was published as M. E. Vasilieva, "Zapiski krepostnoi," *Russkaia Starina* 145 (1911): 140–151.

2. Nikitenko became a well-known academic and censor, and his memoir of bondage was republished in book form in 1893 and 1904; it has been translated by Helen Saltz Jacobson as *Up from Serfdom: My Childhood and Youth in Russia, 1804–1824* (New Haven, CT, and London: Yale University Press, 2002).

3. The only other one I know of is A. G. Khrushchova's in *Vospominaniia Russkikh Krest'ian XVIII–Pervoi Poloviny XIX Veka,* ed. and intro. by V. A. Koshelev (Moscow: Novoe Literaturnoe Obozrenie, 2006), 94–107.

4. See main introduction.

explanation of how the author learned to read and write, and an account of changes of status within bondage (here, the narrator's move from the cattle yard into the manor house). Perhaps because the "abolitionist" imperatives are absent for Vasilieva,[5] her specific examples of landowner sadism, kindness, and indifference seem almost as much manifestations of personality type and individual difference as systemic consequences of unfree labor.

Most unusual (and quite possibly a result of the termination of the tale with this first installment) is the "child's- (and *orphan*'s)-eye view" taken by the narrator. The conventional comparisons between the narrator's formerly unfree and currently free condition are missing; nor is the serf child represented as straining at every point toward liberation. For this reason, the serf-holding family here is not primarily the "owner," not an obstacle to freedom, but rather the continual object of mixed terror and fascination. Only at the end does a strong voice of specifically *collective* protest emerge, but it is a protest against a callous indifference to poverty rather than against bondage as such. Of course, readers will find their own points of comparison between the great slave narratives and this bitter, ironic, and eloquent sketch.

I

I am a serf maiden belonging to the Bolotin family.[6] Our masters were important people; my old *bárin*,[7] Petr Georgievich, often told his daughters how their grandfather, Georgii Nikolaevich, was greatly favored during his time of service at the court of the Tsaritsa Ekaterina Alekseevna.[8] After the empress's death, bárin Bolotin resolved never to serve anyone else, and moved to his village, called Dubovoe,[9] where he lived until his death.

---

5. Although it is not entirely clear that the piece was written *after* emancipation; see note 6.

6. Note in original: "The surnames have all been changed." Although the text is written in the past tense, the opening sentence indicates that the narrator is *presently* a serf.

7. Landowner, master.

8. Catherine the Great.

9. Pronounced "doo-BOH-vuh-yuh"; the word means "of oak" but also (figuratively)

Before he died, Georgii Nikolaevich built a church in the village in honor of Saint George the Victor and Saint Catherine the Great Martyr. To this day, the priest makes mention of the church's builder, the *boliarin*[10] Georgii, every Sunday during the prayer for the repose of the soul. But the elderly house serfs, ancient old men, said other things about bárin Georgii Nikolaevich: that he was cruel and would flog not only his own peasants but those of the neighboring landowners as well. The police didn't dare so much as show their noses on his premises; to greet them and other uninvited guests, two bears and six hunting dogs were kept chained outside. The bárin would order the dogs to be released as soon as the footmen announced the arrival of a district police officer or police chief at our main gate. They'd learn their lesson then—they might not be bitten, but would certainly be scared to death, and their clothing torn to shreds.

Before his death, Georgii Nikolaevich began lamenting his sins and refused to die before summoning all his peasants and asking forgiveness of them.

Our own former bárin, Petr Georgievich, had a character different from his papa's—he was quiet, timid, and compassionate to his peasants. He was no longer young (about forty years of age) when he married a Circassian princess, Varvara Ivanovna; she was a beauty on the outside but had a cruel heart.

After his marriage, our bárin began obeying his wife in everything, and life became bitter for us peasants.

For many years, our masters lived every winter in Moscow; in spring, when the bird-cherry tree blossomed, they would come to Dubovoe with their children and servants, living there until the arrival of the first light frosts. . . .

I was brought to the masters' village at the age of five. My parents were peasants; I was born in a village within four versts[11] of the masters' estate. When my mother and father both died within a single week, the village

---

"coarse," "thick," "rock hard," "bullet-like," "inedible." There was a village with this name about fifteen kilometers from the town of Ranenburg (now Cheplygin), southwest of Moscow and between Voronezh and Riazan'; it had about seven thousand inhabitants in 1902. See V. P. Semenov, ed., *Rossiia: Polnoe Geograficheskoe Opisanie Nashego Otechestva* (Saint Petersburg: A. F. Devrien, 1902), 2:415.

10. An archaic title meaning "noble master."

11. One verst (in Russian, *versta* ["vyair-STAH"]) is equivalent to about 1.06 kilometers.

elder came to our hut, took me in his arms, and brought me to Granny Ustina, who lived in the cattle yard at Dubovoe.

Our masters had instituted the practice of bringing any and all orphans—whether foundlings or legitimate peasant children—onto the estate and turning them over to the care of Granny Ustina.[12] I remember her as an already very old woman, though still able to work. In summer and winter she would help the herd women with grooming the master's cattle. Seated on a bench in the evenings, when the torch would be lit inside the hut, Granny would weave the master's linen on the spinning wheel or twist out threads on the spindle.

Our hut was divided into two halves by a small, low fence: on one side hung the cradle where the little ones slept, while we older children lolled around on the straw strewn on the floor; on the other side were calves, which were fattened for slaughter and then sent to the masters in Moscow. We children loved to watch as Granny fed some of the calves with milk, while the others skipped about beside her. During the day, the older children babysat the younger, and our lives were good. As orphans we received a monthly ration of a measure of rye, a measure of buckwheat groats, and every day (as a rule) two pitchers of fresh milk from the master's cows.

During the time that our masters were absent from the village, we ran not only all over the yard, but in the master's garden as well. When our steward, Nikanor Savel'evich, opened up the windows of the manor house in the spring, we would surround him and beg that he show us the masters' rooms; fed up with our pestering, he would say: "Come along with me, piglets, just make one promise, a promise dearer than gold: don't touch a thing!"

Nikanor Savel'evich was kind to us orphans, for he had suffered much himself in his time. After serving our masters for fifteen years as a footman, he eventually went deaf from the mistress's blows to his head, and the bárin sent him over to us to work as a steward. We children were [. . .] overjoyed

---

12. Peter Kolchin suggests that a concern for orphans was widespread among landowners. "Noblemen . . . ordered [stewards] to make sure that orphans and children of those unable to provide adequate support were cared for. Count Orlov instructed his steward to find homes for abandoned illegitimate children, adding that 'this matter is pleasing to God' and promising that 'for the support of such infants' the steward would 'receive praise from me'" (*Unfree Labor: American Slavery and Russian Serfdom* [Cambridge, MA: Belknap Press of Harvard University Press, 1987], 77).

that Nikanor Savel'evich allowed us to follow him; and when we would enter the lord's mansion after living in the cattle yard, we thought we'd landed in heaven. The master's house was huge, with bright rooms, parquet floors, gilded furniture, and marble columns in the hallway.

Nikanor Savel'evich not only showed us the rooms, but took us onto the balconies as well, of which there were four. From one of them an oak grove could be seen atop a high hill, below which a narrow river wound along like a white ribbon; from another we could see the church with its golden cupolas, and the field where we would run after cornflowers in summer; the third opened onto a wide road planted with oak woods; while the fourth looked onto the courtyard.

For two years running, our masters had been absent from their village, but during the third year our steward received a letter from the bárin, relating that he and the mistress had decided to move permanently to Dubovoe.

The master wrote: "Check, Nikanor, to make sure that the whole house is in good condition so that we'll be able to live in it during the winter as well as the summer." This set off a rush of activity. Peasant men and women were herded into the courtyard; the men cleaned up the garden, which had fallen into neglect, while the women plucked grass in the yard.

Nikanor Savel'evich walked around the whole house with his hammer, tapping the walls. In the office he noticed that one wall was cracking and bulging forward, and immediately sent a courier into town for the stonemasons. As the masons began breaking down the wall, they noticed a human figure immured there between the bricks; they took fright, stopped working, and ran to the steward.

"We must send for a priest, Nikanor Savel'evich," they said, and the steward went himself to fetch Father Vasilii, our priest. He was an ancient old fellow who remembered our bárin's father.

When Father Vasilii saw human bones stuck inside the wall, he crossed himself and began to pray. "Lord, lay this murdered man, your slave, to rest; take his name, Lord, into account. . . ." Later, he pointed to a large portrait in a golden frame of a handsome bárin with curly gray hair. "That is the builder of our church, the boliarin Georgii," said the priest. "I remember how he would flog his own peasants to death. The Lord alone knows the sins of men; we Orthodox people shall pray for both—for the slain one and for boliarin Georgii." After the offices for the dead had been performed, the priest ordered the bones to be taken out of the wall, placed in a box, and carried to the cemetery. He himself walked at the head of the procession to the graveyard, just as though he were wearing a chasuble and carrying a censer.

Later, Nikanor Savel'evich summoned all the house serfs, strictly ordering them to hold their tongues about all that had happened that day.

II

The bailiff received another letter, indicating that our masters would be arriving on Whitsunday; we began preparations for their arrival.

The day before, young birch trees cut from the forest were planted in the courtyard. All the cripples and old people on the estate poured into the courtyard early in the morning on Whitsun, so as not to miss the arrival of the masters and to have time and opportunity to bow down to them. Few of the house serfs went to mass that day; the only ones who attended were those who had enough money to give a special offering to the health of the master, the mistress, and all their kin. Then they would leave with the communion loaves they had received and present them to the masters.

Nikanor Savel'evich brought all of us children into the garden and cut each one a large bouquet of lilacs. He then had us stand on either side of the master's porch; from there we were to give the flowers to our mistress, Varvara Ivanovna, when she got out of the carriage. . . .

Our masters didn't arrive until after lunch.

We were all standing by the porch holding our flowers when two carriages, each drawn by four horses, flew into the yard.

In one of the carriages sat the master and mistress. Petr Georgievich was already old, with hair white as snow. Varvara Ivanovna was no longer young, though still stately in appearance; her respectable moustache made her look more like a man than a woman. The young bárin Egor Petrovich sat opposite the two elder masters, and Son'ia Petrovna (the younger daughter), Praskov'ia Petrovna (the older daughter), along with the governess (Anna Vasil'evna) and dry nurse (Ol'ga Ivanovna) came in the other carriage.

Our mistress petted us on our heads when we presented the flowers to her, all the time chatting with Granny Ustina, who, on the double occasion of Whitsun and the masters' arrival, was wearing a *shugai*[13] of yellow nankeen, the very same dress in which she was married.

13. A kind of dress.

The mistress asked her how many new orphans had arrived that winter and how many calves were still alive.

The old bárin ordered a footman to pull a traveling provisions hamper out of the carriage; right there on the porch he treated the male house serfs to some vodka.

I was preoccupied with the young masters and paid little attention to their elders. Both of the young mistresses were wearing round straw hats and yellow burnouses. The older one was at that time in her fourteenth year. She was rather thin but entirely pleasant and bowed to the house serfs with an affecting smile; all of us liked her very much.

The younger daughter was nine years old, with a complexion cracked by scrofula. It was said that she was sickly, and one of the footmen carried her out of the carriage and set her on the porch. When she suddenly threw a tantrum about something, Anna Vasil'evna, the oldish-looking governess, scurried over to her; we could hear how she told the young mistress: "It's naughty to throw fits, Sonechka[14]—all your serfs are looking at you."

The fit intensified; Son'ia Petrovna stamped her foot at the governess and began spitting on us children.

The young bárin, Egor Petrovich, tarried longer in the carriage than any of the others. Dressed in a black jacket and wearing a peaked cap with a red band, he was at the time sixteen years old, and the very picture of a bárin: tall, slender, with black arching eyebrows and an oblong pink face.

He went past the house serfs proudly, as though he didn't even notice how everyone around was bowing down to him; he turned around only once to give a smack to his shaggy-haired dog and then, playing with his cane, went into the house.

III

It became more cheerful in the village after the masters moved back in.

I would often run over to the servants' quarters to watch the footmen and maids and to listen in on what they were saying about our masters. The mistress, Varvara Ivanovna, received no praise from the domestics; she was very rude and not only beat her servants but criticized her husband for

14. That is, the younger daughter, whose name is later revealed to be Sof'ia Petrovna. She is referred to as "Son'ia," "Sonechka," and "Sof'ia"; "Son'ia" and "Sonechka" are familiar forms of Sof'ia.

not doing the same. The old bárin was a quiet man and hated fighting, but when his wife set the dogs on someone, he would walk up to him and shout until he grew hoarse, all the time beating his walking stick on the floor. But no one feared him—they knew that he only shouted and would never resort to blows.

The mistress was also censured for not loving her older children while lavishing attention on her youngest daughter. The son did not fear his mother and gave her no quarter; she was, in fact, rather afraid of him. On the other hand, she nursed her eldest daughter (Praskov'ia Petrovna) with slaps to the face, all because she would intercede on behalf of the servant girls. Nasty, capricious young Son'ia Petrovna was hated by all the domestics; any careless word pronounced in her presence would be reported to mommy, and the culprit turned over for a whipping with a birch rod.

Although the maids liked the young bárin Egor Petrovich for his beauty, they complained that his "endearments" were painful. He would caper around pinching them and lashing them with a switch that left behind bloody welts on their flesh. The young bárin carried himself proudly in the presence of common people; he'd sometimes share a chuckle with the maids, while the footmen heard nothing from him except "take this—give me that."

One time the domestics were talking about the young bárin, and our steward joined in. "As far as appearance is concerned, Egor Petrovich and that portrait of his grandpa, Georgii Nikolaevich, are as alike as two drops of water," said Nikanor Savel'evich. "And his character, too, will be exactly like that of his grandpa, who flogged people to death. Once, when he was eight, the young bárin tried to set me on fire. I was his tutor at the time and had a terrible time with him; and I dared neither to put a stop to his behavior nor complain about him to the mistress. In the maid's room, he once crawled under the tambour[15] and began piercing the girls' bare legs with pins. The maids were crying and didn't know what to do: they couldn't complain to the mistress because she'd only slap them across the face and wouldn't stop her son in any case.

"So I went into the maid's room, and they beseeched me: 'Nikanor Savel'evich, take the bárin's son out from under the tambour—he's made our legs bloody with all his pricks.' I pulled Egor Petrovich out and,

15. An embroidery frame.

grabbing him by the ear, told him 'go, complain to your mommy and daddy about me.'

"The whole day I awaited the mistress's blows, but what ended up happening was something different. At dusk I lay down on the leather sofa in the footmen's room and nodded off. Luckily, I soon woke up and noticed that my head felt hot and that the room was filled with a stench like that of burned hair. I grasped my head and, finding it aflame, seized a sofa cushion and extinguished the fire. I was thinking 'how did my head catch fire?' — when I looked around and saw the bárin's son standing behind a wardrobe, watching me and laughing; he had a box of sulfur matches in his hand."

After such stories, I began to fear the young bárin, but wanted to look at him all the same. I would run over to the fence surrounding the master's garden, hide in the bushes, and observe how Egor Petrovich trained his dog to carry things along the path lined with lime trees. The young master harassed his dog as well; he carried an iron-tipped lash that left a bloody stripe each time it touched the dog's shaved hindquarters. And God protect the dog if he were ever to snap or show his teeth: then Egor Petrovich would flog him with all his might, and the animal could do nothing but yelp and howl. The young master would eventually throw the lash down and, after walking up and down the path for a couple of minutes, called the dog (who was hiding in the bushes) and began petting him.

My arms and legs would sometimes shake with fear as I watched the young bárin beat his dog; but I still remained at the fence and would run there again to await him the next day.

On another occasion, Egor Petrovich came to the garden with a rifle in order to shoot birds. He preferred wounding them to killing them immediately. When a bird would fall to the ground, its little wings quivering, the young bárin would bend over and stare as though he were feasting his eyes on it; he would then grab the bird by its legs, shake it, and hurl it against the fence. He killed my tomcat in the same way.

Vas'ka (the cat) got into the habit of following me to the master's garden. While I stood by the fence, he would climb onto it and sit there sunning himself.

At first the young bárin didn't notice Vas'ka. But one day he suddenly took aim and fired in my direction, and the cat fell over into the garden like a thunderbolt. At first I thought that Vas'ka had jumped off the fence, but when the young bárin lifted him by his legs and hurled him in my direction against the fence, I realized that Vas'ka had been killed and ran over to him.

P. Bezsonov, "Portrait of a Lackey Sweeping," 1836. (courtesy of the State Historical Museum, Moscow)

Seeing that the cat was goggle-eyed like a crayfish, I began to howl at the top of my voice.

The bárin saw me and shouted:

"Come here, pretty little girl, come over to me!"

I picked the cat up in my skirt, took to my heels, and ran to the cattle yard without looking back once.

Soon after that, Egor Petrovich went to Saint Petersburg to finish his education and for seven or eight years never cast a glance in the direction of his village, Dubovoe.

IV

I was brought to serve inside the house during the first winter after the arrival of the masters.

The young mistress Son'ia Petrovna was once out walking in the courtyard with her governess, and I, chancing to meet them there, bowed to them. The young mistress called me over to her; she asked me where I lived and what my name was, and right then and there told the governess: "I want to play with this girl in my room."

Later in the evening on the same day, while Granny Ustina was still weaving and we children, by now played out with running around in the courtyard, were soundly sleeping side by side on the floor, Granny overheard someone groping along the wall inside the porch, looking for the door.

Granny rose and opened the door. The maid Aksiuta came in wearing a large kerchief. She said that she had been sent by the mistress to fetch Akul'ka the orphan girl, to whom the young mistress Sof'ia Petrovna had taken a liking to that day while out for a walk.

"The young mistress won't go to sleep without your Akul'ka," said Aksiuta. "She's throwing a fit and scratched the dry nurse's face all over till it bled. 'I want Akul'ka to sleep next to my bed,' she says, 'on the floor, like a little dog.'"

Granny then and there shook me awake and set me on my feet. I stood there half-asleep like a dunce and hadn't any idea what was going on. . . . Granny tied my hair into a braid, Aksiuta pulled one of the young mistress's old dresses out from under her kerchief, and together with Granny put the dress on me.

When I saw that I was wearing a pink dress with two flounces, I was so happy that all my doziness immediately vanished. Aksiuta took me by the

207

Nicolas de Courteille, "Portrait of Anna Borunova" (a serf singer owned by Prince Nikolai Iusupov), 1821. Borunova's brother was the architect I. E. Borunov.

hand and we left the hut. I could hear Granny beginning to wail, as though for a dead woman.

It was freezing outside, and I had nothing on except for that light cotton dress. When Aksiuta covered me with her large kerchief, it became difficult to walk, so we took to chasing one another in order to warm up. The run made me feel downright hot.

When we arrived to the master's house, Aksiuta led me to mistress Son'ia Petrovna's room. She was lying in bed, still not asleep; the dry nurse stood next to her, trying to persuade her to stop acting up. The young mistress beat on the grille railing around her bed with her arms and legs and cried: "Bring me Akul'ka, bring Akul'ka!"

"Look, Sonechka, there's your Akul'ka standing over there," the dry nurse Ol'ga Ivanovna told the young mistress as I entered with Aksiuta.

Son'ia Petrovna rose up on the bed, looked at me sleepily, and without saying a word, lay down again, turning her little face to the wall. Ol'ga Ivanovna said to me in a whisper: "The mistress will fall asleep now, and you, Akul'ka, sit here on this chair and don't budge."

I sat down, and the dry nurse extinguished the candle. It was tedious, sitting there in the dark, and I began listening to the voices in the next room, the door to which wasn't tightly closed. Through the crack I could see a light, and could hear how something heavy was being carried into the neighboring room.

Suddenly someone in that room shouted: "Dry nurse, where's the sponge I ordered you to dry out?"

Ol'ga Ivanovna picked up a sponge from the stove bench and put it in my hand. "Take this sponge to the mistress in her room, through that door," she said.

As I went in, my attention was seized by a large green bathtub standing in the middle of the room. Two footmen were pouring buckets of water into it; not far from them, the mistress was sitting on a sofa, entirely naked except for one leg from which the stocking had not yet been removed. Aksiuta was sitting on her knees in front of her, trying to unravel some lace from the stocking's suspender. I bowed to the mistress, handed her the sponge, and already wanted to leave when she stopped me.

"Akul'ka," she said, "since you've woven threads with Ustina, surely you know how to untie a knot. This fool"—and here she gave Aksiuta's face a jab with her foot—"made the knot so tight, that it will have to be cut open."

I prostrated myself before the mistress and with my teeth unraveled the knot in a second. Lifting my head, I saw the old bárin in the room.

He was wearing a Bokhara housecoat and carried a newspaper. The footmen were still in the room, bustling around the bathtub.

Frowning, the old bárin looked around the room, glancing cursorily at the footmen, at me, and finally resting his gaze on the mistress. "You might have thrown at least a sheet on yourself, Varvara Ivanovna," he said in a gentle voice.

"Why?" she replied. "It's warm in this room."

"Well, don't you see," he stammered, looking over at the footmen. "There are men here, looking at you."

"What men?" cried the mistress with surprise. "Here are my serfs, my footmen—do you think they would dare look at me, their mistress? They're no more to me than those two chairs over there."

The bárin shrugged his shoulders, took a candle from the table, and left the room.

And in truth, our mistress Varvara Ivanovna was a shameless woman. She not only appeared naked in front of the footmen, but did other things in their presence as well. . . .

From that evening forward, I lived inside the manor house. At first I played with dolls together with Son'ia Petrovna; as she began to learn to read and write, I also learned to read and write in order to help give her a taste for study. In the evenings, after the lamps were extinguished in the living room, the mistress and her eldest daughter sat at a table and worked. The governess taught Son'ia Petrovna how to dance, and had me doing all the poses and practicing the steps along with her.

Son'ia Petrovna didn't like studying and often did not learn her lessons; for this, I, not she, was punished. The mistress would clutch my head between her knees and beat me until I bled. Praskov'ia Petrovna, the eldest daughter, often fought with her mother over me.

"You have no shame, mama," she would say. "Son'ia is lazy, and you give beatings to Akul'ka."

In response, the mistress would give her such a slap in the face that poor Praskov'ia Petrovna would have to go around for a long time with a bandage on her cheek.

Anna Vasil'evna, the governess, pitied me as well, but was afraid to say a word. When the mistress would leave me behind in the room with eyes overflowing with bitter tears, the governess would come to me on the sly, away from Son'ia Petrovna, and pass me a candy or piece of gingerbread.

Once Son'ia Petrovna did see this, however, and tattled to her mommy, who rushed up to Anna Vasil'evna and said: "You don't understand that I beat Akul'ka in order to make Sonechka ashamed of her laziness; that's the way I arouse noble feelings in my daughter."

But the mistress was not telling the truth—she did not beat me in order to shame her daughter with my tears. She beat me because she passionately loved beating children, a fact known and observed by everyone. She would generally pick on any and every boy or girl who approached the courtyard fence, claiming that they were plucking berries off the bushes. After ordering the gardener to chase the children into the garden, she would beat them until they either turned blue from crying or fell silent and stupefied. For this reason the children feared the mistress like fire—a fear that led, however, to a certain incident, after which our mistress grew more quiet.

It happened like this: the windows of the master's dining room opened onto the garden, and when the weather was good, our mistress loved to drink tea by the open window. One day she poured herself a cup of tea, took a bun from the breadbasket on the table, and sat down by the window.

While this was going on, a boy named Seriozhka was helping the gardener transplant some hollyhocks into the flowerbed. The gardener went off somewhere, leaving behind Seriozhka, who stayed there watching the mistress drink tea.

Seriozhka was an orphan and lived in the cattle yard with Granny Ustina. After the masters returned to the village, the monthly ration for the orphans was reduced, and by this time they were always going around hungry; even the older children went begging in the countryside on Sundays. When Seriozhka would chance to see me in the garden he would ask: "Akul'ka, bring me at least a crust of bread—I'm horribly hungry."

Now, like a hungry dog, Seriozhka fixed his gaze on the mistress as she ate her bun and poured cream into her tea. As ill luck would have it, for some reason the mistress left the dining room, leaving her half-consumed cup of tea and half-eaten bun behind on the windowsill. Seriozhka could see that there was no one in the dining room, and that he could grab that piece of bun; from within the garden he would have only to stretch out his arm to reach it. He ran to the window, seized the bun from the windowsill, but hadn't managed to put it in his mouth when the mistress came back in.

Seriozhka was so frightened that he even forgot to hide the bun; he stood there holding it and staring at the mistress, like a fool. "You piece of trash—why did you steal my bun?" queried the mistress. Seriozhka, quaking with fear, was silent. The mistress saw the gardener and shouted to him:

"Avdei, cut me a switch!"

Only then did Seriozhka come to his senses and took to his heels as fast as he could. "Girls, people—catch that boy!" cried the mistress from the window. The maids' window, like that of the dining room, opened onto the garden; we had seen how Seriozhka had stolen the bun, and watched now as he took off down the path like a shot.

When the mistress shouted at us to catch him, Aksiuta (who was always ready to worm her way into the mistress's good graces) was the first out the window; so as not to fall behind her, we also hopped out and ran after Seriozhka. But Seriozhka wasn't running—he was flying, and all that flitted before our eyes were his naked heels.

The gardener Avdei was chasing along with us, but suddenly Seriozhka made a turn and we lost sight of him in the trees. When we reached the turn, Seriozhka was nowhere to be seen; in one spot near the fence, some high, unmown grass had been trampled down.

"Did Seriozhka vanish here into thin air?" asked the girls, looking at the crumpled grass. "Surely he's not a wood goblin," said old Avdei, scratching his head. "He must have crawled over the fence right here. But there's a well here next to the fence—just today Seriozhka and I drew some water from it to water the cucumbers. I'll climb the fence, girls, but not you," he told us. "Go around the fence and over to the well."

We still hadn't reached the well by the time Avdei met us, running as fast as he could for a boat hook. "Seriozhka is in the well!" he cried to us without stopping. It had rained continuously for the last while, and the water had risen to the very top of the well. Little bubbles could be seen rising in it, rising and falling. By the time they had brought boat hooks and extracted Seriozhka, he had already succeeded in giving his soul over to God.

When they laid the drowned boy on sackcloth and lifted him up, one of the footmen noticed that Seriozhka had something clutched inside his little fist; they unclasped it and found the piece of bun. All the house serfs wept and said in a single voice:

"A person has died for a few crumbs of bread."

Index

Index

Wisconsin Studies in Autobiography

William L. Andrews
General Editor

Robert F. Sayre
The Examined Self: Benjamin Franklin, Henry Adams, Henry James

Daniel B. Shea
Spiritual Autobiography in Early America

Lois Mark Stalvey
The Education of a WASP

Margaret Sams
Forbidden Family: A Wartime Memoir of the Philippines, 1941–1945
Edited with an introduction by Lynn Z. Bloom

Charlotte Perkins Gilman
The Living of Charlotte Perkins Gilman: An Autobiography
Introduction by Ann J. Lane

Mark Twain
Mark Twain's Own Autobiography: The Chapters from the North American Review
Edited by Michael J. Kiskis

Journeys in New Worlds: Early American Women's Narratives
Edited by William L. Andrews, Sargent Bush, Jr., Annette Kolodny,
    Amy Schrager Lang, and Daniel B. Shea

American Autobiography: Retrospect and Prospect
Edited by Paul John Eakin

Caroline Seabury
The Diary of Caroline Seabury, 1854–1863
Edited with an introduction by Suzanne L. Bunkers

Cornelia Peake McDonald
A Woman's Civil War: A Diary with Reminiscences of the War, from March 1862
Edited with an introduction by Minrose C. Gwin

Marian Anderson
My Lord, What a Morning
Introduction by Nellie Y. McKay

American Women's Autobiography: Fea(s)ts of Memory
Edited with an introduction by Margo Culley

Frank Marshall Davis
Livin' the Blues: Memoirs of a Black Journalist and Poet
Edited with an introduction by John Edgar Tidwell

Joanne Jacobson
Authority and Alliance in the Letters of Henry Adams

Kamau Brathwaite
The Zea Mexican Diary: 7 September 1926–7 September 1986

Genaro M. Padilla
My History, Not Yours: The Formation of Mexican American Autobiography

Frances Smith Foster
Witnessing Slavery: The Development of Ante-bellum Slave Narratives

Native American Autobiography: An Anthology
Edited with an introduction by Arnold Krupat

American Lives: An Anthology of Autobiographical Writing
Edited with an introduction by Robert F. Sayre

Carol Holly
*Intensely Family: The Inheritance of Family Shame and the Autobiographies
of Henry James*

People of the Book: Thirty Scholars Reflect on Their Jewish Identity
Edited by Jeffrey Rubin-Dorsky and Shelley Fisher Fishkin

G. Thomas Couser
Recovering Bodies: Illness, Disability, and Life Writing

John Downton Hazlett
My Generation: Collective Autobiography and Identity Politics

William Herrick
*Jumping the Line: The Adventures and Misadventures of
  an American Radical*

Women, Autobiography, Theory: A Reader
Edited by Sidonie Smith and Julia Watson

José Angel Gutiérrez
The Making of a Chicano Militant: Lessons from Cristal

Marie Hall Ets
Rosa: The Life of an Italian Immigrant

Carson McCullers
*Illumination and Night Glare: The Unfinished Autobiography of
  Carson McCullers*
Edited with an introduction by Carlos L. Dews

Yi-Fu Tuan
Who Am I?: An Autobiography of Emotion, Mind, and Spirit

Henry Bibb
The Life and Adventures of Henry Bibb: An American Slave
Introduction by Charles J. Heglar

Suzanne L. Bunkers
Diaries of Girls and Women: A Midwestern American Sampler

Jim Lane
The Autobiographical Documentary in America

Sandra Pouchet Paquet
Caribbean Autobiography: Cultural Identity and Self-Representation

Mark O'Brien, with Gillian Kendall
How I Became a Human Being: A Disabled Man's Quest for Independence

Elizabeth L. Banks
Campaigns of Curiosity: Journalistic Adventures of an American Girl in Late Victorian London
Introduction by Mary Suzanne Schriber and Abbey L. Zink

Miriam Fuchs
The Text Is Myself: Women's Life Writing and Catastrophe

Jean M. Humez
Harriet Tubman: The Life and the Life Stories

Voices Made Flesh: Performing Women's Autobiography
Edited by Lynn C. Miller, Jacqueline Taylor, and M. Heather Carver

Loreta Janeta Velazquez
The Woman in Battle: The Civil War Narrative of Loreta Janeta Velazquez, Cuban Woman and Confederate Soldier
Introduction by Jesse Alemán

Cathryn Halverson
Maverick Autobiographies: Women Writers and the American West, 1900–1936

Jeffrey Brace
The Blind African Slave: Or Memoirs of Boyrereau Brinch, Nicknamed Jeffrey Brace
as told to Benjamin F. Prentiss, Esq.
Edited with an introduction by Kari J. Winter

Colette Inez
The Secret of M. Dulong: A Memoir

Before They Could Vote: American Women's Autobiographical Writing, 1819–1919
Edited by Sidonie Smith and Julia Watson

Bertram J. Cohler
Writing Desire: Sixty Years of Gay Autobiography

Philip Holden
Autobiography and Decolonization: Modernity, Masculinity, and the Nation-State

Jing M. Wang
When "I" Was Born: Women's Autobiography in Modern China

Conjoined Twins in Black and White: The Lives of Millie-Christine McKoy and Daisy and Violet Hilton
Edited by Linda Frost

Four Russian Serf Narratives
Translated, edited, and with an introduction by John MacKay

Mark Twain
Mark Twain's Own Autobiography: The Chapters from the North American Review, second edition
Edited by Michael J. Kiskis